FAIR SHARES
*The layman's guide to buying
and selling stocks and shares*

FAIR SHARES
The layman's guide to buying and selling stocks and shares

Simon Rose

MERCURY
Published by W.H. Allen & Co. Plc

First published February 1986
Reprinted April, May, August 1986
Second Edition (completely revised) February 1987
Reprinted (with revisions) August 1987

Published by the Mercury Books Division of
W.H. Allen & Co. Plc
44 Hill Street, London W1X 8LB

Set in Linotron Palatino by
Phoenix Photosetting, Chatham, Kent
Printed and bound in Great Britain by
Mackays of Chatham Ltd, Chatham, Kent

ISBN 1-85252-010-8

To Jane –
The best editor
a man could have

CONTENTS

PREFACE TO THE SECOND EDITION

'All you need to be an investment genius is a rising market and a short memory'
Anon

The speed with which the attitude of the general public towards the stock market has changed is really quite extraordinary. When I wrote the first edition of *Fair Shares*, I felt rather in the apprehensive position of a missionary who arrives in the middle of some curious, but nonetheless extremely sceptical natives. Was all this interest in shares a flash in the pan, I wondered, a fad that would disappear as quickly as hoola-hoops and skateboards?

It seems not. I appear now to be preaching to a converted people. The number of shareholders in the country has increased by leaps and bounds with each big new share sale. Before British Telecom tempted a new generation of investors, the ranks of shareholders mustered only about two million people. BT increased that to some three million. Just over two years later surveys suggest a figure nearer to ten million, an extraordinary *quarter* of the adult population. About half of this new wave of shareholders are under the age of 45 and many are far from being thought of as well-off.

Yet one wonders what lies behind this sudden upsurge of interest. Is it really a desire to take a stake in British business that motivates these new investors? Or is it simply that they see the big share sales as being money for old rope, an easy way to make a quick killing. With BT tripling some investors' money in less than six months and TSB offering a 60% profit on the first day of dealing, it is easy to see why such a view might have taken hold. The government, eager to launch yet another company on the privatisation slipway and thus swell the Treasury coffers, does nothing to correct this opinion, nor do any of the financial institutions who are so eagerly soliciting the business of novice investors.

Yet old stock market hands look at this new-found enthusiasm for the business of investing in shares with some dismay, even though they know that their warnings that it will all end in tears go unheeded. Swept along by the belief that you can't fail to make money in the stock market, investors are clambering onto the bandwagon without even the most basic understanding of what they are letting themselves in for. Few of us would dream of spending our hard-earned cash on a hi-fi or a car without doing considerable homework first, perhaps checking the opinions of various magazines, asking advice from the experts and discussing it with friends. Yet such elementary caution is thrown to the winds by some people when it comes to using their money to make more money. They cheerily hand over hundreds of pounds with scarcely more than a moment's thought.

Investing in the stock market without the slightest notion of what you are buying is nothing less than a gamble, pure and simple. It is not investment. It is fortunate for the newcomers that the privatisation programme has coincided with a long period of rising stock market prices. Yet shares do not go on climbing for ever. When the market turns savagely downwards, as it surely is going to do at some stage, many investors new to the stock market, who have perhaps over-reached themselves, won't have the slightest idea of what has hit them.

Buying a share in one or two privatised companies – and over half of stock market investors have no greater involvement than that – can give no real idea of what the stock market is all about. *Fair Shares* should show that there is a good deal more to investing in shares than that, that it is about selling shares as well as buying them, and that it is an activity within everybody's reach. It is an activity not without risk, but those who comprehend most of what is in this book will have a distinct advantage over those who keep their heads in the sand.

The Government and its advisors, despite their laudable intentions of trying to make us all share owners, have done nothing to help educate the public about the stock market. Ensuring that these issues are a success appears to be all that they are worried about. The 20 million pounds that was spent on advertising the British Gas sale may have done what it set out to do, but where in all those posters, television ads and glossy brochures was the health warning, explaining the possible risks, as well as the rewards of the stock market? The Janet and John booklet on shares knocked up in an afternoon by the Stock Exchange hopelessly over-simplified the whole thing.

The media and the City, the one terrified of losing its advertising, the other of missing out on its massive commission revenues, somehow neglect to criticise the government for 'share pushing', an activity that would be completely illegal were it attempted by any other body. Lamentably, first-time buyers learn as much about the workings of the stock market from the brochures handed out with government share issues as they do about sheep-farming from listening to a recitation of 'Little Bo Peep'. This is a rather short-sighted view on the part of the authorities. In that arrogant manner fairly typical of the 'Nanny' school of government, we are told something is good for us and that we should simply take the medicine and not ask awkward questions. It is possible to learn about the stock market from trial and error, but such a method of tuition could prove very expensive to the pupil. If the climate changes and investors lose, rather than make, money it will hardly be surprising if Nanny finds herself on the receiving end of some tough words from her formerly docile charges.

It is a great pity that the upsurge in share ownership coincided with the so-called *Big Bang*, the far-reaching, and often extremely confusing, changes to the way the stock market in this country operates. From the private investor's viewpoint, the method of dealing in stocks and shares remains pretty much the same. But the conflicts of interest which the new system has thrown up make it all the more imperative that investors do not involve themselves in the stock market without a basic understanding of the way in which it works. The majority of investment businesses in this country are run by honest, upright individuals but there are always bound to be some less reputable people preying off the ignorance of gullible investors.

The introduction of what Nigel Lawson – with that catchy way with words for which he is so renowned – has called 'people's capitalism' has added another dimension to the picture. Personal Equity Plans, which allow individuals to invest up to £2,400 a year tax-free, are being sold more aggressively than soap powder has ever been, with many of the advertisements for the product as misleading as they can be without actually breaking the law. In discussing PEP's I shall explain why investors new to the market should think twice before getting involved.

[3]

I shall also show that for those investors who arm themselves with the requisite knowledge before getting involved in the stock market, there has never been a more exciting time to deal in stocks and shares. The market is more welcoming to the private investor than for many years. The big financial institutions thrown into being by Big Bang are simply crying out for your business, opening up shops in the High Street and offering dealing services of the greatest simplicity. But are they really concerned for your welfare? Are they determined, as good stockbrokers of yore were, to make you money? Or are they just keen to have your commission for a while, before you tire of them and move it elsewhere. The easier it is made for investors to deal on the market, the more cautious they should be.

In the words of that most wise of stock market saws: 'Mind your eye.'

1

THE FINANCIAL COWARDICE OF THE BRITISH

The decline and rise of the private investor

'There was a time when a fool and his money were soon parted, but now it happens to everybody.'
Adlai Stevenson

There is no doubt that Britain is slowly but surely becoming a nation of capitalists. Irrespective of political affiliations, people are increasingly aware of the importance of investment as a way of enabling them to safeguard and build upon their capital. This trend is most obviously visible in the massive increase in home ownership; a staggering two-thirds of homes in this country are now owner-occupied, or at least they will be when the mortgages are finally paid off.

For most of us, our homes will be the most substantial investment we will ever make; one that is made more attractive by the seemingly inexorable rise of domestic property prices and by the lucrative tax breaks available for mortgage borrowers. But investors are becoming steadily more sophisticated right across the board, increasingly willing to experiment with new forms of investment. The choice available to them is wide indeed – life assurance, annuities, endowment policies, pension plans, high-interest accounts, National Savings, gold, premium bonds and building societies, to name just some of the most popular.

A few years ago the stock market wouldn't even have been considered by most people as a suitable home for their money. Owning shares was a pretty lonely pastime and if you ever tried to start up a conversation with a stranger about the stock market, you might as well have been talking about philately or astronomy for all the response you were likely to get.

Now all that has changed, and stock market investment is once more back in vogue. British Telecom, sold off in the dying months of 1984 with all the subtlety and refinement of a second-hand car auction, was undoubtedly the catalyst, creating around a million first-time investors in one go. To the surprise of itself as well as everyone else, the government uncovered an extraordinary enthusiasm for shares among the British public. Indeed so popular is it becoming that the government has put aside its earlier eagerness for making us all homeowners and is now concentrating on making us all shareowners instead. The privatisation programme, Personal Equity Plans, employee share schemes, all are designed to swell the numbers still further.

In fact, although the numbers of shareholders seems to be increasing all the time, the influence of the private investor in the affairs of the stock market as a whole is still fairly negligible. Most of those who apply for the giant share issues don't seem to want to get any further involved in buying and selling stocks and shares. Those who hold just one or two shares do just that; once they have bought them they tuck them away somewhere and virtually forget about them. The trend towards wider share ownership does not seem to have been paralleled by a rise in the level of stock market activity by individual investors. The proportion of market turnover accounted for by private clients dropped from 28% as lately as 1983 to 19% by mid-1987. We may be becoming a nation of shareholders, but we are very far from becoming a nation of regular stock market investors. There is a very big difference.

Private investors used to be vital to the stock market. As recently as 1957 individuals owned two-thirds of all shares quoted on the UK Stock Exchange. By 1981 that figure had fallen to just 28% and the latest estimates place it at less than a fifth, despite the privatisation programme. There's been much hot air spouted as to why that should be. It certainly can't be because of disillusionment with it as an investment, for over the past thirty years an investor's money would have increased thirty-fold on the market!

Whether or not you hold any shares in your own name, you will almost certainly have participated in the stock market's performance. For if you belong to a private pension scheme or a trade union, or if you have a life policy or insurance of any sort, then you are financially involved with the fortunes of the Stock Exchange. It is this indisputable fact that makes the dismissive attitude of so many people towards regular investment on the stock market so surprising.

After all, when you come to retire, you expect to do so in comfort, thanks to your pension. And when you make a claim on your insurance policy you fully expect the sharks to settle up. But what do you imagine the trustees of your pension fund, or the managers of your insurance company have been doing with your money in the meantime? They sure as eggs haven't been trotting round to the building society on the corner with it each month. If they had, your nest-egg would have shrunk considerably and they would be out of a job. Instead they've been investing it, with a large proportion of it directed towards the world's stock markets.

So even if you are fairly hostile towards the idea of the stock market, you almost certainly do have a vested interest in the fate of the Stock Exchange. As the role of the private investor in the stock market has been steadily declining, so the savings of the great British public have become increasingly institutionalised. As the chart shows, back in 1957 when the private investor was dominant the institutions cowered in their caves, controlling as they did less than a fifth of the shares quoted on the stock market. But the dinosaurs have triumphed, growing in size and influence until, at the last count, over 60% of UK shares were owned by these vast, impersonal institutions. The biggest investors in the land aren't individuals, they are bodies such as the National Coal Board and British Telecom Pension Funds. They are

OWNERSHIP OF UK QUOTED SHARES

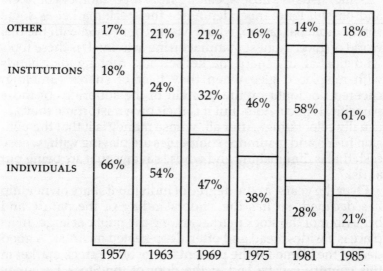

STOCK EXCHANGE, P&D

immensely powerful, with total assets of well over £250 billion; a decade ago they controlled less than twenty billion. Greatly assisted over the years by tax advantages denied to us ordinary mortals, a handful of big investing institutions are among the greatest powers in the land.

The shares these giants own in their portfolios may not have your name on them, but they are yours nonetheless. It is your money they are investing, but you try telling them what to do with it and see where it gets you.

The public disdain for the stock market

'It is Enterprise which builds and improves the world's possessions . . . if Enterprise is afoot, Wealth accumulates whatever may be happening to Thrift; and if Enterprise is asleep, Wealth decays, whatever Thrift may be doing . . . the engine which drives Enterprise is not Thrift, but Profit.'
John Maynard Keynes

Many Britons have a rather snooty attitude towards the City, and the stock market in particular. They have no objection to money *per se*, but find the City's wanton interest in it rather improper. The attitude still remains widespread in Britain that money isn't really a suitable subject for discussion.

Some, usually those speaking from a position of complete and blissful ignorance, denounce the stock market as some sort of capitalist casino, which has no connection with the real world of good, honest manufacturing activity. It is these fools who gloat at any sharp market setback, rubbing their hands with misplaced glee when they hear of shares tumbling, cheered no doubt by the thought of the sufferings of those parasitical speculators. But it is their own misfortune they are usually celebrating. After all, whose money is it that the pension funds and insurance companies are playing with, whose cash that is diminishing and whose savings that are being put at risk?

Over the years, as the degree of individual share ownership has declined, so has the understanding of the nature and behaviour of the stock market among the public at large. In its place is a widespread and often deep-seated mistrust. A good deal of the blame for the present image of the stock market in this country can be laid at the door of the Stock Exchange itself. Frightened that by making itself conspicuous it would merely draw criticism, the Exchange has generally preferred to maintain a low, if not completely invisible profile. As a result, private investors have often felt unwanted, while the critics of the system have had virtually free rein.

The criticism that the stock market has nothing to do with the hard graft of industry ignores the fact that the manufacturing base in this country was financed and made possible by the stock market. Even the nationalised industries were originally brought into existence by private capital. The majority of British companies rely on the stock market's efficient functioning to raise capital; the government needs it to borrow immense amounts of cash; the institutions need it to safeguard the savers' money which is, through the market, channelled into industry.

The City is accused of harming the economy by investing funds abroad instead of earmarking it for British industry. The UK's overseas assets have risen from 12.5 billion pounds in 1979 when exchange controls were lifted, to something like 90 billion pounds. However, less than a third of this increase came from new investment made by the institutions and others. The rest was pure profit resulting from capital gains and the benefits of exchange-rate movements.

The regular income from this nest-egg is substantial and much of the capital will be brought back to Britain when its investors feel the time is right. By being invested abroad, the wealth of the nation as a whole is far greater than it would have been had the funds remained in the UK. The City – not just the Stock Exchange, but the whole financial sector – is one of the most successful areas of the UK economy, and has been for years. Its place as one of the world's pre-eminent financial centres is extraordinary when you consider Britain's relative decline in virtually every other area. In 1985 our financial institutions earned over £7½ billion overseas, contributing two-thirds of those invisible earnings which do so much to prop up our less healthy trade account. In 1986, the City's overseas earnings even outstripped our income from North Sea Oil. In addition 14% of our national income in 1985 came from financial services, a sector which now employs almost 10% of the UK workforce.

Such considerations matter little to the City's opponents who attack it for its blinkered concentration on the profit motive. In marked contrast to the position in America, profit is still a dirty word in Britain. Somewhere in the same sentence in which the critic spits out the word 'profit', you are also likely to find a reference to that abhorred practice of 'speculation.' In Britain, both words are emotive and derogatory. In America, they're emotive and praiseworthy.

In the United States, profit is the driving force of the economy. So it is here, but few are willing to admit it. It is true that the Americans are all far more besotted with money than we restrained British are – besotted with making it, keeping it and with spending it. Money there means position and power, and in the search for the American Dream the striving for profit is more important than anything else, while entrepreneurs in the transatlantic mould are still fairly rare creatures in Britain and even the most hardened and successful businessman will rarely admit that the justification for his activities is the quest for maximising profit.

This distaste for the baser roots of money extends to, and is often centred upon, the Stock Exchange. After all, what is the rationale behind the stock market if it isn't the maximisation of profit? Rather than soil their hands with good, honest, blood-sweat-and-tears labour, so the argument goes, the denizens of the City prefer instead to make money out of little bits of paper, moving them hither and thither in order to prosper, living like parasites on the backs of those who toil in industry. In fact, the survival and prosperity of much of industry has been made possible only because the companies concerned have been able to raise money on the Stock Exchange. Companies which were already quoted on the stock market used it to raise £5 billion in 1985 and almost £7 billion in 1986.

Yet it is the capitalists who are often accused of undermining the economy, of preventing industry from succeeding, of starving it of funds. And it is the speculators who are always accused of distorting the behaviour of the financial markets – leeches, the lot of them, say their critics.

At this point, I can't resist telling one of my favourite jokes. The Russian leader dies and, even though he has always refused to believe in an afterlife, he is sent to hell. He is given a choice though. He can be sent either to the capitalist hell or to the socialist hell. As you don't get to run the USSR by being dumb, he not unnaturally opts for the capitalist hell. There he suffers the appalling agonies of unbearable heat with blistering flames licking at him constantly.

He pleads to be allowed to transfer to the socialist inferno and finally his request is granted. On arrival, he is bewildered to find the damned relaxing in easy chairs, looking cheerful and content and giving little sign that their souls are in torment. Noticing that the place is pleasantly cool, he asks for an explanation. One of the attendant devils enlightens him: 'Well, comrade, we're waiting for some spare parts for the furnace, we ran out of sulphur last month, haven't had any deliveries of brimstone for a year or so now, and of course you can't get boiling oil for love nor money. But we're forming a committee to see what can be done about it.'

Speculation or investment?

'It is speculation when you lose; investment when you win.'
Anon

On one particular point the critics of the system are perfectly correct. The City does thrive on speculation. The place is over-run with speculators; they ooze from every nook and cranny. But just who are these greed-crazed monsters? In the foreign exchanges, where the speculator undoubtedly holds greatest sway, there are such notorious examples of the breed as Barclays Bank, together with Lloyds, Natwest and Midland; then there are such impetuous and rash companies as British Petroleum, General Electric and ICI; not to forget the governments of such countries as West Germany, the UK and the United States. And let's not leave out one of the sharpest financial speculators of them all – the Soviet Union! Even Communist China is now jumping on the bandwagon, tapping and exploiting the Western capital markets and happy to be doing so.

All are speculators. They might prefer to call themselves investors, but the two are inextricably entwined, for there can be no investment without speculation.

The word 'investment' is rarely used correctly these days. It used to mean 'the sacrifice of certain present value for unknown future value', but somehow the goalposts have since been moved. Many so-called investments nowadays are nothing of the sort. In fact, the safer an investment is claimed to be, the less likely it is to merit the name at all. Correspond-

[11]

ingly, the greater the promised or hoped-for return, the riskier the investment is likely to prove.

It isn't surprising that the correct meaning has become lost in the mists of time. Even the Stock Exchange, whose rulers would, were they in politics, undoubtedly earn the epithet 'wet', tries to play down the element of speculation in its market. This is simply silly, for it reinforces the view that investment and speculation mean separate things and encourages the belief that there is something inherently wrong with the concept and practice of speculation.

The whole American ethic is built upon the concept of speculation; those who are prepared to take risks in the hope of an eventual reward are society's idols. The ideas of financiers being the heroes of films or books – or even, come to that, the villains – must strike many Britons as being faintly ludicrous. Money isn't felt to be interesting enough in Britain. Not so in America, where every self-made millionaire dashes off a 'How to Make a Million' book and promptly makes another. Over the past few years, businessmen and entrepreneurs have regularly topped the best-selling lists in the United States.

The public attitude towards the stock market there is very different. It is accepted as an integral part of the economic fabric of the nation, not some alien creature preying off it. Nearly one in three of all adult Americans directly owns shares and, unlike their British counterparts, they actively trade them. The stock market there is a matter of national concern. Every news bulletin carries the latest information from Wall Street. In fact, several TV and radio channels carry nothing else. The market is discussed everywhere as avidly as middle-class Britons discuss house prices. The market-orientated Yank not only buys and sells shares, but is quite happy to buy shares with borrowed money and may even commit himself to selling shares he doesn't yet own. Speculating is as American as blueberry pie.

The element of risk in investment

'Jesus Saves'   (Grafitto)
'. . . and Moses Invests'   (Later addition)

Although Britons spend more time and money on what is generally called investment than ever before, we are still a nation terrified of risk. The uncertainty of the stock market's behaviour is the principal reason most savers shun it. After all, you can never know with certainty from day to day what your investment will be worth.

Instead we favour the 'safer' investments such as National Savings and the building society. At least they tell you exactly how much your money will earn. Its proponents argue they must therefore be far less risky. Unfortunately that isn't usually true. Such investments rarely provide sufficient protection for capital; building society deposits have proved to be one of the worst possible investments over the years, failing to keep pace with rising prices, and leading to a sharp reduction in the real value of capital left there for any great time.

All investments are, to a greater or lesser extent, a trade-off between risk and return. The least risky thing you can do with your money is to stuff it into a mattress, providing you can keep it safe from the attentions of moths and burglars. But however secure it is against physical attacks, it won't be proof against the ravages of inflation; in fact it will earn you a negative real return because it will steadily decline in purchasing power.

Building societies offer to give you interest on any money you deposit with them and find favour with millions of investors, including many non-taxpayers who don't even realise that basic rate income tax is deducted from their savings. Yet although you know each day how much interest your money will earn, you don't know what the rate will be in a month or in a year's time. You are also taking on some risk by giving a building society your cash. Although the institutions themselves must seem safe enough, that safety rests solely on the maintenance of public confidence. And building societies take quite extraordinary risks with their savers' money when you think about it. Their *raison d'être* is to provide home loans and they do this with their depositor's money. In an effort to compete, they are sometimes less than cautious about who they lend to and how much they are willing to advance. They also place some of their funds on the 'speculative' money markets where, it is hoped, they will earn more than the rate of interest they are promising their depositors.

Those depositors expect to be able to call back their money at any time, but in the event of a 'run' on a building society there is insufficient cash to match the figures in more than a few of their passbooks.

An understanding of the perils of leaving your cash with an institution that specialises in 'lending long, borrowing short' would come quickly to those woebegone investors left outside when a society shuts its doors. There is no way all depositors can be satisfied at once. Much of the money has been lent to home owners. Mortgages would need to be called in to pay back savers, homes repossessed and then sold. That would take an enormous time and have a catastrophic effect upon the housing market.

Of course that is an extreme example. The building societies that have run into trouble have usually been bailed out by the others, terrified that a panic might spread through the whole system. American savers have not always been so lucky over the past few years. Several of their 'savings and loans' have run into difficulties through imprudent lending. The worst may never happen in Britain, but that does not mean that there isn't a risk inherent in getting your extra return on your capital. The new powers given to building societies to make them more like banks only increase the potential risks. The banks, of course, take quite extraordinary gambles with their client's money, lending it to Latin American countries even though they realise they are very unlikely ever to have earlier loans paid back. This imprudence is financed to a great extent by customers giving the banks their money for free by leaving it gathering dust, but no interest, in current accounts.

The whole structure rests upon investors' trust and faith. This is true also of the savings we plough into life assurance and pension funds. The return expected is greater than that offered by a building society and to achieve that return our money is subject to an even greater risk. As you now know, your savings with these institutions are channelled in large part into the stock market. To reduce the risk to you, they won't pay all the money they make straight out, but keep a surplus as a cushion during any future lean years.

The surpluses of the pension funds and of the life assurance companies reduce the risk to you; even in times of declining markets there should still be plenty in the pot. Of course that reduction of risk tends to mean that the total return to you is also somewhat smaller than it would otherwise be.

There is thus some element of risk in every investment. The ones with the greatest risk tend, over time, to be the ones which give the greatest return, although that obviously can't hold true all the time.

It is probable that savers have lost much of the interest in the stock market that they once had because many of them are now simply too frightened to contemplate the uncertainties involved. They would rather somebody else made all the difficult investment decisions for them; if someone else is looking after their money investors can easily put to the back of their mind the thought that there is any risk involved. But the saver who believes that by giving his money to a stranger to manage he is playing safe, has his head in the sand and is too timid to admit responsibility for his own cash. At least if something untoward happened to his money, he can blame the building society, or the bank, or the insurance company, or his pension fund managers and trustees. It won't get him his money back, but it might make him feel a bit better.

The desire by savers for absolute safety often leads them into some very rash investments. They get involved in very risky ventures because some less than upright salesman guarantees them a fabulous return on their money way in excess of anything that they can get elsewhere. They fall for it hook, line and sinker without asking themselves what the salesman is doing with their cash in order for him to make all that money and a bit more on top for himself. As often as not, they find out only once the company has gone bust or departed for sunnier climes. In investment you should be very, very wary of 'guaranteed' returns.

A nation of gamblers

'In gambling the many must lose in order that the few may win.'   George Bernard Shaw

It is odd that the British are so averse to the idea of risk in investment, so unwilling to speculate to accumulate, for we, after all, are a gambling nation. 'Having a bit of a flutter' is a national pastime, if not a disease. A massive six billion pounds is said to be wagered in Britain every year. By way of comparison, that is even more than the net amount all the giant pension funds and insurance companies together put into shares on the UK Stock Exchange each year!

Gambling has an air of respectability that the members of the Stock Exchange must envy. How peculiar that their contribution to the efficient functioning of British business life should be frowned upon, while betting seems to meet with general approval. It is even stranger when you realise that the punters have to lose in the longer-term if the nation's bookmakers, casinos, amusement arcades and bingo halls are to stay in business.

Gambling's respectability is only enhanced by the regular racing 'tips' given on television and radio. Yet those same organisations who help to line the bookie's pockets by promoting gambling on the airwaves and who, by tipping, let him know in advance which horses the punters are likely to bet on, would never dream of allowing anything so salacious as stock market 'tips' into the ether. Heaven forbid that anyone should receive advice on such things on air and use some of their money to back British industry. Good honest gambling is all right though, especially with the authorities. Like cigarette smoking, it will never meet with governmental disapproval while it keeps bringing in revenue to the Exchequer.

2
THE STOCK EXCHANGE

Why invest on the stock market?

*'A youth and middle age spent on the London Stock
Exchange had left Lester Carmody singularly broad-minded.
He had to a remarkable degree that precious charity which
allows a man to look indulgently on any financial project,
however fishy, provided he can see a bit in it for himself'.*
P. G. Wodehouse, *Money for Nothing,* 1928

I could give you several reasons why you, as a solid, respectable citizen might consider investing in the stock market. I
could tell you how the Exchange exists to provide capital for
British business, how it is responsible for the very existence of
most of the country's largest companies, how it financed the
Industrial Revolution, how it made possible the construction
of Britain's infrastructure – the railways, canals, water, gas,
electricity – and how it has helped in the development of our
oil industry. I could tell you how the government relies on the
Stock Exchange, borrowing enormous sums of money by
selling gilt-edged stock there, how the local authorities also
tap the market for funds, and how taxes and rates would be
unpleasantly higher if they weren't able to do so.

But this would not provide you with a compelling argument for investing in the market. Convincing you of the
public service the Stock Exchange performs is not going to
have you reaching for your chequebook so that you can show,
in some small way, your appreciation of the market's contribution to Britain. At least I hope it doesn't. We can be thankful
of the role the Stock Exchange has played, and continues to
play, in the development of the economy, but that is no
reason to be rash and foolhardy with our hard-earned capital.

There is, however, one compelling reason why it would
have made good sense for you to have invested in the stock
market over the years; a reason so compelling and simple that
it is rather surprising that everyone isn't playing the market.
Investment in shares has, for the best part of the century,

been immensely profitable. It has had its ups and downs, its indifferent, bad and horrific years, but these have been offset by a greater number of satisfactory and stupendous years. Short-term investment has proven to be every bit as risky as one might have expected, but the investor with the longer time-horizon will have good cause for feeling satisfied with the stock market.

That holds true even when the effect of inflation is taken into account, as of course it should be in all investment calculations. Since 1918 the *average real return* on UK shares, or equities as they are also known, has been a massive 7% per annum. If that doesn't sound a lot, think again. It is seven per cent even after the effects of inflation are taken into account. Seven per cent on average, even if you were unfortunate enough to have held shares during the stock market crash of 1973 and '74.

If you had played safe in 1946 and invested £1,000 in the building society, that money would, if left untouched since,

FUNDS INVESTED IN EQUITIES & BUILDING SOCIETY SHARES WITH NET INCOME REINVESTED

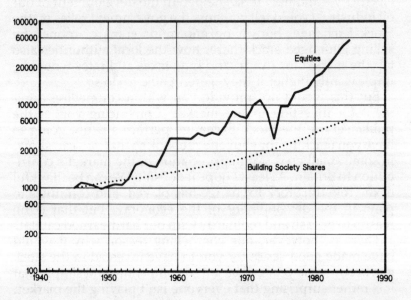

SOURCE: BARCLAYS DE ZOETE WEDD

have risen to £7,210 by the beginning of 1987. On the stock market, however, a basic-rate taxpayer would have seen his £1,000 grow over the same period to £83,977.

Once inflation is brought into the picture, the building society investor's position looks even less rosy, for that money would have shrunk to just half of what it was worth in 1945. In real terms, the stock market investor ended up with 5½ times his original stake.

If Personal Equity Plans had been in existence in 1945, freeing investors from the iniquity of having to pay income tax on their dividend income, that same £1,000 would have mushroomed to £167,000, assuming (ha!) no dealing costs.

With hindsight, it is clear that we would all have done very well by the stock market. Unfortunately we can't invest our present capital using hindsight and no-one can guarantee what the behaviour of the stock market will be in the future. There are times when it is more sensible to hold investment funds in the form of 'cash', when the interest received on it outweighs the expected return from shares. The building society should not always be spurned by alert investors, but they ought to be aware of its limitations as a long-term home for their money.

Yesterday's stock market

> 'In the evening, Lupin, who was busily engaged with a paper, said suddenly to me: "Do you know anything about chalk pits, Guv?" I said: "No, my boy, not that I'm aware of." Lupin said: "Well, I give you the tip; chalk pits are as safe as Consols, and pay six per cent at par." I said rather a neat thing , viz: "They may be six per cent at par, but your pa has no money to invest." Carrie and I both roared with laughter. Lupin did not take the slightest notice of the joke.'
> George & Weedon Grossmith, Diary of a Nobody

The stock market is generally thought to be rather a dry and dull place, with those characteristics rubbing off onto those who work there. Stockbrokers, along with most of the other denizens of the City, are often considered a social liability, believed to possess a conversational ability ranking on a par with officials of the Inland Revenue.

Whatever the popular opinion of the Stock Exchange and

its inhabitants now, the market has certainly not been lacking in interesting characters in the past. Indeed, so colourful were many contributors to the Stock Exchange's history that some of the present incumbents would no doubt prefer not to be reminded of their exploits. They forget that it was the behaviour of the most disreputable scoundrels who made necessary the tightening up of the rules of the Exchange into a code of which most present members are rightly proud.

To a very great extent we owe the might of the British Empire to the invention of 'shares'. They originated over 400 years ago in the days of merchant venturers, galleons and Good Queen Bess. Early voyages of trade and discovery proved extremely expensive to finance and although they frequently benefitted the Crown, Queen Elizabeth was not going to dig into her pocket if, with only a little arm-twisting, the London merchants would provide the cash instead.

The merchants wanted the benefits from trade, but were loath to take on excessive risk. Although such expeditions could bring enormous wealth, many ships sent out from England with high hopes were simply never heard of again and the steadily mounting cost of such voyages made it ever more difficult for one merchant, no matter how wealthy, to finance them.

The origins of the Stock Exchange lie in the solution to the problem hit upon by the merchant-venturer Sebastian Cabot in 1553. He founded the first known 'company' in which public shares were issued. The aim of the 'Mysterie and Companie of the Merchant Adventurers for the Discoverie of Regions, Dominions, Islands and Places unknowen' was to seek out the Northeast Passage which led, so they believed, to the Orient and the Indies.

The company fitted out three ships in the hope that at least one would survive the trip; only one did. To defray the cost of the expedition among the London merchants who sponsored it, the necessary sum of six thousand pounds was split into shares of twenty-five pounds each 'lest any private man should be too much oppressed or charged'. Instead of discovering the Orient, they discovered Russia and the company thrived, going into the history books as the first 'joint-stock company' where the owners were not necessarily those who ran it, but whose capital was employed in return for a share in the profits of the firm.

There can have been little aversion to risk capital in those days, for the Muscovy Company, as it was renamed, turned out to be the first of many such bodies including the Turkey Company, the East India Company and the Hudson's Bay Company. They opened up for trade places such as Persia, the South Seas, Japan, India, the Spice Islands, and of course America, sparking off a long and golden era for British trade.

Providing a company didn't founder, it made more sense to keep the share structure in place all the time, rather than re-form companies for each expedition. Gradually dealings began in the shares, for those who had subscribed in the initial stages might want to sell out, while there might be others who regretted missing out on the setting up of a company and who wanted to participate later on. Over the two centuries following the conception of the Muscovy Company a market in stocks and shares gradually arose. It was centred on Threadneedle Street, which is still the base for the Stock Exchange.

There was no Exchange as such then. Transactions were carried out in the various coffee-houses that littered the City. There you could find out what enterprises were starting up or already in existence and find someone who would sell you, or buy from you, shares in those companies. The present generation of stockbrokers hasn't completely forgotten its origins. The most famed of the coffee-houses, Jonathan's, has lent its name to the members' bar at the present Stock Exchange while another, Garraway's, is now the name of a popular City wine bar.

During this period of development, companies were set up for other purposes than foreign trade – mining, armaments, water supply and provisioning, for instance, 'The Governor and Company of Adventurers of England trading into Hudson's Bay', or the Hudson's Bay Company, beloved of *Boy's Own* adventure stories, was set up in 1668. It is still quoted on the Stock Exchange today, making it the oldest existing listed company, though its operations are now run from Canada.

In 1694, the Bank of England was set up by London merchants, again as a joint-stock company. Its purpose was to lend money to the state and act as a national bank. It continued to perform this role as a private company until 1946, for it was only then that it was brought into public ownership.

Most interestingly, perhaps, 1694 was also the year of the wonderfully named Million Adventure. Parliament wanted to borrow one million pounds from the public, which it did by offering ten-pound 'tickets' to the Adventure, a form of lottery. There was £40,000 a year to be given away in prize money but irrespective of this bounty, the Adventure paid 10% interest for sixteen years. In some respects it was a little like the more modern premium bonds except that your capital was not returned to you. This slightly disreputable-sounding method of raising funds was the origin of what we know now as the National Debt.

The development of the stock market took its most considerable knock in 1720, the year of the greatest of the scandals the market has had to endure. The 'Governor and Company of Merchants of Great Britain trading to the South Seas and other parts of America, and for encouraging the Fishery' had been set up in 1711 by the Chancellor of the Exchequer as a means of discharging the National Debt. It was originally intended that the company establish trade with South America, but the South Seas company lost money from the word go. This wasn't, unfortunately, made clear to the public, who poured their money into it. Its semi-official status no doubt encouraged them to support it, and they did so like no other company before or since, at least until British Gas came along. Instead of ceasing to trade as any insolvent company ought to do, its board, a mixture of fools and scoundrels, pulled in more and more cash by offering ever more shares. And so the 'bubble' swelled.

By 1717, the South Seas Company was valued at twelve million pounds. This was hardly chickenfeed, being double the value of the Bank of England and three times that of the United East India Company.

Becoming ever more desperate to keep afloat, in 1720 the directors planned to merge the National Debt with the South Seas Company. Little serious thought appeared to be given by the public to the common sense of the idea; they were too busy ploughing their money into it. The price of the shares seemed to show that they were right in doing so, for they rose from £129 in January of that year to £1,000 in July, buoyed up by the incredible demand. At one stage, it is thought that almost half of all the country's investments were in that one insolvent company. Like even the most skilfully blown bubble, however, it had eventually to burst. An insolvent company cannot go on taking in money for ever. The price of the shares crashed, plummetting to £174 in September and dropping as low as £124 by December.

Almost overnight shares lost their respectability as thousands of punters lost most of their savings. The loss of confidence was made worse by the fact that many of those connected with the South Seas Company managed to sell out near the top, an early example of insider trading. It wasn't as popular then as now for the bosses of defunct companies to abscond to the Costa del Sol, and the directors found most of their estates confiscated, while the Chancellor of the Exchequer was even imprisoned in the Tower of London. The whole episode left a nasty taste in the public's mouth that was not to disappear until after the onset of the Industrial Revolution.

The affair did not stop the government from refining its methods of raising money from the public. The lottery method slipped into abeyance (until revived in 1956 through Ernie), and as the eighteenth century progressed, gilt-edged securities took their place, with the government borrowing money and promising in return to pay a certain amount of interest each year. The most renowned of these, Consols, became part of every investor's portfolio. According to Alan Jenkins, in *The Stock Exchange Story*, 'the Victorians believed in them as they believed in God, the Queen and the empire'. At least they were backed by the government, and lacked the speculative tinge that had burnt so many fingers earlier.

By the beginning of the nineteenth century the populace had largely forgotten about the South Sea Bubble. Shares were back in fashion as the most popular means of raising capital for an enterprise. Dealings in stocks and shares had been centralised as early as 1773 in a house in Threadneedle Street, with the brokers attempting to shrug off the image of a profession that did all its business in coffee-houses. It was not until 1801 that they built their first ever 'Stock Exchange' but already by then they were trying to distance themselves both physically and in the public's eye from the more 'creative' sort of broker who tended to bring the profession into disrepute.

During the Napoleonic Wars there were several panics, both into and out of stocks, depending on the nature of the rumours. It is from this time that one of the more famous stock market stories dates. Communications were poor and nervousness was at a peak when the market got to hear of the commencement of a gigantic battle at a little place called Waterloo. The Rothschilds, pan-European traders of some standing, had a messenger system second to none. When their dealers came onto the market floor, looking gloomy, unease spread like wildfire. The Rothschilds started to sell what looked to be all the shares they owned, presumably because they had heard of a victory for Napoleon. Their appearance caused a market collapse as everyone tried to unload their stocks. Knowing full well of the British victory, the Rothschilds merely bided their time and when the market was at its lowest ebb, stepped in and bought everything in sight. The manoeuvre is said to have vastly swelled the already substantial Rothschild fortune, but sadly there is little evidence that the story has any truth in it. That won't stop it being passed on to each new generation of stockbrokers, apocryphal or not; good yarns are always admired in the profession.

The Industrial Revolution was the occasion for another investment boom, this time in canal and railway shares. Many, if not most, of the shares in these new companies were dealt in outside the Stock Exchange. The members of the Exchange were wary indeed of becoming involved in any new ventures that weren't solidly respectable for, in public relations terms, their standing in the country was at a pretty low ebb. Nevertheless, there were fresh scandals, as was only to be expected at a time when projects would be hatched to lay rails to hamlets with little more than a man and his dog in residence. Many schemes were substantially over-funded, with more money being raised that could possibly be needed for ventures which were pretty unsound to begin with.

The greatest railway promoter of them all, George Hudson, was a man whose vision blinded him to the need or the wisdom of keeping his books straight. When the great Railway Bubble burst at the end of 1845, Hudson controlled nearly a third of Britain's 5,000 miles of railway tracks. While it is undoubtedly true that he left a legacy consisting of much of the present rail network in this country, he also left a great many small investors a good deal less well off and regretting that they had ever heard of Mr Hudson.

Despite such setbacks, the Exchange's reputation grew throughout the nineteenth century as it became apparent to investors that it was rather safer to invest there than with those dealers operating outside its authority; the Stock Exchange's phrase for the shady characters who took advantage of unwary investors was 'bucket shop', which has since passed into the language with a rather broader meaning.

The most important boon to those small savers wanting to

invest in shares was the adoption of limited liability which, after early strong resistance, had become fairly commonplace by the end of the 19th century. Before this, if a company failed, an investor might be called on to provide extra cash to fund that company's liabilities. When the unlimited City of Glasgow Bank collapsed in 1878, for instance, around two hundred spinsters with an average holding of £240 in shares were each asked to provide another six and a half thousand pounds! A company with limited liability provided a much-needed safety-net for investors; henceforward all they could lose was the amount they had already committed, which is still the situation today.

As the new century dawned, there were already listed on the Stock Exchange many companies whose names are familiar today; BSA, John Brown, Dunlop, Rover, Cunard, Bass, Ind Coope, British Electric Traction, Harrods, Rolls-Royce, Claridges Hotel, Courtaulds and Explosives Traders (now ICI). The development of the Stock Exchange this century has been rather more sedate and the number of scandals rather fewer and less dramatic, although the Marconi case, another affair of mysteriously profitable dealings in shares by those 'in the know', did involve the up-and-coming young Cabinet minister, David Lloyd George.

With a boom in the market after that War To End All Wars, it would have been surprising if there hadn't been a setback for shares at some stage. When Wall Street crashed in 1929, the showbiz newspaper, *Variety*, marked the occasion with one of the most famous headlines in the history of journalism: 'Wall Street Lays an Egg.' The UK market, too, took a dive, dropping by almost 50% in three years, much to the chagrin of many first-time investors who had been drawn into the market by seven years of rising prices.

It wasn't until the early 70's, however, that Britain's own egg was well and truly laid. 1973 and '74 was the time of property collapses, of the secondary banking crisis, of a miners' strike and of the three-day week. Many UK shares plunged to just a fraction of their previous values and for a time it seemed there might be no end to the market's slide earthward, with the prospect of widespread bankruptcies in British industry a terrifying possibility. The trough came just before Christmas 1974 when, at a meeting whose details still remain cloudy, a group of leading financial institutions decided to buy shares aggressively. This sparked off a rise almost as sharp as the earlier fall, as confidence returned to the market at the start of what turned out to be more than a decade in which share prices rose almost continually. The Stock Exchange issued no medals for those veterans who survived 1974, but they still haunt every stockbroking firm, reminding the cocky, brash, youngsters that they have yet to experience a 'real bear market', of the sort that puts hairs on the chest.

It wasn't all that long ago. It may never happen again, but it should act as a reminder to all investors that the whole system is founded upon collective confidence and little else.

The modern stock market

'All work and no play makes Jack a dull boy – and Jill a wealthy widow.'   Evan Esar

I don't suppose I am alone amongst those who know the City in believing that while its financial markets have steadily become more sophisticated and exciting, the Square Mile itself has been becoming even duller. There seems less room these days for the more florid characters and less time to be spared for horseplay. The work itself is far more involved than ever before and is taken a good deal more seriously; with both competition and volatility on the increase, there is no room in today's City for those who don't pull their weight. But in the days of rather slower communications than we have now, members of the market frequently found attractions other than dealing in stocks and shares to occupy their time. In 1920 for instance, the ruling council had to ban the playing of roulette on the market floor. Many of the less successful members would also double as bookmakers. Time was less important in the business of share dealings then and older members still recall the days when there were comfortable armchairs in the market available to assist in the digestion of lunch, and when all present in the Exchange used to sing 'Jerusalem' at the end of every account. Markets moved at a much more sluggish pace, and there was less chance of missing something by being absent from one's post. You had to keep a wary eye out though, for practical joking on the market floor was common.

One jape that seems never to have palled for its perpetrators was to find some old buffer relaxing in an easy chair, reading a newspaper. It was but the work of a moment to apply a match to the base of the outside pages. You could be half-way across the market before the rag really caught alight, evading the obvious fury of the old gentleman who suddenly discovered *The Thunderer* had turned into an inferno in his hands.

Dress was more stylish in the market's earlier days too. While there are still some dapper dressers around now, there are few hats – not even bowlers – to be seen any more. Some dealers in the gilt-edged market sport toppers to this day, but they serve only to highlight the shabbiness of what is beneath them. A senior stockmarket dealer delighted in telling me the tale of one particular top-hatted gentleman of an earlier vintage, who was immensely proud of a splendid example of this headgear which he had just purchased. So proud was he that his colleagues decided generously to go out and purchase for him two more top hats, identical in all respects bar the size; one was a size smaller and one a size larger. They derived endless hours of amusement from beholding the puzzlement of the chap who found that his hat was at one time too big for him, and at another too tight. Their mirth became unrestrained when they discovered that he had eventually consulted his doctor, believing that it was his head that was constantly changing in size!

Occasionally unsuspecting members of the public would wander into the Exchange, no doubt curious about what went on in The House, as it was known. A cry of 'Fourteen Hundred' would go up at the sight of the stranger and the poor chap would be lucky to escape with his trousers. The shout is said to date back to the days when the Exchange had 1,399 members: the 1,400th person therefore had to be an intruder.

Before property fetched such a premium in the Square Mile, and before the architects who built the monstrous blocks that now disfigure its skyline were out of nappies, the City was a vastly different place. Many of the narrow, twisting, alleyways that had been a part of the City for centuries were still there, their pavements scattered with an extraordinary variety of shops. As rents have steadily mounted many of them have had to move on, or close completely. Although there are a few fine old tobacconists, men's outfitters and hairdressing emporia left, the brokers with longer memories still hark back nostalgically to the days when Throgmorton Street had a chemist smack-bang opposite the Exchange that offered comfort for a particularly recurrent complaint; its proprietor, Mr Douch, would mix hangover cures which were apparently invariably efficacious, enabling many a broker to face a day that would otherwise be too horrible to contemplate, and in his own way contributing to the smooth running of the stock market.

Although times were changing and some of this had to rub off on the stock market, a good deal of its character was destroyed at a stroke when the Stock Exchange moved to its new building in 1972. This is one of the more unedifying creations in a hideous panoply of modern architecture that pollutes the City of London. Swathed in dull, grey, concrete from top to bottom this 26-storey blot on the landscape, coffin-shaped from the air, is immensely depressing merely to behold. There are those who feel the stock market's collapse shortly afterwards was in some way related to the new building. At least its title as the worst building in the City has now been taken away from it by the new Lloyds.

Despite the changes being wrought in the City, where the constant search for office space has made the term 'Cubic Mile' seem more appropriate than 'Square Mile', I would still recommend it as a fascinating place to stroll round, either during the hectic working week or at the weekend when it resembles a ghost town, because there are so few residents.

The potential for horseplay in the stock market was very much reduced in the new Exchange building because of the presence of a glass-walled visitors' gallery; a senior partner taking important guests to the market would scarcely be happy to see his members of staff making asses of themselves on the floor below, even if they were only mirroring his behaviour forty years earlier. Yet the gallery proved to be a boon to outsiders wanting to catch a glimpse of what went on inside the Stock Exchange. Before Big Bang you could, from the gallery, see the bustle of share dealings below. The floor is littered with hexagonal 'pitches', which used to be the province of the jobbers – the share wholesalers. The scurrying men, and just occasionally a woman or two, rushing between the pitches, were the stockbrokers' dealers. They were, if they were performing their job conscientiously, trying to find the best dealing price in a share for a client, or perhaps just checking out the price for him.

[28]

The market at times resembled a rather boisterous minor public school. There was a well-defined pecking order on the floor of the 'House' with the unauthorised clerks, or 'bluebuttons' at the bottom of the heap. On their first day at work, these unfortunates would be sent hither and thither in search of prices in such imaginary shares as Venetian Tramways, Icelandic Banana Plantations and Newton and Ridley (the Coronation Street brewery). Anyone who strayed from the norm would be mercilessly teased. Nicknames were common and everyone stuck to the ingrained ritual of The House. There was a strong bond of cameraderie. The market floor was the public school that so many of them never attended, with the major difference in this case that the pupils were in charge.

Even with the viewing gallery open, there were still some pretty rum characters and some flamboyant behaviour to be seen. Take the market dealer who, like any normal commuter, was infuriated when British Rail told him that his train had been cancelled and that the next one to pass through his station wouldn't be stopping. The rest of us would have seethed inwardly, or contented ourselves with grumbling to our similarly furious neighbour. It is unlikely that we would have jumped off the platform and headed off down the tracks, waving our brolly in the air at the approaching through-train as this chap did. I don't believe an umbrella waved from side to side is a signal British Rail teaches its drivers to recognise, but it served its purpose: the train stopped. While it was stationary, the platform emptied of delighted commuters. Our hero was not unnaturally detained on arrival at the terminus, his back bruised from repeated hearty patting from his fellow passengers. By the time he finally arrived for work, word of his great deed had spread right round the market. He was received with the acclaim normally reserved for such momentous events as the relief of Mafeking and transported round the market floor on the shoulders of his comrades, to the amazement of the visitors gaping from the gallery. Thereafter he would frequently be serenaded on the floor by two jobbers, blowing whistles and waving green and red flags.

These days, however, it has all changed. Most people have left the floor and now work from their offices dispersed around the City. The floor is no longer used for trading ordinary shares. The jobbers have become market-makers, sitting in their offices in front of television screens which display the latest prices, doing all their deals over the telephone.

[29]

The dealers too, no longer need to be fleet of foot. There is no more rushing between jobbers' pitches. Everything they need is on the screen in front of them. The new market works pretty efficiently, more so than anyone can have imagined when it was still in the planning stage. But the floor of the Stock Exchange is well nigh deserted by comparison with former times, apart from those boisterous traders in one corner dealing in Traded Options, and it isn't only the old-timers who miss the friendly, more carefree, days.

The creatures of the market

'The trouble with the rat race is that even if you win, you're
still a rat.'   Lily Tomlin

The stereotype stockbroker is a dapper, lean and lengthy gent, bedecked in a pinstripe three-piece suit with immaculately shiny black brogues, a bowler perched on his head and an umbrella over an arm which is also grasping the *Financial Times*; no doubt he will have been to Eton or Harrow and probably Oxford or Cambridge as well. He's upper-class, a rather dim sort but assisted by being born with a silver spoon in his mouth.

That popular image of a stockbroker has faded somewhat over the past couple of years, to be replaced by the picture of a tough, flash, upwardly-mobile, Porsche-driving youngster. This has been helped by the fascination of the media with the lifestyle and telephone number salaries of the new breed of City slickers. Although frequently wildly exaggerated, there is no doubt that salaries have soared in the City in the past few years, with some 25-year-olds being paid sums that would have seemed princely to a senior partner not so long ago, and still seems obscene to many of those outside the Square Mile.

Yet almost everyone in the Square Mile knows that the boom cannot possibly last. The financial conglomerates that have bought up stockbroking and stockjobbing firms have invested fortunes to become big players in the securities industry. Everyone wants to be a major player. But it is not feasible for the UK stock market to support all these new entrants. At the end of the day, the business is profit and if profits are being squeezed because there are too many firms, some are going to have to withdraw or go to the wall. When demand for young dealers was at its peak, the prices paid often seemed crazy. Yet unlike most other areas of the economy, the labour market in the City is very efficient and if demand drops off, salaries will plummet. Much of the remuneration of stockbrokers is in the form of bonusses anyway, which will only be paid out if the firm has had a successful year. With everyone certain from the start that the golden days were numbered, it is hardly surprising if they squeezed from their employers everything they could.

The new breed of dealers working for the big securities houses are very tough and combative. To survive, they need to be very bright. The City is teeming with rats all fighting to win the race. The hours are far longer than they used to be with 7.30 starts, breakfast in the office and 12-hour days now quite common. The rewards for success may be great, but there's little compassion wasted on those who don't come up to scratch.

There are plenty of stockbrokers who have been to public school or Oxbridge, but still more who haven't. In fact, for some time, the more respectable English families looked down on the City. The Stock Exchange was a profession of last resort, almost as bad as going into 'trade'. Now everyone has woken up to the fact that the opportunities and rewards in the Square Mile are quite extraordinary and it has become quite the 'in' place to be.

But education or social standing isn't really terribly important. Securities firms need people who are going to be good at their job and the magic of the old school tie no longer works the wonders it did in the old days. There are people with all sorts of backgrounds working in the City. No-one can afford to carry dead weight on board and so, alongside the rather pukka and refined stockbroker may sit a street-wise East Ender. Both remain in work only because of their quickness of mind and their ability to make instant decisions in which thousands of pounds are at stake. You either have those talents, or you don't – they can't really be taught. The City is an egalitaian society where talent almost always wins out.

The stock market is a market like any other and most brokers are in essence nothing more or less than salesmen. If they weren't in the City, many of them would probably be earning their crust instead as street-traders or as second-hand car dealers. Indeed there are a few who tried their hand at that first. Earlier this century, when the stock market proper shut for the evening, trading would still continue in the surrounding streets; Wall Street was just starting up for the day and for those who wanted to deal in American shares, a street market was necessary. In the days of instant, global, communications, that is no longer needed, but the cries and shouts you hear in one of the big City dealing rooms are virtually indistinguishable from those of the traders in Petticoat Lane just a few hundred yards away.

There are many stockbrokers who aren't part of the massive financial supermarkets, who toil in smaller firms both within the Square Mile and in the rest of the country. Although they use the same modern trading methods, their lifestyles are not so frenetic as the young turks. They are frequently far more interested in the private client than the bigger firms and, to be perfectly honest, rather better at serving his or her needs. They are the remaining link between the old world of service and courtesy and the modern one of speed and competition.

3
SHARE TALK

Just what is the stock market?

'In no sense is the stock market a great gambling enterprise like a lottery. But it is an exercise in mass psychology, in trying to guess better than the crowd how the crowd will behave.' Adam Smith, *The Money Game*, 1968

When discussing the origins of the stock market, we saw that shares were devised as a means for a company to raise capital. As ventures became more and more expensive, it became less likely that any one individual could shoulder the entire cost himself. Companies that otherwise could not have been financed – for this was an age long before banks existed – saw the light of day only because investors agreed to parcel out the necessary finance to get the business going among themselves. Each had a 'share' in that business, a stake in any eventual rewards. If a merchant subscribed for a tenth of the shares in a trading company, he would be entitled to a tenth of the profits that company subsequently made, if it made any at all.

Things haven't changed all that much since 1553. Despite the sophistication and complexities of modern markets, a share is in essence exactly the same thing it has always been; a stake in a company on which an investor hopes to see a positive return for his willingness to take the initial risk. From the company's point of view, the raising of finance by the issuing of shares is an alternative to bank borrowing.

Borrowing from banks has the inconvenience that they demand to be paid back interest at regular intervals and the gall to want the capital eventually returned to them. Shareholders are rather more flexible, and often less demanding; companies don't need to promise them anything in return for their money. Obviously if they expect to attract the necessary funds they do need to dangle some sort of bait in front of them; there are only so many mugs in this world who are happy to hand over their money without ever expecting to see it back. So a company will usually give shareholders a dividend each year, a few pence paid out on each share which is taken from the firm's profits. The advantage to the company of this method over bank borrowings is that in lean years shareholders can be given less than in times of plenty, or even given nothing at all. As they are part-owners of the business, they should prefer to see what money there is available retained to help the company succeed, rather than see it founder because it has paid out too much in dividends.

Despite the belief of many of the City's critics, most shareholders take a long-term view of the companies in which they are involved, even if companies are sometimes irritated at having to report so frequently to them. It is often the banks, rather than the shareholders, who tend to panic in times of crisis, foreclosing the minute there is some doubt about a company's future in case their money should vanish. On the other hand, unlike borrowing from the bank, a company has to live with its shareholders for ever; at least it can pay a bank to get it off its back.

For the companies who have their shares listed on the stock market, the ability to use it to raise capital by the issuing of shares is the most important of its two main roles. Nearly £5 billion was raised by companies making their debut on the stock market in 1985. Those know-alls wishing to display their intimate knowledge of the subject may refer to this facility as the Primary Market.

But the raising of capital isn't the function that people usually think of when talking about the stock market. They are more likely to be referring to the trading of shares, the visible transactions we used to see being made from the gallery, or on television whenever the *Financial Times Index* has soared or plum·neted. This is known as the market's secondary role, and it is the one which occupies most of its time. In 1986, almost £200 billion worth of UK shares were traded on the Exchange with an average of 30,000 deals done every day. That has been boosted considerably by Big Bang, since when there have been days with over 60,000 deals done and more than £2 billion worth of shares traded.

It is a common misconception that when shares are bought or sold, companies in some way benefit or suffer from that activity. In fact, once a company has launched itself onto the Stock Exchange the antics of its share price may leave it completely indifferent. It already has its money, which was raised when the shares were initially sold. The gyrations of the share price may amuse the company, bemuse, irritate or please it, but unless it returns to the stock market to ask for more cash, it may find all that activity to be totally irrelevant. Once the shares begin trading, anyone who decides to buy them will be purchasing them not from the company, but effectively from someone who already holds them. For each buyer there has to be a seller. The company doesn't get any more money just because its shares have changed hands on the Stock Exchange. The only people who benefit from the transactions there, apart from either the buyer or the seller, are the stockbrokers, market-makers and, of course, the government.

If this is so, it seems a sensible question to ask what is the point of all that frantic activity? This is a question which is frequently levelled by those critics of the stock market who wish to prove that the activities of the Exchange are parasitical and unrelated to the real world of graft and industry. Unfortunately for them, it is a very easy question to answer. The trading of shares, or the Secondary Market, is essential to the existence of the Primary Market. Would anyone have considered buying shares in British Telecom, TSB, or British Gas if they knew they would not be able to sell them later on the stock market? Imagine the difficulties shareholders would face if they had to find buyers for their shares themselves. Even if someone was found willing to buy them, the seller would have to haggle over price and arrange all the necessary paperwork.

The Stock Exchange acts as a central marketplace, a place where buyers and sellers of shares can find each other easily. Each listed share has a quoted price, which is given every day in the newspapers, so that investors have a pretty fair idea at all times of how much their investments are worth. Without the Secondary Market, companies would find it very tough indeed to raise money by selling shares to the public.

It is an over-simplification, however, to say that once a company has raised its capital, dealings in its shares don't affect it. Even after its initial launch it can return to ask its shareholders for more cash, which they may or may not choose to give. The traditional method of doing this is through what is called a 'rights issue', although the new-fangled 'vendor placing' is fast growing in importance. In 1985, companies whose shares were already trading on the stock market raised an extra £5 billion from investors, while in 1986 the figure was nearly £7 billion.

Companies can also use their shares as a sort of currency, almost like cash. For the stock market places a value on each firm that has its shares quoted there, giving the perceived opinion of what the business is worth. At the end of 1986, all the UK shares listed on the Stock Exchange were valued at £1,500 billion.

Suppose Morpheus Engineering – a rather dull manufacturer in a sleepy corner of the stock market – has ten million shares in issue and each is quoted at a pound (though somehow things are never quite that simple in real life); then it is said to have a market capitalisation, or value, of ten million pounds, i.e. the number of shares multiplied by the price of each. Companies that are expanding can utilise the value the market places on their shares by offering them instead of cash when they want to buy another company. The success story of Saatchi and Saatchi, growing from an insignificant little ad agency to the world's largest in just a few years, owes much to the way in which the company was able to use its shares to buy up other companies. This was only made possible because investors on the stock market valued the shares so highly, and persisted in that opinion for most of the time that it was expanding. If Saatchi had had to use real money all the time, such phenomenal growth would have been considerably more difficult to achieve.

Of course, the converse of this is true as well. If the stock market places a low value on a company by shunning its shares, that company may find itself vulnerable to a takeover bid. If over the years the share price of Morpheus engineering slipped to just twenty pence, then its market capitalisation would have fallen to two million pounds. The management might prefer spending more of their time at their club and on the golf course than trying to put the business to rights. Another company, however, might find Morpheus a very tempting prospect at its depressed level, feeling that by injecting more dynamic management it could be made to thrive, or simply reckoning that by buying Morpheus it could gets its hands on assets such as land and buildings that it thought undervalued.

It isn't only the investors who take risks when shares are floated on the stock market. It is the companies as well.

What is the point of owning a share?

'"What's the market gonna do, sir?" "Fluctuate, my boy, just fluctuate."'
J. Pierpont Morgan and an elevator operator in
conversation

If you own any shares in a company you are, in effect, a part owner of that company. It matters not a jot whether you have ten shares or ten million; the fact that you're a shareholder means that some part of the business is yours. That is the case even if you weren't one of the founder shareholders. Shares listed on the stock market are easily transferable. Should one of the original owners of the business want to sell out, he is unlikely to find any willing buyers unless the purchaser has the same rights and benefits as the seller. You may feel that if you subscribed for shares when the company first came to the stock market then you should in some way be viewed more favourably than some upstart who merely joined in the fun later on, when any fool could see the attractions of the business that you spotted right at the beginning, but things don't work like that. The only exceptions are some of the large privatisation issues which offer the original shareholders bonus shares if they hold on to their shares for a certain period, usually three years.

We've already seen that share ownership entitles you to a proportionate share of a company's profits; usually most of the profits are ploughed back into the business but a successful firm will pay out the rest to shareholders in the form of dividends. When things are going well, the shareholder's lot is a happy one. The company will raise its dividends each year and the share price ought to rise roughly in step.

In addition to this you are, as an owner of a share of the company, entitled to a say in the way its affairs are run. It may appear that large companies are run by the managing director, the chairman, and the board of directors. But they are merely acting on behalf of the shareholders who appointed them. The shareholders aren't able to involve themselves in the day-to-day running of the business; it may be one of only many investments for them. It is far more sensible for them to find someone trustworthy and efficient to manage the company on their behalf. However much it might like to forget it, the board of directors is always answerable for its actions to

[37]

the company's shareholders. Each limited company must send reports on the state of its affairs regularly to shareholders and must hold a General Meeting of shareholders at least once a year to explain its actions and be prepared to be quizzed upon them.

It isn't only directors who fail to understand the relationship between the two. There are always shareholders at the British Telecom AGM, for instance, who complain to the board about the increase in the price of telephone calls and who ask if the company is not making enough profit as it is? They don't seem to grasp that the profit BT makes belongs to the shareholders who own the company.

The most prevalent sort of shares in the UK are known as 'ordinary' shares. That is no comment on their quality, though the Americans call their equivalent 'common' shares, which sounds even worse. They have the lowest ranking in a firm's capital structure. Should a company fail for any reason and be wound up, it is the holders of ordinary shares, the owners of the business, who are the last to see any money. Indeed, this is true even while a company prospers. The company's employees, its creditors, its bankers and those who hold loan stock and preference shares; all these have a prior call on the company's money. The ordinary shareholders are entitled to what is left after everyone else's claims have been met.

That might not sound very satisfactory but, if a company is thriving, what is left after the others have taken their share may be very substantial indeed. Shareholders have to accept the potential risk involved in their chosen form of investment if they expect to participate in those greater returns. The same company may also have issued a fixed-interest loan stock, borrowing capital from investors as with shares, but in this case promising to pay back a fixed level of interest each year. In times of hardship, the owners of that loan stock may be doing rather better than the holders of ordinary shares. But however well the company may do, all the loan-stock holders will see is that same level of interest, year in and year out. They will not reap the rewards if the company becomes phenomenally successful. The beneficiaries of this success will be the ordinary shareholders, whose risking of their capital made it all possible.

If disaster does strike, then initially shareholders may miss their dividends, as a company tries to conserve its cash to see

[38]

it through. If the firm actually goes bust, then whatever assets are remaining will go to the company's creditors first. Only when they have all been satisfied will shareholders see a penny, assuming there is anything left.

At least every company quoted on the stock market has limited liability, so that shareholders are never putting at risk any more than their original investment. Were a concern not a limited company, then anyone owning a stake of the business would be personally liable for its debts if it were to go under, or trade at a persistent loss. With a limited company, the shareholder can rest assured that he can never be compelled to provide extra funds, unlike the poor spinsters ruined when the City of Glasgow Bank shut its doors (see page 25).

Having said that, very few companies quoted on the stock market ever find themselves in this position. You should, however, always remember that money invested in shares is risk capital and is not backed by any guarantees.

Why do share prices move?

'There are two fools in every market; one asks too little, one asks too much.'
Russian proverb

The day-to-day movement of share prices is perhaps the one aspect of the stock market that puzzles new investors more than any other. After all, why should the price of a share be constantly fluctuating? It all boils down to that most basic of economic laws: the influence of supply and demand. Once a company has issued its shares on the stock market those shares are in limited supply; in our example of Morpheus Engineering, there are ten million in issue. Like other commodities, the greater the demand, the higher the price. A seller of shares not unnaturally wants to get the best possible price for his holding. A potential purchaser would like to pay as little as possible. For every share there is a level at which the needs of buyers and sellers at that moment are perfectly matched. The people making a market in those shares will try to set the price around that level, so that orders to buy and sell are in rough equilibrium.

But however well the needs of buyers and sellers may be matched at an equilibrium price, the attractions of a share change. The price depends upon investor's expectations, their hopes and their fears. If a company is thought to be doing well, producing exceptional profit growth year after year, its shares are likely to be in demand. If it invents a new product, breaks into a new market, takes on new management or if the industry it is involved in suddenly becomes fashionable in the City – all these things might increase the demand for a company's shares. But the sellers who, before conditions changed, had been perfectly happy to sell their Morpheus Engineering shares at fifty pence, say, are hardly going to do so if Morpheus lands a big order to supply their main product, let's call them Thingumajigs, for installation in every civil servant's office in Whitehall. That one order could bump Morpheus' profits up substantially and sellers might change their minds and hang on. They might not sell at fifty pence, nor even at fifty-five, but a few might decide to do so at sixty. By the time the price reaches sixty-five even more potential sellers might be ready to unload their shares, but the buyers waiting in the wings might feel the price has gone high enough and settle for the shares they were able to get hold of at lower levels.

The bright young analysts at various stockbroking firms will have been working out the prospects for Morpheus since they landed the big Thingumajig order from the government. They might conclude that if the government is so keen to have Thingumajigs, then others might want them as well. Once these thoughts start spreading, the price of Morpheus might start moving ahead again. Or alternatively someone might discover after the initial flush of enthusiasm that the government has in fact specified left-handed Thingumajigs, whereas until now Morpheus has only produced right-handed ones, and that the retooling necessary to make left-handed ones will cost Morpheus virtually all the profit they will make on the one order. In that case, the price might well have a relapse.

Sometimes a company can perform exactly as anticipated and yet still see its share price move out of line. British Telecom is an excellent example of this. The popular belief seems to be that BT shareholders have made an absolute killing. True though that may be for those who sold out in the earlier heady days, those investors who stuck with the company for a couple of years may well have rued their tenacity.

Floated at 130 pence, the shares hit a high of 278p in April of 1986. But then thoughts of what competition from Mercury might do to BT's profits – and, even more importantly, the fear of what could happen to BT if Labour returned to power – sent investors running for cover. With too few buyers around willing to take up the shares of a growing number of sellers, the price tumbled 100 pence from its earlier peak.

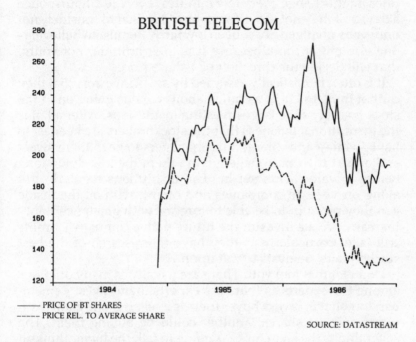

BRITISH TELECOM

—— PRICE OF BT SHARES
----- PRICE REL. TO AVERAGE SHARE

SOURCE: DATASTREAM

The lower line shows how BT's share price performed in relation to the stock market as a whole. Relative graphs are very valuable. If they slope upwards, then a share is performing above the average. If they turn down, then it is doing worse than the general market. This one shows that BT began its fall from favour, not in April of 1986, but rather in the autumn of 1985. From that moment on, one would have done better to have got out of BT than stuck with it, for the mood of the crowd was beginning to turn against the company. Those who missed out on the flotation and who decided to buy BT shares in the market would have done better over the two-year period to have left their money in the building society. Despite this, a survey of BT shareholders in late 1986 found that 80% thought that, in buying shares, they were incurring only a low risk or none at all. Just over a half thought it was no more risky than keeping their money in a building society!

It is important to realise that there is never a 'right' price or a 'wrong' price for a share. The current price is merely a distillation of collective opinion about the company, opinion that can be extremely varied. That opinion is as volatile as that of any crowd, and it will determine the price of a share. That price might change every few minutes, every few hours, once a day, or it may not move for weeks. It is vital to consider, not only your own views about a company, but also what everyone else might think because it is their attitude, not yours, that will decide the direction of a share price.

It is often fatalistically assumed by small investors that they cannot hope to know as much about what is going on in the stock market as the large investing institutions. After all, it is the institutional business that the stockbrokers are keenest to have, wining and dining fund managers to keep them sweet and attract their patronage, giving them the low-down long before private clients get in. The institutions regularly trot along on visits to companies and ought, with all the inside gen they pick up, to be able to forecast with greater certainty than any private investor the future path a company's profits will take, particularly as they have the research of the best stockbrokers' analysts to call upon.

Don't let that fool you. There are usually as many opinions among the experts as there are experts themselves. Remember, too, that for every buyer there is a seller. If one giant institution sells its shares, another could be buying them. The seller thinks the share price is going to fall, the buyer thinks it will rise. Both believe they are right. But one has to be wrong. Only time will tell which chap made the sensible decision and which will regret his actions. The all-powerful, see-everything, know-all institutions can be just as fallible as you or me, and frequently are. Over the past few years, the UK portfolios of most pension funds have performed less well than the All-Share Index, the broadest measure of the market's behaviour. Don't immediately jump to the mistaken conclusion that if the professionals can't do any better, then the private investor doesn't stand an earthly. Think about it. The All-Share Index measures the average performance of over 700 leading shares. If the pension fund managers do worse than that average, then it stands to reason there have to be a good many other people who are beating it. So don't let fear of the so-called professionalism of the institutions keep you away from the market.

4
BIG BANG AND THE PRIVATE INVESTOR

Daddy, what is the Big Bang?

'The Big Bang was such an awesome event to contemplate, being all-embracing in its massiveness, violence and creativity, that physicists might have been forgiven for shrugging it off as a kind of impenetrable chaos.'
Nigel Calder, *The Key to the Universe*

What is the Big Bang? That was the question that everyone working in the City dreaded being asked. The whole thing seemed so complicated that the more one tried to explain it, the more difficult it became to understand. In retrospect, of course, it is far easier to see what the important aspects of Big Bang were than it was at the time.

For four years, until July 1983, the Office of Fair Trading was gunning for the Stock Exchange, accusing it – like various other professions – of numerous restrictive practices, such as the system of fixed commission levels and the admission to the market of Stock Exchange members only. The Exchange mounted an expensive defensive against the OFT's attack, which many of its members expected it to win. However, there was increasing concern that the battle was delaying important reforms which were needed if the Stock Exchange was to meet the challenges of ever more complex international markets and the ever increasing competition from overseas financial institutions.

The Exchange had missed out entirely on the extraordinary growth of the Eurobond market, which has its centre in London. In 1985 the volume of trade in these professional financial instruments was £2.25 billion against the £370 billion of business done in stocks and shares within the Exchange. The rather parochial Stock Exchange rules meant stockbroking firms couldn't join in, while British banks seemed less willing to tackle the new market than overseas banks with active London branches.

In addition, the stockbroking fraternity was concerned that many leading UK shares were already actively traded in America, with over half of the business in ICI, for instance, taking place outside the Stock Exchange. Trading in stocks and shares was becoming increasingly international in scope as technology enabled deals to be made between borders and continents just as easily as within the Square Mile.

The need for a strong European financial market in between the important time zones of the Far East and North America was obvious to the crystal-ball gazers who foresaw the advent of a 'Global Market' in which the securities of big international companies are traded twenty-four hours a day, with the baton being handed from Tokyo to London to New York and back to Tokyo again, following the sun. The government and the Stock Exchange both wanted to ensure that London retained its position as the pre-eminent European financial centre and that the UK financial institutions played a leading role within it, rather than seeing the business taken almost entirely by foreign groups as has been the case with Eurobonds.

So an agreement was reached in July 1983 by which the Government called off the OFT in return for a promise that the Exchange would institute certain internal reforms, including abandoning fixed commissions. The relief among the rank-and-file of Stock Exchange members was short-lived, however, for these seemingly minor concessions set off a chain reaction, bringing about a revolution in Britain's financial markets on which the dust has yet to settle.

Until Big Bang, there was a distinct and unique separation between the roles of stockbroker and stockjobber, a system which was known as 'single capacity'. Despite the OFT's view, it was one which worked very much in the investor's interest. Your stockbroker had no shares to sell you. He would buy them on your behalf from a jobber, a sort of wholesaler of shares who was not allowed to deal with the public directly. As stockbroking firms were not permitted to deal in shares, their investment advice could be relied upon to be dispassionate. Stockbrokers had to compete on service. Price was not a consideration, when commissions were fixed.

If their commission levels were going to be squeezed by competition then many stockbrokers realised that their future income would be insufficient for them to survive unless they, too, could make markets in shares like the jobbers. So the principle of single capacity was abandoned and the Stock

Exchange geared up for 'dual capacity', whereby brokers could not only deal on behalf of investors, but could 'make a book' in shares too. However, to make markets in a competitive environment needs immense amounts of capital and so a rush of marriages took place in the City as banks, insurance companies and the like offered quite extraordinary sums for stakes in the larger broking firms.

As if this wasn't enough, the Stock Exchange also decided that the time had come to abandon its traditional, and admittedly somewhat archaic, methods of dealing and take a leap into the computer age by creating the present screen and telephone system, thereby giving its technical experts the near-impossible task of building the whole thing from scratch in just over a couple of years.

Considering all the noise that was made about Big Bang, it is perhaps surprising how little has changed from the private investor's viewpoint. Much of the business of buying and selling shares is exactly the same as it was in the old days and the ways of going about picking shares have not altered one iota. What *is* different, however, is the relationship between investor and stockbroker. Far less can be taken on trust than in the past, for within the gigantic new financial conglomerates, or securities houses, there are potentially some massive conflicts of interest. These firms may not only be making markets in shares, but they could be managing large pension funds, acting as advisors to companies and dealing in shares for themselves as well as playing the more traditional role of dealing on behalf of their clients and giving them investment recommendations.

It is important for the investor to realise just what some of the potential problems are in the new environment. The stockbroker can now be both principal (dealing for himself) and agent (dealing for the investor), in effect acting as both broker and jobber. He might receive a big selling order from a favoured instututonal client. Whatever his views on the shares, it might be politic to deal for such a client, giving the broker a large chunk of some shares he may not want at all. The cost of hanging on to such a holding is massive and it is conceivable that he might attempt to reduce that risk by peddling the shares to his other, smaller clients. It is impossible to believe that such things won't happen from time to time, though a broker is under an obligation to tell his client in what capacity he is acting. Even those firms which aren't 'market-makers' may buy and own shares which they can sell on to clients, although they must disclose that they are doing so. Brokers' profit margins have been much reduced by Big Bang – the days when money simply dropped off the branches of trees straight into the brokers' wallets have disappeared. Unfortunately reduced profit margins have meant a need for increased turnover and that, in turn, has occasionally meant rather less impartiality and care on the broker's part.

To cope with the problems created, a new regulatory system has been set up to oversee the City. Even though the Stock Exchange has always policed itself in the past and, on the whole, done it fairly well, it is no longer able to do so on its own. A system of supervised self-regulation has been introduced by the Financial Services Bill, not only to govern the Stock Exchange, but to oversee every investment business in the country. The legislation is hideously complicated, so much so that many smaller firms are already wondering if their business is successful enough to cope with the burden of the extra administrative costs they are facing. It still remains to be seen whether its prime intention, that of protecting the investor, is achieved any more successfully than in the past.

Overseeing the whole shebang is the Securities and Investments Board. Every investment business in the country (except Lloyds of London) has to be registered, either with the SIB, or with one of several Self-Regulatory Organisations whose duties are to supervise their own members in the day-to-day running of their business and ensure that they comply with the enormous numbers of rules and regulations which are intended to bring about justice and fair play for all investors.

There were originally two SROs governing securities transactions with the Stock Exchange supposedly overseeing the domestic market in stocks and shares and another, ISRO, governing international dealers and their activities. There was a fear that a split in securities dealing in Britain could develop. So, after a great deal of discussion, the two bodies merged. It seemed a fairly practical arrangement as many members of ISRO had already bought up Stock Exchange firms in the run-up to Big Bang. At the same time, the Stock Exchange abolished its ownership structure. From its creation until 1986, individual members had owned and governed the Exchange. This was amended so that it is now the corporations who are the owners of the Stock Exchange. The merged

SROs are now known as The Securities Association. Others cover life assurance and unit trust managers, investment advisers, licensed dealers, the futures market and so on. Some organisations are, because of their complex nature, members of more than one SRO. A central compensation fund has been created, subscribed to by all the SROs, which can be drawn upon in the event of a firm going out of business. This has caused some irritation at the Stock Exchange which has maintained a compensation fund for years, many times the size of this new fund. It is concerned that its members, and other well-established businesses in the financial community, may have to shell out cash as a result of the inadequacies of upstart bucket-shops in other areas of investment with which they have no connection at all.

Just in case anyone was worried that there weren't enough acronyms around in the new investment world, the SIB also recognises a variety of Investment Exchanges. These have been set up to provide orderly, efficient and fair markets in which to deal. The Stock Exchange is only one of these Recognised Investment Exchanges (RIEs), others being for things such as commodity and futures trading.

Within each Stock Exchange firm will be a compliance officer, who is there to make absolutely certain that the so-called Chinese Walls which are supposed to exist between the various departments develop no chinks and that their activities are kept entirely separate. To ensure in the new order that investors always get a fair deal, all contract notes on share deals must show what time a particular deal was done. The Stock Exchange's computers keep records of the movements of all share prices and can ascertain that the price at which someone has dealt was the 'best execution' possible at the time. Investors who feel they may have been the victim of funny business and who consider that they have a justifiable complaint should direct it, when other avenues have been exhausted, to 'The Deputy Chairman' at the Stock Exchange. There is also an Ombudsman covering Stock Exchange matters.

Investors in other fields who have complaints which they feel are not adequately being dealt with by the particular company concerned should contact the relevant SRO. There is an obligation for all investment firms to tell you to which SRO they belong. If you still are having problems, try the SIB itself on 01-283 2474. Daunting though the regulations this body produces on paper are, they appear to be an extremely helpful organisation to those who find the system they have created confusing. They also produce an excellent free guide, called *Self-defence for Investors* which ought to be made compulsory reading for everyone buying a financial product of whatever sort.

For many investment businesses, this degree of regulation is something quite new. The Stock Exchange, however, has had rules in force to protect investors for many years and their reputation for self-regulation is still outstanding. Whatever the provisions of the Financial Services Bill, it still seems likely that if you want to deal in stocks and shares, the safest way to do so is through a firm that is a member of the Stock Exchange.

How to grab yourself a stockbroker

'Those whose opinion I value will not volunteer it; those who volunteer it I find of no value.' Bertrand Russell

For those who had never dealt in shares, it used to be quite difficult to find a stockbroker, for they were shy, retiring, creatures who hid their light under a convenient bushel. Even when advertising was permitted by the Stock Exchange very few took advantage of it. Nor did the Exchange itself consider it necessary to go and 'sell' the concept of the stock market to the general public, leaving such vulgar activities to the banks, building societies and insurance companies and wondering, in its own naïve way, why they proved much more popular with private investors. It was hardly any wonder that the public ignored the stock market, sheltering as it did behind a veil of mystery that only reinforced the opinion of the uninitiated that investing in shares was an horrendously sophisticated and difficult form of investment.

In the age of Popular Capitalism, of course, that has all changed and we are now being pulled, prodded and shoved into the stock market like cattle being sent for slaughter. It isn't only the government that is doing the pushing. With commissions from the big institutions sharply reduced by Big Bang, stockbroking firms have suddenly found the private investor an attractive proposition again. Large City outfits that wouldn't have given you or me the time of day a few years ago now have outsized private client departments eagerly awaiting our business.

Having spent fortunes on buying up stockbroking firms, the High Street banks are now trying to recoup their expenditure by tempting customers to dabble in the market. Even the building societies are getting in on the act. Share shops are the latest thing, the idea being that you can wander in off the street and buy a company or two like so many pairs of socks or a tin of car wax.

I may be being a little cynical, but I tend to believe that the more eager someone is to offer you a service, the more sceptical one should be that that service is just what you need. Just because someone has the financial muscle to have a presence in the High Street does not mean that they have the interests of the private investor at heart.

It is true that many investors feel it would be less daunting to go into their bank or building society and discuss investment than contact a stockbroker. Yet the services that have been offered in the High Street until recently have been fairly restricted. My bank has enough trouble just coping with the complexities of my current account, and the idea that I should do all my dealing in stocks and shares through them strikes me as being faintly ridiculous. Why should I use a middleman whose knowledge about the stock market is likely to be rather vague when I can save time, expense and hassle by using a stockbroker directly? It doesn't make sense.

Despite the popular misconception it is not, and has never been, difficult to use a stockbroker. To buy a share all you need to do is to pick up the telephone, call your broker and give him your order. You will be sent a contract note setting out the details of your deal and then, after a short while, you'll be sent a statement showing how much you owe. You write out a cheque and that's that. I can't see that it is any easier popping into some share emporium with your hands full on your way back from Marks & Spencer.

Having said that, your most difficult deal will be the first one, for you have to establish a relationship with a stockbroker first. The problems one can encounter here are on a par with trying to find a solicitor, or a dentist or even a plumber. They are, each of them, difficult to locate in the first instance but, having found them, it is then appreciably easier to use them in the future.

Much the same is true of stockbrokers. As with solicitors, it is preferable to have one recommended by a friend who has been content with the service given to him. If you can't find anybody to recommend a broker, then you must shop around for one, stopping only when you come across an individual with whom you feel comfortable. If you write to the Stock Exchange Information Department in Threadneedle Street, London EC2, they will furnish you with the names of some stockbrokers in your area. You may find one of the many advertisements in the press appeals to you.

Alternatively you could ask your bank which stockbroker they use whenever they have any share dealings to perform for clients, although increasingly this will be the City firm the bank has bought. There's no earthly reason why you can't just look a stockbroker up in the Yellow Pages. They are listed somewhere in the vicinity of Steel Stockholders, Steam Cleaning, Stationery Retailers and Stone Masons. I have included a list of firms happy to accept private client business at the back of the book and suggest you try one or two of the numbers there.

On initial contact a stockbroker will ask you to sign one or two documents and may want to take up references but this is only a one-off thing, much like opening a bank account.

Like a solicitor, a stockbroker is a member of a professional body. It does not mean he will be the ideal person to deal with you. As in any profession, the quality of individuals varies considerably, sometimes alarmingly so. If you feel the particular firm you are using is fine, but that you and your contact don't get on like a house on fire, then ask to speak to someone else before you go to the bother of trying to find a different outfit.

If you live outside London you may find that you can get a better service than those who inhabit the capital, which makes a change. For the large London stockbrokers have massive staffs, rents and overheads. Despite their publicity, they are rarely as keen as their smaller brethren to take on the private client, unless he is particularly well-heeled. Even if one of the big firms *is* willing to take you on, bear in mind that from its point of view, you are probably a very small fish. It makes more sense to find a smaller London broker, or one based away from the capital, to do your dealing for you, and you should find it comparatively easier to strike up a stronger relationship there. Many of the big London firms now have offices around the country, so if you do want to be with the

[50]

crème de la crème, why not contact one of their out-of-town branches?

There are still quite a few London firms with the far-sightedness to take on very small new clients, in the hope that some of them at least will turn into giants one day. But in general, the bigger the firm, the more likely they are to want to institutionalise you, to force you into a straightjacket so that you conform to their requirements. Unless you are well and truly wealthy, and that usually means only a few degrees off stinking rich, the large firms are not going to want to talk to you very often and would prefer never to hear from you. If you want to be an active investor, then you are going to want to talk to your broker fairly regularly, so choose someone to whom you are not going to be a major irritation. If you find a decent broker and get on well with him or her, then you would hope that they contact you from time to time to recommend interesting investment ideas.

Another advantage of dealing with a smaller stockbroker is that the possible conflicts of interest are going to be that much less. You ought to check first but it is unlikely that smaller firms will have market-making arms. As so-called 'agency' brokers, they will almost certainly have no ulterior motive for recommending a particular share. They will be able to deal in stocks and shares themselves as principals, but are under an obligation to inform you if they have a position in a particular security. Small brokers probably won't have a string of companies for whom they act on corporate matters, either.

If you really are terrified of talking to a stockbroker, then in your initial explorations of the stock market perhaps you would be happier walking into your bank or building society and asking them to transact business for you. But don't expect them to have the in-depth knowledge and comprehension of the market that a broker does. It isn't only the buying and selling of shares that matters, but also understanding how to track down errant share certificates, or cope with settlement problems. If you think some parvenu in your local High Street is going to be able to cope with all this adequately, then fine. If you aren't sure, then you ought to start the process of finding yourself a stockbroker.

The High Street may be convenient, but unless you have some very detailed investment requirements, there is probably no necessity ever to meet your stockbroker. It should make very little difference to you where he is located in the country. One of the great advantages of the new Stock Exchange trading system, with its video screens and telephoned orders, is that a broker in the north of Scotland can deal just as effectively and with the same speed as one in the heart of the City of London. They won't face the same high office costs as their cousins in the crowded Square Mile and so are likely to be able to charge you less for your deals. There's nothing to stop you using a broker at the other end of the country, even if you do live in the capital. Don't look down your nose at the regional firms. They can be ideal for the private investor.

The simplicity of the complexities of share investment

'When a stockbroker phones you up and says you must buy this stock, you can bet it's on the way up. When two or three stockbrokers phone you up, you can bet it's reaching the overvalued stage.'   Raymond Johnstone

Once having found a stockbroker, there is still that nagging feeling that you are getting involved in a business that is terribly complex, where the small man who knows only a little about the subject is going to be eaten alive by the professionals who have so much more time to concentrate on the market. Yet you wouldn't dream of staying put in your present house for ever, simply because moving would involve you in the complexities of conveyancing or because you are frightened of getting in touch with a solicitor. You might be apprehensive about the sheer frustration of moving, but at least you know that a solicitor is going to handle the financial and legal details for you. After all, that's what you're paying him for.

The same should be true of a stockbroker. You are paying for the services of someone who thoroughly understands the stock market. The stockbroker will know his way around the Stock Exchange's voluminous rule book. There is certainly no need for *you* to wade through it before attempting to deal in shares. Understanding its innumerable intricacies is quite frankly unnecessary. If you give a stockbroker an order to buy, he will execute that order at the best possible price and send you the bill. The only area where you need to develop your knowledge of the stock market is in deciding what shares to buy or sell, and when to do so.

Your stockbroker may give you very good service; it is in his interest to make you money. He wants you to keep coming back for more, preferably in bigger and bigger sizes. You should always give a good deal of thought to a share purchase, or indeed a sale, rather than commit yourself without a moment's thought. A share purchase should be considered as carefully as any other item you're buying. You would hardly buy a hi-fi or a new car on impulse, nor anything else costing a few hundred pounds or more. You are more likely to spend days or weeks examining brochures or reading consumer reports to see how your potential purchase matches up to others, before committing yourself.

Why should shares be any different from other expensive goods? Consider what you are doing extremely carefully, even if you are being advised by someone whose opinion you respect. It is far more sensible to wait a short while until you are certain that you want to own a particular share before giving an order. That might mean you end up paying a slightly higher price, but better that than acting hastily and repenting it at leisure. You can't return shares simply because they aren't performing in the way you expected. There's no one-year warranty on them, nor any guarantee.

You should also realise that the service most stockbrokers offer is by no means confined only to stocks and shares. In fact, they are among the best all-round financial advisers available and, in my opinion, a good deal more trustworthy than many so-called independent intermediaries whose judgement on life assurance and so on is all too often clouded by the amount of commission offered on differing financial products and by the parties and overseas 'conferences' to which they are invited. You should be able to turn to your broker for help on tax, school fees, insurance, retirement advice, passing capital onto your offspring, pensions, the Business Expansion Scheme and many other areas. In the new era, it is possible that brokers will charge for some services which might have been free in the old days, but the days of getting something for nothing are now dead and buried.

5

THE DEAL

The Stock Exchange Account

*'The game of professional investment is intolerably boring
and over-exacting to anyone who is entirely exempt from the
gambling instinct; whilst he who has it must pay to this pro-
pensity the appropriate toll.'*   John Maynard Keynes

Before going into greater detail about what you should look
for in a potential share purchase, it might be helpful to go
through the actual procedure involved.

Having opened an account with a stockbroker, if the
references prove satisfactory you may then deal at any time.
Under the new investors' regulations, all investment firms will
have to set out the basis of their relationship with their clients
in a customer agreement letter. This will set out the func-
tions or services the firm is to provide and its responsibilities
and obligations, and need to be signed by investors before
dealing can commence.

The Stock Exchange calendar is divided into a series of
'accounts', periods which are usually two weeks, but every so
often three weeks, long. All your transactions made with any
one stockbroker during this period are lumped together so
that if you buy five hundred pounds' worth of shares, and sell
one thousand pounds' worth of a different share in the same
account, a balance cheque will be due to you and you need
never write out a cheque for the purchase.

All the deals are totted up by the broker and the balance due
or owed to them needs to be satisfied by Settlement Day, generally the second Monday after the account ends. In this way
it is possible to deal in shares 'on tick', as it were. If you
bought a thousand pounds' worth of Morpheus Engineering
on the first day of the Stock Exchange account, you might
decide to sell them before that account ended on the Friday
after next. If you did so and sold them for £1,150, the stockbroker would have to pay you the difference of £150 less commission even though you never had to produce any money.
Of course the reverse is also true; should your sale of

Morpheus show a loss of £150 then you must pay up the difference on Settlement Day.

Details of the accounts, their commencement, conclusion and their Settlement Days, are given in most newspapers that carry financial news, though they'll be tucked away somewhere. Your stockbroker will help you if you can't find them there. He may even send you a copy of the yearly Stock Exchange calendar – no beautiful pictures, I'm afraid, just the list of dates.

There is a quite widespread feeling that since Big Bang, the need to have a Stock Exchange account at all has diminished considerably and that it may be done away with altogether. This would necessitate a drastic overhaul of the settlement system at the Exchange and, after the upheaval of Big Bang, it is likely that brokers will be given some time to adjust themselves to the new order before any further revolutions are wrought.

The order

To deal, you need do nothing more strenuous than telephone your stockbroker and give him your order. Do make sure that it is repeated back to you so that you can be certain the broker knows exactly what you want him to do. Certain shares have very similar-sounding names, such as BATs and Bass. By the time you discover a mistake has been made, it could be too late to do anything about it.

You may be content to give an order and put the phone down straight away. It is more likely that you'll want to have some idea of the price at which the share is trading. On the stockbroker's desk will be a TOPIC screen, a video terminal which is linked to the Stock Exchange's price information computers. On it, within seconds, the broker can call up virtually any actively-traded share price. These used to be recorded by clerks wandering the floor of the Exchange. Now, under the Stock Exchange's Automated Quotation System (SEAQ), market-makers input the prices at which they are willing to deal directly into the system. On the screen in front of him, your broker will be able to see the prices quoted by all those who are making a market in that particular share. He will deal at the best possible price simply by calling the market-maker offering that price on the telephone.

[55]

In actively-traded shares the market-maker will be obliged to deal with your broker at that price, although for smaller companies the price on the screen will only be an indication of the level at which the market-maker will trade. If you are not happy about the available prices, then you can always leave a 'limit' order with your broker, telling him the price at which you are willing to deal. Once you have given him an order, however, the matter is entirely in his hands. You cannot change your mind a few minutes after he has carried out the deal simply because you have got cold feet.

The new SEAQ system has speeded things up considerably. No matter where the broker is located, he has access to exactly the same information as every other stockbroker in the country. In the old days brokers had to contact their dealers on the floor of the Stock Exchange by means of a radio-phone or telephone. This dealer would then walk briskly, one hoped, from jobber's pitch to jobber's pitch until he located the one offering the best price.

One of my favourite stockbroking stories, as unprovable as all of them, dates from those olden days long before Big Bang when everything was done through the telephone. A stockbroker and his dealer were old sparring partners, indulging in what they felt to be bold and incisive repartee.

The broker telephoned down to the dealer.

'Right, you reprobate. See if you can't get me a price in ICI if it isn't too much trouble. And don't be all day about it; I've got a lunch appointment in a couple of hours.'

'I'll see what can be done, you fish-faced fool, but if you spent a little less time lunching, and a little more getting orders I'd stand a chance of being able to remember which jobbers are quoting a price in them.'

This badinage over, the dealer promptly sought out the best price and rang the broker back. 'If you haven't packed up early for your lunch, you lazy slob, I might just be able to provide you with the price you wanted.'

There was a sharp intake of breath on the line. 'Do you know who you are talking to, young man?'

The dealer, suspecting a leg-pull, replied: 'The Queen of Sheba?'

'Don't be facetious. I am the senior partner of this firm.'

There was a brief silence from the other end. Then the dealer asked: 'Do you know who *you* are talking to?'

'No I do not.'

'Well, thank heaven for that,' confessed the dealer, slamming the phone down.

The execution

A stockbroker has an obligation to deal for his clients at the best possible price available. Using the wonders of SEAQ, of course, it is a good deal easier for him to locate the most attractive price than it used to be be. Once he calls up the requisite page on his TOPIC set he will see a list of all the market-makers who deal in that particular share, together with the price they are all making, and the size in which they are willing to deal at that price. The system is used, naturally, not only for private client orders, but also for those of the big institutions. In their case, the market-maker could want to widen his price if the deal was in a particularly large number of shares.

From your examination of the newspaper, you might have noticed that Morpheus closed at the end of the previous day at 102. The price given there is a middle price. It does not mean that you can necessarily buy or sell at that level. Were the price to remain at that level on the following day, you might expect to have to pay 103 or to receive 101 for your shares. The more highly priced shares are, and the more inactive the dealings in them, the wider the spread between the two prices is likely to be.

When you ring your broker to deal, the display in front of the broker in Morpheus may look something like this:

MORPHEUS ENGINEERING					
IJKL	UVWX	102–3	QRST	EFGH	
ABCD	102–105	5×5	MNOP	101–104	3×3
EFGH	101–103	1×1	QRST	100–103	2×2
IJKL	102–104	10×10	UVWX	102–105	5×5

Each four-digit abbreviation represents a different market-maker, the successor to the old jobbers. Their job is to act as share wholesalers. They survive by charging more for the price of shares they sell than they are prepared to pay when buying them. The expression 'jobber's turn' refers not to some fainting spell that attacks members of the fraternity, but to what is, in effect, the market-maker's profit margin. Being able to make markets profitably is a considerably difficult task, one reason why the talents of these individuals is so much in demand.

The broker can see that market-maker ABCD is quoting 102p to 105p. That means he can buy the shares at 105 and sell them at 102. 5×5 means that the market-maker is willing to both buy and sell 5,000 shares. Two market-makers, QRST and EFGH, are willing to sell shares at just 103, making them the most attractive for a purchase of shares. For a seller, IJKL and UVWX offer the best price. To spare the broker the difficulty of looking through each price, the 'touch' is given to him at the top of his screen. He knows from looking at the second line that he can sell shares at 102p and buy them at 103p. If his firm has a market-making arm, he can only do the business through it if it offers the best price. Outsiders may be surprised at the degree of animosity that sometimes exists between market-makers and salesmen within the same firm. Rather than living in peace and harmony, both can on occasion see the other as a hindrance to the successful completion of their own business.

If the share is one of the 600 or so most actively traded shares in the market then the price shown by the market-makers will be fixed. The broker can call the market-maker and demand to deal in the stated volume at the price shown on the screen. These categories of shares, 'alphas' and 'betas', will be discussed in greater detail later.

If the share is a 'gamma', of which there are about 3,000, then the prices may only be an indication, not a firm dealing price. The broker will ring up and ask for a dealing price without admitting to the market-maker whether he is a buyer or a seller. Only when he is quoted a satisfactory price will he clinch the deal.

It is worth noting that at least one bank offered an instant dealing facility to the public during the British Gas sale which went, not through a stockbroker as usual, but was linked up directly to the bank's market-maker. Although on a sale that size most market-makers were giving out similar prices, it meant that those dealing this way could not be guaranteed 'best execution.' Yet another reason for going to a stockbroker, raher than an organisation with a vested interest in ensuring the business goes to one particular firm.

[58]

SEAQ is a price information system, not a dealing system. However, the Exchange plans to introduce yet another acronym, SAEF, the SEAQ Automated Execution Facility which will enable firms to carry out deals in relatively small sizes at the touch of a button. Brokers won't even need to check which market-maker offers the best price. The computers will perform this arduous task for him. If it proves satisfactory, it is hoped gradually to increase the size of orders that can be traded in this way.

My favourite market-maker story dates from the Saturday before Big Bang when the stockbroking fraternity was forced to abandon its leisure pursuits and head into an otherwise deserted City to take the new dealing system through its paces. One dealer rang a market-maker in a particular share and said: 'You've got them 297–300 in 10,000 on your screen, I'll sell 10,000.' The deal was struck and the phone replaced. The market-maker adjusted his price on the screen which now showed 296–299 in 10,000. Once again he received a call from the same broker, who sold him 10,000 at the firm price shown on the screen. The market-maker adjusted his price downwards by another penny only to receive yet another call from the same broker wanting to sell 10,000. It happened again, and again. At last the market-maker's temper broke.

'Look this is supposed to be a realistic rehearsal. How long is this farce going on?'

'As long as you like old boy. The price you're showing is a pound too high.'

It was fortunate for the market-maker that, on that day at least, they were not playing for real money.

Unlike other markets, nothing actually passes from hand to hand in dealings on the stock market. Everything is done on trust. The Exchange prides itself on its motto *dictum meum pactum* though, as many brokers' Latin is a trifle rusty, you are more likely to hear it as 'My word is my bond.' Although a little hard to believe, that is exactly what is meant. A stockbroker or a market-maker is compelled to abide by his word in his dealings. This may sound a rather effete and gentlemanly way of going about things in the twentieth century, but it has enormous advantages for the efficiency of the stock market. The dealer buying Morpheus shares simply notes down the deal; the market-maker selling does exactly the same. Later the broker claims the shares from the jobber, paying the requisite amount.

As a result of the entry to the stock market of many firms and individuals for whom the system is a novelty and who may not have been brought up in a similar trusting climate, many firms now record all telephone conversations, just in case anyone is tempted to forget that their word really is their bond, even in the new, tough, competitive environment.

Were the two parties to a deal not able to trust each other's word, the procedure might be significantly slower. Imagine how laborious the whole process would be were the market-maker compelled to hand over the shares there and then, and the dealer forced to write a cheque for them. It would hardly make for a smoothly functioning stock market.

The contract note

Over the years, the procedure for buying shares has been gradually refined to the point where it is now a doddle for the private investor to deal in the market. The stockbroker handles all the paperwork that in days of yore you might have had to do yourself.

After the bargain has been struck – Stock Exchange trans-actions are referred to as 'bargains' no matter how disastrous the deal may turn out to be – the next step is for you to sit back and wait for the contract note confirming the details of the deal. It is very important to realise that having given an order to a stockbroker to perform, you have already made a contract with him. If events turn against you, you cannot expect him to undo the whole thing for you simply because you've changed your mind. Your word is taken to be your bond. This was a common mistake made by novices dealing with shares like British Telecom and British Gas. They declared over the phone to one broker that they would sell their shares at a certain price, only to try and sell them to another broker later on when they saw that the shares had risen still further. I need hardly point out that you can't sell something you own twice over without being a bit of a fraud. In several cases the stock-brokers concerned pursued the tyros using the full might of the law. The brokers had, after all, to produce the shares their clients had committed them to selling.

People who default on deals with one broker will find them-selves shut out from the market altogether. Although they like to keep it fairly quiet, any stockbroker considering an application from someone to become a client will make discreet enquiries to the Stock Exchange Mutual Reference Fund which keeps what is, in effect, a blacklist of investors who have done down their brokers. You have been warned.

The contract note should take just a day or two to arrive, Post Office permitting. On it will be set out all the details of your share purchase or sale. These pieces of paper may vary in size and style between different stockbroking firms, but the essentials will be the same. In polite, but brusque, English you will be informed that your stockbroker bought on your behalf, say:

a) 1,000 Morpheus Engineering 25p ordinary shares @ 103p	1030.00
b) Transfer stamp	5.50
c) Commission @ 1.5%	15.45
d) V.A.T. on commission @ 15%	2.31
	1053.26

a. This is the 'consideration', yet another of the market's buzz words. It has no relevance to the feelings your stockbroker entertains towards you, but is rather the value of the bought shares and the amount which he must pay the market-maker who sold him the shares that you ordered.

b. You can hardly expect the stock market to be a pie into which the government does not dip its finger. It takes ½% in transfer stamp duty, rounded up to the nearest 50p, on every share purchase. It has been reduced in stages from the 2% level at which it stood before the 1984 budget, making dealing in shares considerably cheaper than it used to be. Correspondingly, however, its imposition has been extended. It used to be the case that 'new' shares could be bought for a while without having to pay stamp duty. No longer. After the initial sale, purchases of 'new' shares incur something called Stamp Duty Reserve Tax, the same as stamp duty in all but name. Nor is it possible any longer to buy and sell shares within the same account and escape stamp duty. However, it remains the case that share *sales* are completely free from duty.

c. Commission. The word that gladdens the heart of every stockbroker and infuriates every investor. I've yet to meet one punter who felt his stockbroker deserved the commission he charged. Until Big Bang the Stock Exchange fixed the rates which brokers were able to charge. Now, in theory, you can negotiate a rate with your broker. In practice it is only the large institutions that can do such deals. We lesser mortals have to pay what we are told. In olden days the rate on all deals up to £7,000 in value was 1.65% (see Appendix for comparisons). In this example, the rate is 1.5%. There are lower rates around, particularly from 'deal-only' brokers who will offer the investor no advice at all.

You should be particularly wary of minimum commission levels however. If a 1% deal-only broker set a minimum of £20 a deal, then our purchase of Morpheus shares would be more costly than with the broker charging the higher rate. Virtually every stockbroker charges a certain minimum level which can be as high as £30 at some large firms. The smaller the deal, the more likely you are to incur a minimum charge. If the deal is particularly small, that charge may be quite a significant percentage. If you deal with a large stockbroker and find the words 'minimum commission' on your contract note every time you deal, it might be time to find a different broker.

We'll return to the subject of commissions later, but it is worth mentioning that any deals which you reverse during a Stock Exchange account should be subject to 'closing commission', which is a big fat zero. If you buy some shares and sell them again within the account, or if you sell them and then buy them back, the second commission should not be charged. But don't assume your stockbroker knows that your second deal *is* a reversal of a deal you did only a few days earlier; far safer and quicker to mention it to him when you give the order, so that he can adjust the commission accordingly.

d. The service the stockbroker provides is, I'm afraid, subject to an extra 15% which flows ultimately to the Exchequer. The government does pretty well by share transactions. It isn't completely made of stone though. In the 1985 budget it listened to the pleadings of the city and abolished contract stamp, a tax on the issuing of each contract note. But as the maximum raised at one time from this duty was 60 pence, it was hardly a painful concession to make.

It is possible to avoid VAT if you deal directly with a market-maker, a service offered by one of the High Street banks in the initial days of trading of British Gas shares. As I mentioned before, there are very definite disadvantages to going straight to a market-maker and, for the majority of the time, it is not going to be an option open to you.

The amount at the bottom of the contract note of £1,053.25 is the total cost of your shares to you, i.e. around £23 more than the market-maker received for them. Although the shares themselves cost 103 pence each, in effect the price you have paid for them is 105.3p once all the charges are taken into account (1.053.25 divided by 1,000). It may be a comfort to you if you see the price of the shares rise in the paper soon after your deal, but you will only be showing a profit once Morpheus shares rise to 106. If you want to sell the shares, there will be further, though proportionately smaller, charges to pay. So you should only start celebrating when your new acquisition can be sold for 107 pence; above that it's all pure jam. Obviously these calculations vary, depending on the charges your broker levies.

The contract note will have the date of your deal on it. This is important for tax purposes, though it may be unnecessary for you to pay any CGT at the end of the year. In addition, the time will be logged on the contract note, a great help in the event of any dispute between you and your broker. Whether or not you pay tax, it is worth hanging on to all your contract notes as a record of the deals you have done. Many investors keep a ledger in which they write down all details of their trades, and while that may sound a little fastidious it helps greatly if you hold more than one or two shares. Far better that than the mad scramble each April through your papers trying to find out just what you've done in the year.

Also on the contract note will be printed the Settlement Day for that account. That is the date on which you should settle any outstanding bills for the account or the date on which your stockbroker will write out his cheque to you if you've been a net seller of shares. Before Settlement Day, you should in any case receive a statement from your broker with the details of all the deals you made with him during the account. It will show the amount owed or owing as a result of your transactions and should be settled promptly if you expect to remain on good terms with your stockbroker. Don't leave it as late as the rates or the electricity bill. Remember there will be times when your broker owes *you* money.

The certificate

A few weeks after your deal, a share certificate will automatically be sent to you, duly inscribed with your name and the number of shares you have bought. A few are rather impressive documents, with ornate lettering on beautiful paper. Rather more are pretty dull. The smaller the company, the more basic the certificate is likely to be. On one occasion my purchase of shares in a very young company was virtually completely handwritten; it made me feel as if I were one of the family.

The most unusual certificate of recent years must be that for the Playboy company in America. In the States share certificates need to bear a figure on them, much like banknotes. The organisation decided that rather than stick to tradition and put Hugh Heffner on their shares, they would instead use one of their Playmates of the Month.

All this paperwork has largely been handled by the Stock Exchange on your behalf, including contacting the company's registrars to inform them of the change in the shareholder's register. The Exchange's computerised Talisman system, introduced in 1979, has speeded up the process considerably. The buyer of the shares no longer has to receive the certificate physically from the seller. Instead all transactions are placed into a central pool and matched off.

It is quite important to hang on to your share certificates and keep them in a safe place, although if they do get lost it is possible to prove ownership of the shares, so you don't risk losing your right to your holding. But a lost certificate takes time and a good deal of bother to replace. You might want to ask your stockbroker or your bank to look after your share certificates for you.

When you sell shares you will be sent a Talisman Sold Transfer Form. This initially seems a rather confusing piece of paper. It has to be signed by you in the relevant place as confirmation that you relinquish your rights to the shares. When you have completed this onerous task you should return it together with the relevant share certificate to your broker. Share sales are marginally more demanding than purchases.

If a share certificate to which you are entitled doesn't arrive, you shouldn't worry unduly. Remember that your broker's word is his bond; his contract note setting out details of the deal with you obliges him to get the shares and the certificate for you, even if he has made a mistake in effecting the transaction. And just because you have not received your certificate there is no reason why you shouldn't sell the shares concerned either, although it might be worth mentioning to your broker when you deal that you are still waiting for your shares to arrive; the Talisman Sold Transfer Form provides space for you to point out that the certificate is not yet in your possession. If it does turn up later, simply forward it on.

You should not think you can't sell part of your holding in a company, simply because the share certificate is for the whole amount. After a year or two, your 1,000 Morpheus shares might have doubled in value (it's only an example). You may then feel that you have got rather too much money tied up there and want to lighten your holding. Simply give the order to sell the number of shares you want; when the Sold Transfer Form arrives, send your certificate for the entire holding back and a new, smaller one will be issued to you in due course.

When you buy shares for the first time in a particular company, the Stock Exchange will inform its registrars of your name, address and your holding. For not only does the company need to send you your shares certificate but also a copy of its annual report and accounts, and details of the half-year and full-year results. You will also receive an invitation to the Annual General Meeting at which you can, if you so desire, make known your views about the performance of the company. If you change address, you will need to inform each company in which you hold shares of your new address, although if your broker handles your portfolio for you, he might be prevailed upon to do this for you.

The Stock Exchange is at present developing a system, known as Taurus, for doing away with share certificates altogether, thus cutting down still further on the paperwork associated with stock market investment.

6
THE BASICS

'October. This is one of the peculiarly dangerous months to speculate in stocks. The others are July, January, September, April, November, May, March, June, December, August and February.'   Mark Twain

Even if the government is happy to push millions of people into share ownership without caring one jot whether they know what they are doing or not, I am not so sure that it makes any sense for anyone to consider investing on a regular basis without at least a basic understanding of the way the market works. It isn't the aim of this book to deal with every last detail the investor might encounter. If you find that you are becoming more involved with the market, there are some far weightier tomes around to consult. I don't want to kill any interest you have stone dead by drowning you in a sea of information. The detail in this chapter *is* important, but if you want to skip it for the moment, you can always come back to it later.

Stocks and shares Referring to the activities of the market, we must all of us have used the phrase 'stocks and shares' without realising what they are. In general stocks are fixed interest securities, things like government stocks, or local authority bonds, or company debentures and loan stocks. They differ from shares in that they are usually quoted in terms of the current value of £100 of stock, though the actual value of that stock can vary in exactly the same way as shares. This is explained in greater detail in the chapter on gilts.

Having said that there is a distinction between stocks and shares, that distinction is these days rather blurred. Some companies call their ordinary shares 'stock', and the Americans refer to all their companies' shares as 'stock'. As a result it is really becoming too complicated to differentiate between stocks and shares all the time, and the difference is hardly worth bothering about any longer.

As we have already seen, a company issues Ordinary shares. (There are other kinds beyond the scope of this book.)

These shares are frequently referred to as equities, the two terms being completely synonymous. The shares of the greatest and mightiest companies in the land, such as ICI and GEC, are often referred to as 'blue chips', as are the companies themselves. Blue chips are theoretically the ones that, if not as safe as houses, are at least as safe as the more solid sort of bungalow. To qualify for their blue-chipness a company simply has to be massive; the sort of business that is hardly going to vanish overnight. There is no set list of blue chips, although the category of shares under the Stock Exchange's new trading system known as 'alphas', less than a hundred of them, would probably all fall in the category. From an investor's point of view, the only thing blue chips might have to commend them is their perceived safety. But even that is not permanent; Rolls-Royce was once a blue chip, as was Dunlop. And who now remembers Murex or Maple or Fine Spinners? There is a school of thought, whose views will be considered later, which says that private investors actually do better avoiding blue chips, for these companies have become so big that their room for future growth is more limited than that of smaller companies.

Par value This probably causes more confusion to beginners in the stock market than anything else, mainly because it has no relevance at all to investors. You may recall that on your contract note for the purchase of Morpheus Engineering, the shares were described as 'Ordinary 25p' shares. That 25p is their par value, a term which is nothing more than a book-keeping exercise for the company. Generally the par value of a share is 25p, but some are £1 shares and others may be 1p, 5p, 10p or 50p. The Americans avoid such complications as practically all their shares are of 'no par value.'

The imagined difficulty in Britain arises because investors seem to think the price they pay for their shares should bear some relation to the figure for par value. But simply because a share is said to be a 25p share does not mean that the actual price traded has ever been 25 pence. British Telecom shares, you may recall, were launched at a fully paid price of 130 pence. This had nothing at all to do with the par value which was, and still is, 25p. Yet some people seemed shocked that '25p shares' were being offered to the public at £1.30, as if someone was somehow pocketing the vast difference.

[67]

Share price The share price is, on its own, a completely irrelevant piece of information, a meaningless number, a set of digits without length, breadth or height. Believing in the importance of the absolute price of a share is one of the most common mistakes made by newcomers to the stock market and one which can prove extremely costly if not rectified.

Investors with little knowledge of the market sometimes believe that the lower a share price, the 'cheaper' that share is. But if it were true that those with low prices were cheap and those with high prices 'expensive', then surely wise investors would simply sell the heavyweight ones and buy those with low prices until every share on the stock market was at exactly the same level.

TSB, for instance, sold 1,500 million shares at £1, a price thought 'cheap' by some people. They could just as easily have opted for 750 million at £2, or 375 million at £4. Each would have raised exactly the same amount of money for the company. Experienced investors would have come to just the same decision about the shares. They would have bought a different number in each case, but their total investment would have been identical.

You need far more information than just the price to decide upon the merits of a share. It is possible for a share costing £10 to be 'cheap', and consequentiy worth buying, and one costing 10p to be 'expensive', to be shunned like the plague. Some investors believe that because they can buy more lowly-priced shares they are better off than if they buy a few pricey ones. But the investment is exactly the same and if both shares climb 10% the profit is identical.

The share price is just one piece in a jigsaw. It is useless without the other pieces, just as they are of little value unless they are related to the price of the shares.

Dividend While the price of a share is determined by the supply and demand for it, like any other free market commodity, there are several factors which determine that demand, and therefore the share's price. The level of dividend a company pays on its shares is one of these, being the only real link between the profits of a firm and the price of its shares. It is of far greater importance to the big institutions than it is to most private investors, but even if income is not a major consideration with you, you should realise that because other investors pay close attention to it, it is a vital influence. As you now know, companies pay a dividend to their shareholders which is taken out of profits, or out of the company's reserves if the profits in the current year aren't up to it. The payment usually happens twice a year, once at the interim profits stage when the half-year results are announced and again at the end of the year. This final dividend tends to be rather larger than the interim.

The price of a share will fall to take account of a dividend payment, losing roughly the same amount as the net dividend. Before that fall, the shares are said to be trading 'cum dividend' (cd) and those buying them are still entitled to the payment. But when they go 'ex dividend' (xd) and the price falls, those buying the shares are no longer entitled to the payout and must wait another six months or so for the next one. Someone who sells 'xd', even if he has not yet received the dividend, is still entitled to it.

The potential investor is interested in the total dividend for the year, expressed either as a net or gross figure. Companies may quote it as either, so a little care is needed when examining the numbers. As an investor, your dividend will be paid to you net of basic-rate income tax, much as any income you receive from the building society or bank. With it you will be given a tax credit, showing the amount the company has paid on your behalf, based on the assumption that you are a basic-rate taxpayer.

Take, as an example, Morpheus's dividend. Its total gross dividend for the present year is 5 pence, all paid at the end of the year for some reason. When shareholders receive their money the cheques will be for 3.65 pence on each share, i.e. after basic-rate income tax of 27% has been deducted. On the 1,000 Morpheus shares bought earlier, there would be £36.50 income received. Accompanying the dividend is a tax credit for £13.50. In effect, the company has paid this, 27% of the gross dividend, to the Inland Revenue on your behalf. Convenient though this may be for basic-rate taxpayers, if you are subject to higher rates of tax you should be prepared to pay the rest due at the end of the year. Dividend income and the tax credits given need to be declared on your tax return, so you should keep a record of them somewhere. If you are in the fortunate position of escaping the income tax net altogether, the tax paid by the company on the dividend will be refunded to you, unlike income from a building society or bank where the deduction is lost forever.

[69]

DIVIDEND RECEIVED BY HOLDER OF 1,000 SHARES IN MORPHEUS ENGINEERING

Gross dividend 5p	Net dividend ...3.65p	Tax credits 1.35p
Gross payment £50	Investor gets .. £36.50	Total tax credit £13.50

Yield The investor is interested not only in the amount of dividend a company pays out but also in its relation to the current share price. For while a 5p dividend for a company like Morpheus, with its shares standing at 103p, may be significant, it would be peanuts for a share of, say 800 pence.

To calculate the dividend yield of a particular company is simplicity itself. It is simply the gross dividend multiplied by 100 and divided by the current share price. If maths really is your weak point, you may find your calculator has a percentage button on it which will perform the sum for you. If you still can't cope, then most serious newspapers will give the yield as one of the pieces of information on their share prices page. In Morpheus's case, the dividend yield is obtained thus:

GROSS YIELD ON MORPHEUS AT 103p

$$\text{Yield} = \frac{5p \text{ (gross dividend)} \times 100}{103 \text{ (share price)}} = 4.9\%$$

Yields are always calculated on gross dividends, so that one can compare easily the yields of different companies. Obviously the yield is a function not only of the dividend, but also of the share price. If Morpheus rose to 200p, its yield would fall to 2.5%, making the income received from it rather less attractive for investors. That wouldn't matter materially to our investor who was lucky enough to buy it at the lower level, for he is still receiving a gross yield of 4.9% on his original purchase price, though not of course on the present value of his investment. However, most companies try to increase their dividend each year and an initial yield on an investment may increase over just a few years into something quite substantial.

The board of a company, acting on behalf of its shareholders, determines what level of dividend should be paid for the year. An investor should not necessarily be happy if the company pays out too high a level of dividend. For that portion of net profit that isn't paid out is ploughed back into the business; if too much is paid out then the business might suffer as a result.

It might be worth your while checking the **Dividend cover**, which shows the number of times the actual net dividend *could* have been paid out of net profits of the company. The higher it is, the further profits can fall before the payment of the dividend comes under threat. If the ratio is less than one then the company is having to dig into profits retained from earlier, better years, in order to pay the dividend. Obviously that can't continue for long without the company running itself into the ground. A company might decide to keep the level of dividend unchanged in bad times if it thinks it can weather the storm. It might be felt that such an action is desirable to retain the loyalty of shareholders. Whether that will work or not depends very much on the general perception of the company's future. If investors at large are less optimistic than the board, they might feel the directors are being unnecessarily profligate with their money and cash in their chips while they have the chance, or try to replace the board.

On the other hand, the directors might find it necessary to cut the dividend to drive home to investors the seriousness of the company's trading position. For a company with a long growth record, and a reasonably straight-talking management, a decision to chop the dividend is not one to be made lightly. If their public relations people are doing their job properly, investors ought not to feel miffed, but ought instead to understand that the board is taking the necessary tough measures to put the company back on its feet. It also gives the company extra leverage in its bargaining with the workforce if the shareholders have been seen to suffer.

Earnings per share No investor ought ever to look at one year's figures from a company in isolation. But its growth record is extremely important; is the company growing steadily or is it showing signs of fatigue? Rather than look merely at the most generally followed figure in a company's statements, that for pre-tax profits, it is also worthwhile examining the earnings per share. It is possible for profits to climb even though earnings per share remain stagnant, particularly if the company takes over other businesses or if it issues more shares. If the rate at which profits or earnings are growing merely matches the increase in the number of shares in issue, then each shareholder will see no real benefit; though the company is making more money, his proportionate stake in the company is declining as it does so.

The earnings per share figure enables the investor to check how the growth of the company has affected his holding. Like the calculation for dividend cover, it is based upon the amount of profit that can in theory be paid out to shareholders – the after-tax earnings of the company. The earnings per share figure is arrived at by dividing these after-tax earnings by the number of shares the company has issued.

Let us say that this year, through Herculean efforts, Morpheus has produced £2.3 million pre-tax profits. It isn't a terribly complicated company, having never felt the need to diversify away from turning out Thingumajigs. Of these profits 35% are earmarked to be paid in tax to the Exchequer, leaving £1.5 million in net profits which can, in theory, be paid out to shareholders. With ten million shares in issue, the earnings per share (eps) figure is 15p.

MORPHEUS ENGINEERING

Pre-tax profit	£2.3 million
Corporation Tax at 35%	£0.8 million
Post-tax profits or net earnings	£1.5 million
Earnings per share (10m in issue)	15p

To take a real example, Saatchi and Saatchi have issued, over the years, a phenomenal number of shares, but they have been able to increase profits of the company to almost the same extent. Earnings per share have grown at an annual compound rate of 37% compared with a growth in profits of 48%. But that has still made it one of the fastest-growing companies in the market, with the behaviour of the share price amply reflecting that.

If you are trying to calculate the EPS figure yourself, you will need to find the number of shares in issue. This will be given in the set of Report and Accounts which each company has to publish annually. In the balance sheet willl be a figure for the 'issued' or 'called-up share capital'. This usually shows the number of shares in issue at the time. If it doesn't, take the figure given for share capital, in pounds, and divide it by the par value of the shares. You will thus easily be able to

[72]

SAATCHI AND SAATCHI – GROWTH RECORD

	Pre-tax profits (£m)	EPS (p)	Net dividend (p)
1977	1.2	2.1	0.6
1978	1.8	3.1	0.8
1979	2.4	4.2	1.3
1980	3.0	5.1	1.7
1981	3.6	6.4	2.0
1982	5.5	9.3	3.0
1983	11.2	13.1	4.4
1984	18.3	19.8	6.9
1985	40.4	31.5	9.8
1986	70.1	38.1	12.2

SOURCE: PHILLIPS & DREW

determine the number of shares in issue. This figure is vital to any analysis you do, so if you are having problems finding it, just ring the company concerned and ask the company secretary for the figure. He ought to know it.

If you examine the Report and Accounts, you will also find a five-year record of the firm's progress. It is frequently very instructive to see just how steady the rate of growth has been. If there are any hiccups in the rise in profits or earnings per share, can they easily be explained? If earnings are steadily increasing, but the company's turnover, or sales, remains fairly static, just how are they improving margins and can they continue to do so?

Price-earnings ratio The most important of investment calculations is the price-earnings ratio, usually referred to as the PE. It is necessary to have a yardstick by which you can measure the merits of shares against each other. By comparing them using their PEs, analysts can attempt to determine which shares are 'cheap' and which 'expensive'. Once you have found, or calculated, the earnings per share figure for a company, as described above, the PE ratio can be determined simply by dividing that number into the current share price. In the case of Morpheus, currently standing at 103p, with earnings per share of 15p, the PE is 6.9 (103 divided by 15). An alternative way of saying it is that Morpheus's share price is currently standing 'at seven times its earnings.'

This may all sound nothing more than mathematical mumbo-jumbo, but it is important to understand the concept of PEs as their use is so widespread. The figure shows the extent to which the share price is supported by the real earnings that the company is making. Or, putting it another way, you could say that the PE represents the number of years it will take the company to 'make' its share price if its earnings remain constant.

If two companies have exactly the same figures for profits and earnings per share, then the one which has the higher PE ratio is expected by the stock market to grow more quickly than the other.

The lower the ratio between the company's share price and its earnings per share, the more soundly are those shares underpinned by the performance of the firm. A PE will decline, either if a company's earnings grow or if the share price falls. If the price falls, but the company's earnings remain constant, it will eventually reach a point where analysts and investors decide that it looks fundamentally undervalued and that the earnings are strong enough to justify a higher PE ratio and thus a higher share price. If the company's earnings are growing strongly, investors are going to reckon that a higher PE is justified because, whatever level it stands at now will be reduced by still greater earnings next year, and the year after that and the year after that one.

A low PE will tend to indicate that the stock market is expecting rather slow growth from that company over the coming years. A high PE, on the other hand, indicates widespread expectations of rapid growth. Perhaps the company is a real high-flyer, involved in the white heat of the technological revolution, rather than in the low-tech manufacture of Thingumajigs. It may have little in the way of earnings per share now but, if it lives up to expectations, those miniscule earnings could mushroom. Investors might be willing to buy the shares of such a company before those earnings materialise, even though it will mean the shares are standing on a very high PE. If growth is likely to continue at breakneck speed for the foreseeable future then perhaps the PE will remain fairly high, with the share price climbing in line with soaring earnings. The greater investors' expectations, the higher the PE ratio they will be willing to countenance. Eager shareholders might be content with this for a while, believing that, as the company expands, its earnings growth will eventually catch up with the climbing share price. However, the higher the PE, the more fragile is the share price. If anything should destroy investors' confidence, such as a collapse in the market for the company's product, or the arrival of a new competitor, it may be more difficult to justify the high PE rating of the shares and they could come tumbling back.

Although PEs are widely used in investment analysis, the calculations made by different individuals or organisations can vary somewhat. To demonstrate this, compare the PEs given each day in the *Financial Times* with those of *The Times*. The reason for the difference is that there are several ways of arriving at the figure for net earnings for a company, and consequently the PE ratio. Many analysts work the numbers out by taking into account the amount of tax a company actually pays on its profits. But others perform their calculations on what is said to be a 'fully taxed basis', which assumes a company pays the standard rate of Corporation Tax, which is 35%. The situation is further complicated if a company does business overseas, because of the wide variety of tax regimes it may encounter.

It is unfortunate that not everybody can agree on earnings figures, but it is only a minor inconvenience. The differences are usually fairly small and, in any case, PE ratios are not to be used as absolute numbers, but for purposes of comparison. It is important to look not at the PE ratio of one company in isolation, but at its relationship to others in the same industry. As long as you compare figures which have been calculated in the same way, there should be no problem. Each sector of the stock market, be it electronics, retailing, oils or engineering, will have its own average PE ratio. The more sluggish sectors have lower PEs than the high-flyers, because future growth is reckoned to be slower.

Near the back of the *Financial Times* every sector is listed, together with the average yield of the shares within it, and the average PE ratio. Do take care when using these figures as some sectors have only one or two shares in them, making them synonymous with the sector. The higher the PE, the faster the growth the market is expecting, both from an individual company and from the sector. If you find a company with a lower PE than the sector average it is probably because its growth rate is believed to be less rapid than the average share in the sector. If you think its growth rate is being underestimated, then you may have discovered a 'cheap' share.

[75]

Because it is the future expectations for a company which are so important in determining investors' attitudes, it is more often than not the 'prospective' PE ratio which is looked at. For this a company's earnings record is extrapolated, with any other known factors taken into account which might influence future profits. The PE ratio is then calculated in exactly the same way. But because the earnings figure has increased (we are assuming there is at least some growth), while the price of the share is taken as unchanged, the PE ratio will decline. Obviously the higher the rate of growth in the company is expected to be, the lower the prospective PE will be in relation to the current one.

Morpheus is a company which rarely surprises the analysts these days, the market for right-handed Thingumajigs being so well established. Profits rose from £2 million last year to £2.3 million this year. To a man, the analysts have pencilled in £2.8 million for next year. This would entail earnings of £1.8 million after tax, or 18p a share, bringing Morpheus's prospective PE down to 5.7. Morpheus is fairly 'lowly-rated', even by the standards of the engineering sector, which is not usually one of the most inspiring areas of the stock market.

However, were all those lunches it gave to civil servants to pay off and Morpheus finally managed to swing that government contract for Thingumajigs, things could change dramatically. The figure of £2.8 million could be scrubbed out, and perhaps £3.4 million put in its place. That would give Morpheus a prospective PE of just 4.7 on an unchanged share price. That would probably encourage buying of the company's shares, with the market believing them to be too cheap. The shares would need to rise to around 125 pence for the prospective PE to be 5.7, the figure that investors were

MORPHEUS ENGINEERING – PROFITS AND EARNINGS				
Share price 103p	Last Year	This Year	Next Year	Revised Forecast
Pre-tax profits (£m)	2.0	2.3	2.8	3.4
Net earnings (£m)	1.3	1.5	1.8	2.2
Earnings per share – 100m. issued (p)	13	15	18	22
PE ratio	7.9	6.9	5.7	4.7

comfortable with before. But it may be that the market's perception of Morpheus has changed completely. Perhaps it is now believed that its growth rate will increase over the next few years and that a PE of 9 or 10 might be considered more appropriate than Morpheus's usual 6 or so. As the company's rating improves, so will its share price.

Asset value One other calculation that determines attitudes towards a share is that of a company's net asset value. This is merely the value of a company's assets – its buildings, plant, land and stocks – attributable to the ordinary shareholders after all prior charges have been met. It is worked out as a value for each share and again is something that can influence the share price. If a company's assets per share are far in excess of the current share price the company might be susceptible to a takeover bid. The predator could be convinced that the company concerned is not utilising its assets efficiently, or even that the company is worth 'breaking up' to sell off the assets. It should be remembered that there is often a large difference between the asset value of a company on paper and the amount that may be raised in reality if a firm has to make a forced sale of its factories, machinery or land. Do take a peek in the report and accounts to see when the property was last valued. If it was a long time ago, perhaps it is worth a good deal more than the figure stated.

There are many other ratios which may prove of use to the investor willing to do some of his own analysis. The **profit margin** is calculated by dividing pre-tax profit by turnover and expressing it as a percentage. An increase in the figure shows either that the company has reduced its costs or that it has increased its prices, or possibly both.

The **current ratio** is an important indicator of the company's solvency and shows the extent to which current assets are available to cover current liabilities. The figure, of current assets (stock, debtors and cash) expressed as a proportion of current liabilities, should generally be greater than one. The problem with this is that stocks cannot always provide cash if it is needed in a hurry. The **acid test** or **quick ratio** gets over this and is calculated as is the current ratio, but with the figure for stocks excluded. There could be grounds for some concern if the number was significantly lower than one. Both these ratios should be steady, if not actually rising, in a healthy company.

[77]

7

HOW TO SATISFY THE CRAVING FOR INFORMATION

Stockbrokers and their analysts

'Economists have successfully predicted 14 of the last 5 recessions.'
David Fehr

There are, I suppose, quite a few private investors who plonk their money into a share, having had it recommended to them, without doing much background reading about the company and without caring very much what the company does. Even if the advice is sound it is rather boring to rely on other people's advice all the time. Even if you are wealthy enough to find a stockbroker or investment adviser who will devote enough of his time to monitor your portfolio of shares for you, it's a pretty dull sort of person who never wants to make any decisions for himself.

You may find you do your stock-picking much along the lines of the punter who only ever puts a bet on the Grand National; his selected nag may run well, but it was only chosen because it had pretty racing colours. But even if you have beginner's luck in the stock market, you're unlikely to continue to do well for long on those lines. Some work has to be put into choosing which shares to invest in. However much assistance you get from the professionals, you really need an adviser who can devote far more time to your investments than any paid lackey ever can – namely yourself. You may not feel your advice is worth listening to at the start, but over time you should be able to pick up enough knowledge to satisfy the needs of any private investor.

It's possible that a potential investor might be put off the idea of having to do any of the background research himself by the thought that he is having to compete with the professionals. Each major stockbroking firm has a large analytical department, with earnest and worthy chaps poring over figures whenever they're not dashing hither and thither visiting companies, all in an attempt to guess – sorry, to

forecast – what results are going to be produce̶
firms this year, next year and maybe even the year a̶
firm may also have a team of economists trying to pre̶
what course the economy is going to take, predictions which
obviously affect the environment in which companies are
operating. There is no way in which you are going to be able to
match up to that sort of operation.

But ask yourself if there is really any need to do so.
However hard stockbroking analysts work, there is usually
still a wide variety of opinion throughout the City on any one
company's forthcoming results. Often no one is correct, with
the results taking everyone by surprise. It is true that in the
majority of cases the consensus is pretty well spot on, but you
ought to realise that just because they devote enormous
resources to their analytical departments, that is no reason to
think stockbrokers are omniscient.

The research done by brokers is often available in some
form or other to the private investor, though it may take some
time to reach him. The first recipients of any new analytical
work will be the big institutions. Most stockbrokers rely on
the commission the institutions' orders generate to survive,
and in consequence pamper and spoon-feed them in a way
the private client could never expect. When a stockbroker
produces a weighty tome on a particular company, it is
usually a 'buy circular'. Rushed round to the institutions as
soon as it leaves the presses, the ranks of salesmen at the
stockbrokers swing into action, dialling all their clients to
'discuss' the learned document and hoping to persuade them
to act upon it. For obvious reasons, it is rare for a stockbroking
firm to spend much time on preparing a 'hold circular'. They
don't like producing anything that won't result in
commission.

If you happen to be one of the lowly private clients of the
broker, you may be sent the circular in due course. But in any
case, the massed ranks of the financial press will almost
certainly receive it. They thrive on such documents, needing
to fill up their pages with something; stockbrokers thrive on
publicity – the more mentions their firm receives in the media,
the happier they will be. The first indication you might have
that a leading firm has produced a circular is in the market
report of one of the main daily papers. These market reports
are becoming more sophisticated and useful all the time.
While those of the *Financial Times* may be a little dry, *The Times*

...n in particular try hard to pack theirs
...es of City tittle-tattle. That is where you
...otherwise inexplicable rise in the price of a
...ou are interested is the result of one of these
...rhaps of a visit by a broking analyst to a com-
...findings are then passed on to the commission-
...esmen, or even a famed 'brokers' lunch', at which
...representatives of the institutions are brought
toge..er with the management of the company in the
stockbroker's offices. The same reports might also reveal the
subjects of the latest bid-rumours in the stock market, for
scarcely a day goes by without some company being tipped as
a likely takeover prospect.

Fuller details of brokers' circulars may be revealed by the
Sunday newspapers, several of which have extensive financial sections, or by the various weekly investment-related
journals. *Financial Weekly* has a regular round-up of the latest
views from stockbrokers.

One slight note of caution at this point. The major
stockbrokers all have corporate clients, whose interests they
represent in matters relating to the stock market. Every company has to have a stockbroker. Some retain the services of
more than one. The blue-blooded firm of Cazenove
specialises in corporate business and the influence this gives it
makes 'Caz' one of the dominant forces in the City. Envious
outsiders believe the firm's success to be due in large part to
the friendships its staff formed at public school or university,
acquaintances renewed in later life when one party is a
stockbroker, the other a leading businessman.

Stockbrokers have to tread a greasy tightrope, trying to
keep their corporate clients happy while at the same time
satisfying their institutional clients. Conflicts of interest may
not prove a problem if the company a stockbroker represents
is doing well, for then its shares can happily be recommended
to clients. There is a slight problem if the company's condition
is not so satisfactory. The broker, as a result of the special
relationship it has with the firm, could be well aware of its
difficulties. What then is it to do? Almost undoubtedly its
institutional clients will hold the shares, possibly at the past
instigation of the stockbrokers' salesmen. Those clients will
cut up rough if they discover they are not being kept abreast of
developments. But if the broker openly admits to those problems and, as a consequence, the share price falls, the com-

pany involved is likely to be extremely upset, to say the least. *In extremis*, they might even decide to switch stock-brokers.

Diplomacy is called for on the part of the stockbroker, though if the firm happens to have a good many corporate clients, the institutions may not want to upset the broker unduly for fear of missing out on some interesting issue in the future. There is an awful lot of back-scratching done in the City. Because few brokers will wish to disappoint their corporate clients, they tend to issue slightly more buy circulars on them than their trading position might otherwise warrant. Whether it has any favourable impact on the share price depends very much on the broker and the company concerned.

Private investors, seeing either the broker's buy circular itself or reference to it somewhere else, should be aware that it is possible the company whose shares are being recommended is in fact a client of that particular stockbroker. That doesn't necessarily mean that the information is in any way invalid. Indeed it may only be that the recommendation itself is just that little bit more effusive then it would otherwise be, but one should be aware that such things are possible. Unfortunately, there is no compulsion for a stockbroker to reveal on its research material whether the companies mentioned are its clients. The financial papers, which also form part of the cozy world of the City, have no wish to irritate the brokers who provide them with good information over such a petty matter as this, so they too neglect to mention when stockbrokers are the 'shop' for a particular company. It may well become compulsory to make such a declaration of interest, but until that happens, as they say in the market, 'mind your eye'.

If not knowing which brokers represent which clients worries you then it is possible to find out from an incredibly valuable publication called *The Hambro Company Guide*. This is rapidly becoming the private investor's bible, for it contains details of every UK company quoted on the stock market together with many lesser firms as well. In addition to telling you the name of a company's financial advisers, it also gives the address of its registrars who will send you copies of the Report and Accounts, the address and phone number of the company, what it does, where in the FT you can find it, when its results are published, when the AGM takes place and, as if this wasn't enough, gives you a five year trading record of the firm. If a company has chosen to pay for an extended entry, there will also be a graph of the share price over the previous 5 years. This indispensable publication comes out every quarter and, at the time of writing, costs a mere £59.50 for the entire year. It has made the life of the private investor a great deal more comfortable than in the past, encapsulating information on companies that could have taken days to amass, and is a mine of incredibly valuable detail. The *Hambro Company Guide* has done much to narrow the information gap between institutional and private investor. It is published by Hemmington Scott who are on 01–253 4106 and should be on the bookshelf of every shareholder right beside *Fair Shares*.

The financial press

Some investors have a junky-like craving for information. Whether the information they accumulate helps them to plan their investments sensibly depends on the use to which they put it. There are certainly plenty of sources to choose from, although their quality is pretty variable.

The more up-market newspapers are steadily improving their financial sections, though whether this is always with the interests of their readers uppermost in their minds or whether it is a ploy to attract more of the lucrative financial advertising is sometimes open to question. Which newspaper you buy is of course a personal choice. If you are concerned to miss nothing of interest, then the *Financial Times* is very much a necessity. It gives the prices of most quoted UK securities, together with information on dividends, dividend cover and yield, the PE ratio and the highs and lows for the share for the year. It endeavours to mention virtually every announcement made by a quoted British company somewhere within its pages, though you may have to look pretty hard on occasion to find information on the smaller firms. The appointments section is worth a glimpse. Many a share has been sparked into life by the arrival of some renowned director on a company's board. Many of the paper's pages are devoted to wider issues than mere company news, which you may or may not find useful.

Although the FT is the City's paper, it isn't really the one that moves the stock market. Like *The Times* in the secular world, it aims to be a paper of record, and tends to shun too much comment, whatever its advertising campaign may claim. However, the *Financial Times* is adding rather more comment on company affairs than it used to. Following the publication of results, there will usually be some detailed comment upon them, which might even be concluded by an opinion about the merits of the shares themselves. The back page of the FT is the home of the illustrious Lex column, probably the most learned of all City financial commentaries, and from time to time also the most unfathomable.

It is perhaps the *Daily Mail* that has the greatest effect upon share prices. It used to be the most commonly spotted paper on the jobber's pitches on the stock market floor, with those estimable gentlemen preferring its more popular style and no doubt its shorter sentences too. The Sunday newspapers can also have a marked effect on share prices, with the occasional article appearing there that can spark off a long-term movement in a particular share or even a sector of the market.

Public announcements have to be made when stakes of more than 5% are taken in a company and at further stages as that stake is built up. Although such a purchase may simply be for investment purposes, the market may perceive it as a prelude to a takeover attempt. Whether or not that is the case, it may affect the share price, as will the disposal of such a holding. Although the *Financial Times* used to list these announcements every day, their coverage is now particularly patchy. It is still worth trawling the back pages of the paper in case there are any interesting share changes. The purchase or sale of stakes in large companies will probably be reported in the other papers too, but the FT is the most likely to mention that some acquisition-hungry group has started taking an interest in one of your smaller investments. There is also an obligation for directors to make an announcement when they are buying or selling shares in their businesses, a useful guide to their own opinions about their companies. If you want to keep a close eye on share purchases and sales, then BRI's monthly guide, *Strategic Holdings for Take-overs* (021-354 8941), monitors stakes in virtually all public companies, while *The Shareholder*, edited by me, publishes lists of directors' share deals.

Keep an eye out for the date on which companies in which you are interested are to announce their results. For many companies this is the time when dealings are most active in their shares. If you haven't spotted details of the date well in advance in the FT, then Saturday's edition gives a list of results to be announced in the forthcoming week.

Another snippet worth watching out for is news that a company is changing its stockbroker. It is likely that the company is making the move because it feels the new broker can do more for it, perhaps because it has a better relationship with institutional fund managers. If the company concerned is a fast-growing concern, it may feel it has outgrown the usefulness of the smaller stockbroker which originally brought it to the stock market. As we saw much earlier, a buoyant share price is useful to a company in several ways. A large stockbroker ought to be able to do more to achieve this, by increasing the general level of awareness about the company and boosting its image.

Do check before before buying any share in a small company that the price is quoted daily in the newspaper you get. None is completely comprehensive in its listings and it is far less satisfying to own a share whose day-to-day movements you can't follow. The *Financial Times* charges for including a share in its list, and whilst most companies find it worthwhile to participate some of the tinier ones can't afford to.

It is extremely useful to monitor the price of shares in which you are becoming interested. Often one might take your eye, but you could be unconvinced of the buying case. Or you might even feel that the price could move lower and want to wait for that to happen. So keep a weekly record of the prices of thirty or so shares, in the hope of spotting when a share is starting to move steadily one way or the other.

There are now several packages you can buy for home computers that will perform the same feat with the benefit of showing prices in graph form. Some will perform clever tricks as well, such as displaying the performance of one share against another, or comparing the movement of a share to that of the market as a whole. If you bought a home computer and have so far found no use for it but playing intellectually stimulating games involving the destruction of little green men, you might consider making your machine legitimate by getting one of these programmes. There are even more sophisticated ones that can be run on personal computers of the sort found lying unused under dust-sheets in offices.

For more detailed comment on the stock market, journals such as the *Investors' Chronicle* and *Financial Weekly* can be valuable. At present, there isn't an investment magazine around that doesn't have serious flaws, but these two should have plenty of instructive information within their pages. The *Investors' Chronicle* aims to cover the results of every company quoted on the stock market and has regular articles on the merits and attractions of individual shares and sectors, besides various features on other forms of investment.

The only way you can find out which newspapers and magazines are suitable for you is to try them for a while. Whichever you do choose, I would recommend hanging on to some of them afterwards. You may find it useful to be able to refer back to old copies, and most investment magazines help by producing quarterly indices which assist greatly in hunting down an article or item which you can only dimly remember.

The Saturday edition of the *Financial Times*, a much more relaxed paper than the weekday edition and aimed far more closely at the private investor, is frequently useful in later months for checking up the prices of shares at particular dates. You will find most newspapers that give share prices regularly also give the highest and lowest level reached during the year. Fine, if the share is at its peak or trough. But if it is somewhere in the middle, and you haven't been following it assiduously, it is helpful to check back to see whether it is passing through the middle from the top down or the bottom upwards.

The report and accounts

Reading the financial press may help to make up your mind on a share, but it may be that you would like to do some more background work into a company which has taken your fancy, before committing any of your funds. Again, it isn't too difficult to get hold of the necessary details. The *Investors' Chronicle*, when analysing results, usually gives a condensed version of the salient figures over the past few years.

This may not be detailed enough for your needs, or you may not have kept your back copies. If you want more information get hold of the company's latest set of Report and Accounts. There is an obligation for every limited company to produce these and they are usually sent out to shareholders a short while after the announcement of results for the company's financial year. Each will contain a profit and loss account, a balance sheet, a director's report and a statement from the chairman. But beyond that they differ greatly. Some content themselves with giving just the bare and necessary details. Others take the process a good deal further, realising that the Report and Accounts offer an unparalleled opportunity to communicate with their shareholders and perhaps also interest hitherto uninvolved parties; the full resources of their public relations agency have been employed in making the company appear glamorous and exciting, with charts and graphs all over the place, photographs of various products, and pictures of their workplaces with invariably happy employees toiling therein. There is a school of thought that believes the greater the effort a company makes to spice up its Report and Accounts, the less concrete financial information is likely to be contained within. But it tends to be the younger companies who produce the glossiest annual reports as they are still striving to bring themselves to the attention of the investing public. Conglomerates, groups made up of various interests in widely differing industries, also have to try hard to convince investors that they have a coherent and viable company policy. For some of the firms involved in advertising, design and marketing, their reports are a chance to show off their skills. Saatchi and Saatchi, for instance, include a graphically illustrated dissertation on the advertising industry each year, which is fascinating for those interested in the subject. The Michael Peters agency has probably produced the most bizarre documents so far; their original prospectus was in the form of an origami kit, while their first year's figures were commemorated with what was apparently the world's only pop-up Report and Accounts!

To get hold of any company's Report and Accounts, which ought to include the trading record of the firm over the past five years or more, you should contact the company's registrars, whose address and phone number will be given in the *Hambro Company Guide* and ask for a copy to be sent to you. If you can't locate the registrars, then the company itself will probably be quite happy to let you have one. If the firm in which you are interested is part of a larger group, or not a public company, then you will be able to find the Report and Accounts filed at Companies House in London where, for a nominal fee, you can pick up a photoco...

Extel publish detailed financial inforn... companies, in the form of small cards issu... stockbrokers will subscribe to the full series... your broker might let you have, or will procu... which you are particularly interested. But th... libraries around the country should also hav... only want to look at a card once, this might be th...

The big libraries also subscribe to the McCart... ...orma- tion Service. This is extremely valuable to anyone wanting to bone up quickly on a company, comprising as it does copies of most articles written in the press on the financial affairs of all quoted UK firms. Again most stockbrokers have copies of McCarthy cards and might help you out with a request, or you could buy the cards on an individual company directly from McCarthy themselves.

If you are having trouble getting hold of some information on a company, you could always try writing to the chairman himself. Such people are a good deal more accessible than one might think, particularly to those who are already share- holders.

The tipsheets

Every investor likes to feel he is occasionally privy to exclusive information. After all, isn't it those who are in the know who really make the big money? That desire to run on the inside track is exploited by the publishers of the various tipsheets, or 'investment newsletters' as they would no doubt prefer to call them, which have proliferated over the past few years. All run extensive advertising campaigns in which their successful tips are loudly trumpeted, whetting potential investors' appe- tites by dangling in front of them the fantastic profits that could have been made if only people had had the good sense to follow their advice.

What's wrong with them? Unfortunately, quite a lot. For a start the publishers of these newsletters are particularly selective when it comes to advertising their product. In giving copious details of the shares they have tipped which have soared in value, they somehow forget to mention those also recommended in the newsletter which have done less well,

...well be the majority. No doubt they feel demand
...publication might be affected if an exhaustive list of
...tips' were given.

Cast your eye down the shares mentioned in their adverts.
You will probably notice that they are all fairly small companies. There is a good reason for this. The reputation and
success of any tipsheet lies in the performance of the shares
mentioned. But tip a blue-chip and the influence of the newsletter will move the price not a jot; there are simply too many
people dealing in the shares in massive quantities. That isn't
so for really small companies. Whereas orders for hundreds of
thousands of shares in ICI are common, smaller companies
will have far fewer shares in issue; dealings in them will be far
more scarce and may be in only a couple of hundred shares a
time. If a newsletter tips the shares of a minor company, it is
easy to see how it needs only a few of its subscribers to follow
its advice to send the price moving sharply upwards. If a
bandwagon starts rolling, the price could shoot skywards
even though relatively few people have been able to buy
shares, for each small purchase will send the price climbing
still higher.

The advertisements for the tipsheets tell you of the increase
in the share's middle price since they were first mentioned in
its pages (or, in a couple of cases, its page). They give the
impression that their subscribers were able to buy the shares
at that price, skating over the unlikelihood of that happening
in reality. For a start, if the share is lowly priced – a 'penny
share' – then the spread between the buying price and selling
price, the jobber's turn, is going to be far more of a problem
than for a higher-priced share. The risk on these shares is
greater for jobbers as well as investors, and only thus can they
protect themselves.

If your chosen stock has a middle price of 6p, it might be 5p
bid and offered at 7p, proportionately a massive spread. You
will have to pay 7p, and to get to the stage where you can get
your money back, the shares will have to climb to a middle
price of 8p. That rise from 6p to 8p for the share is 33% – a full
third of the share's original value, and that excludes any
brokerage charges you will have to pay. You are on a hiding
to nothing from the word go. You may even find the spread
wider than that!

But it is very unlikely that you will be the first to take the
newsletter's advice in any case. Most make a point of the

speed with which they are delivered, often providing a telephone hotline with their latest recommendations. But even so, you are competing with the other subscribers, many of whom will also be trying to act first. It only needs one or two of them to get in before you and the share price could have moved substantially, making the investment considerably less attractive.

The market-makers selling the shares to the brokers aren't exactly dummies either. They subscribe to all the tipsheets that are published, and get them just as soon as anybody else. If a broker approaches, asking to deal in a share that has just been tipped, the market-maker is going to 'read' him as a buyer and may mark the price up accordingly. His living is made from wholesaling the shares. If he has only a limited supply, he may increase the price sharply to dull the demand. He is compelled to make a market in the stocks on his book and if sudden demand for normally dull shares leaves him without any at all, he could find himself in difficulties.

Despite these strictures, the advice given in some of the better newsletters can be perfectly sound. If you find one whose recommendations you respect, my advice would be to wait for a while after a 'tip' before making your purchase. Tipped shares tend to see a bout of enthusiasm which quickly boils over. Many of the bigger share 'traders' prefer to deal only within the Stock Exchange account, selling the same shares that they have bought within that short period so that the amount they have to commit to their investments is far smaller than it would otherwise be. Hold back either until the early froth has subsided, or until the last two days of the Stock Exchange account when others could be selling. If a share really is worth buying, you are unlikely to miss out on much by showing a little patience. Never act hastily.

Amstrad, one of the wonder-stocks of the past few years, took well over a year to multiply itself by a factor of ten. Exactly the same thing applies to the five- or six-line comments on companies made in the Sunday papers. These tell you precisely nothing and you should never act until you have done your own background research. Some of these seem to emanate from market-makers who are 'talking their own book', extolling the virtues of shares which they already hold, hoping they will rise after a mention in the press.

If you insist on slavishly following the advice of tipsheets, ask yourself a question: why are these people being so benevolent as to give everyone else the benefit of their advice? Why don't they keep it to themselves and capitalise on their knowledge? Those in the market think they know the answer as far as one or two of the tipsheets are concerned. After seeing all too often substantial buying of shares shortly *before* they are recommended in some of the less reputable tipsheets, they are convinced that those involved are profiting, not only from the subscription money that flows in, but also by buying the shares in advance of publication, writing them up, and then selling out as the small investors follow their advice. No one knows quite how often it happens, but there have been criminal prosecutions in the past for just this sort of activity, and the private investor ought to be aware of its possibility. A couple of the more venerable newsletters are owned by larger companies which have a reputation to protect; these are undoubtedly on the level, though interestingly, perhaps because of this, the shares they tip tend to be rather less speculative in nature than those of some of their shadier brethren, whose operations may be located in a shared room up a back flight of stairs at an address chosen solely because it looks respectable on paper. These outfits rarely feel confident enough to give subscribers their telephone number, which ought to make one a little suspicious.

Beware in particular of adverts for 'free' newsletters from outfits whose name means nothing to you. These are frequently used as 'come-ons' for gullible investors who, having given their telephone number, are pestered by very plausible salesmen to put their money in totally unsuitable, and frequently unprofitable shares. If the operation is based abroad then, almost without exception, you should ignore it completely. There are some very, very disreputable operators about, who try to persuade investors to buy shares in companies in which they have an interest. These boiler-house operations used to be based in Amsterdam but, now that the authorities have rather belatedly acted, have spread to Luxemburg, Spain and other places with rather lax regulations. Their salesmen make the double-glazing variety look paragons of honesty and virtue. Do not believe them if they 'promise' you great wealth in a very short time. If they are selling you something that is almost completely worthless, it is they who will become wealthy. How else do you suppose that they can afford the cost of all those international telephone calls?

I know of one stockbroker who specialises in private clients who was quite enthusiastic about domestic newsletters and, as this seemed contrary to the usual opinion of brokers, I asked him why. Because, he said, they gave a quick fillip to the price of shares that was frequently quite unjustified, thereby enabling his clients to get themselves out of previously unrewarding holdings.

Before subscribing to any newsletter, consider carefully its often substantial cost. With annual subscriptions that can be well over a hundred pounds a year, you need to be fairly convinced that they will make you at least that much more than you would be able to make yourself.

Inside information – the bad breath straight from the horse's mouth

Whenever you get a tip on a share from an acquaintance, it is probable that he already owns the stock. After all, if you hold a share, it is only natural to try to persuade other people to invest in it as well. The greater the demand, the higher the price. There's also the feeling of security; it somehow feels more comforting to know someone else in the same boat. You can congratulate each other if things are going well and commiserate when they aren't.

There's a natural tendency to exaggerate the quality of the information given. Another punter is far more likely to deal if he thinks the tip comes straight from the horse's mouth. Often such a story is mere hot air. But not always. No company is leakproof, particularly when some big deal is about to be pulled off, for cohorts of professional advisers will have been called in to assist in its preparation. It is not uncommon for someone, somewhere, to let something slip.

If your informant is close enough to the source for you to believe his information to be correct about a forthcoming bid, for instance, or a massive jump in a company's profits, the temptation to act on it can be great. After all, it is far easier to make money from a dead certainty than it is to risk using one's own judgment. But be warned that dealing on inside information is not only against the rules of the Stock Exchange; it also happens to be illegal and transgressors can be fined or even imprisoned.

[91]

A good deal of bandying of inside information does go on in the City and the Stock Exchange frequently report misdeeds to the authorities. However, the ability of professionals to use offshore companies for their activities make it very difficult to prove a misdemeanour and, now that insider dealing is a criminal offence, the proof needs to be conclusive. Those who do get prosecuted tend, on the whole, to be the smaller fry who are less well able to conceal their tracks. The new computerised trading system makes it a good deal easier for the Stock Exchange surveillance department to monitor inside dealing and, while it will no doubt remain very difficult to trap the big fish, the authorities are very keen to prove that self-regulation works.

It is difficult to know what is, and what is not inside information. You should realise that the same rules apply to information that is likely to depress a share price as to information that could lead to a jump in the shares. Selling shares you own because you have heard news of something disastrous in the offing can be an offence. How you choose to behave is up to you. But you should be aware that dealing on what you believe to be inside knowledge is illegal, no matter how far away from the horse's mouth you may be. There have already been successful prosecutions for insider dealing. You could be one of the unlucky ones.

8

TAKING THE PLUNGE

What sort of investor are you?

'All investment carries some degree of risk, whether relating to business or general economic conditions. The existence of SIB no more removes the need for investors to pay attention to where they place their money than the existence of the Highway Code removes the need to look before crossing the road.' Securities and Investments Board Booklet

The theory of share investment is all very well, but just where do you start? You should begin well away from the stock market, making sure that every rainy day you can possibly foresee is well catered for. As you must be aware by now, shares fluctuate in value. If all your spare capital is in the stock market and you need money desperately when the market is depressed, then tough luck. The stock market is, in general, a home for long-term investment, not a substitute for an instant access deposit account. So you would be well advised not to consider building up a portfolio until the rest of your family finances have been sorted out and you have a fund of cash stored away.

However, simply because you aren't yet ready to build up a diversified portfolio of shares is no reason why you can't dabble in the market. The difficulty here is that it is fairly difficult to spread your risk among a number of shares if you are only playing around with the odd thousand pounds or so but, providing you realise this, there is nothing to stop you going ahead. You might look upon your savings elsewhere as being 'safe' and treat the money you use to buy and sell shares as your 'speculative' capital. Alternatively, you could begin by investing in a unit trust or investment trust, where professional managers lump together the savings of thousands of individuals to invest in a range of stocks and shares, giving you a proportionate success in the entire fund. As you will discover later, such trusts have both advantages and disadvantages.

[93]

You must face up to the possibility that you may lose money in the stock market. It is not a sure way to make your fortune, nor can you even be certain that you will come out ahead at the end of the day. You might happen to choose to get involved at the very top of the market and have to wait years before prices return to the levels at which you entered the game.

Are you looking for growth or income from your investments? On the whole, if you are still earning money, then you can afford to take greater risks than those who are not. After all, if the worst does happen, you will be able to replace your losses with your salary or wages. But as retirement nears, making provision for your pension and ensuring you have a satisfactory income once you have received your gold watch will become far more important.

It is expected that over the coming decade, people are going to have a great deal more money available for investment than before. Many homeowners will find they are left another house when their parents die and will suddenly find themselves with tens of thousands of pounds when they come to sell it. In the event of a lump sum falling into your lap, you would be well advised to approach a stockbroker or other financial adviser for advice on how to invest it. If, as would seem sound, he or she recommends a very safe portfolio, you might consider keeping back just a little of the money in order to 'play' the market, just to add that bit of spice to your investments.

One last point, which may seem self-evident. If you are going to invest on the stock market, you will need either a bank or building society cheque account so that you can pay for your shares as and when you need to.

How to choose shares

'There is no shallow end to the stock market where the private investor can dip his inexperienced toe; it's all deep end, but some bits are deeper than others.'   Oofy Prosser

If you are considering investing in shares then sooner or later you are going to have to choose just which companies you will honour by enrolling as a shareholder. The choice is pretty daunting. There are over three thousand companies who have their shares listed on the UK stock market, so variety is one thing that isn't lacking. Cast your eye down the prices page of a newspaper and you'll keep coming across names you know very well – Marks and Spencer, ICI, BP, GEC, British Telecom, TSB, Jaguar, Grand Metropolitan, Bass, Cadbury Schweppes, British Aerospace, Sainsbury, Tesco, Beecham, Trusthouse Forte, Thorn EMI, Ladbrokes – these are just a few of the better known.

Most companies of any size in Britain have their shares listed on the Stock Exchange, though not all. There are a few sizeable ones that have never felt the need for raising capital through the market, such as the Littlewoods Group and Heron. But you'll find quoted equities in virtually every field of business activity: retailing, banking, property, brewing, oil, manufacturing, building, insurance, gambling, electronics, advertising, publishing and the leisure industry.

What exactly are you looking for in a share? No doubt something safe, paying a large dividend, but with immense growth potential as well. Aren't we all? But every investment has to involve a choice, whether to go for safety and accept a lower return, or for a high risk and possible high return, whether to go for a high yield, or whether to plump for a company going hell for leather to achieve growth and which may not get round to paying a dividend for years.

To some extent, the sort of investments you make are going to be influenced by your own circumstances, and particularly your tax position. Although we'll come back to taxation and shares later, basically any income you receive will be taxed at your highest rate, just as the income you receive from most of your other investments. Any net gains you make from selling shares are subject to Capital Gains Tax, which is levied at a flat rate of 30%. Some investors go to extraordinary lengths to try to avoid paying CGT, concentrating on it to such an extent that the attention they give to their investments must surely suffer.

There is an annual exemption for CGT so that for the year 1987–8 investors are allowed to make £6,600 of net capital gains before having to pay any tax at all. Most private investors will never be subject to this tax and should simply forget all about it, a point which makes one wonder about the sense of Personal Equity Plans. Those who do find themselves in the CGT net ought to be proud of their investment achievement. After all, you would need to invest £30,000, see your investments rise 22% in just one year, and sell everything in one fell swoop before CGT would even touch you. With the CGT exemption level raised each year in line with inflation, there should be little fear among private investors that hunting for capital gains in their investments will do them any harm. Having to pay Capital Gains Tax remains one of my life's ambitions.

How *can* you make money out of the stock market? There are innumerable old saws passed down from generation to generation in the Stock Exchange. You will make a pile if you always 'buy too late and sell too soon', if you 'always leave a little for the next man' or if you 'always do the opposite of what the crowd is doing'. Yet although there may be some grains of wisdom in these aphorisms, they are hardly sound enough advice on which to base your investment strategy. You will have to get used to doing some of the work necessary to judge the attractions of shares yourself. Earlier I mentioned that you would need to be fairly wealthy to receive cossetting from a stockbroker. But even if you do find a broker who is regularly giving you good advice, you ought continually to be undergoing a process of self-education, preparing yourself against the day when your broker moves on or retires. If you know what you want to to do without seeking a broker's advice, then you will be able to deal more cheaply and thus keep more of the profit for yourself.

Don't charge into the stock market like a bull at a gate, buying shares left, right and centre indiscriminately. You should immerse yourself in these unfamiliar waters as gently as possible, fully aware of exactly what you are doing and the possible implications of your actions. Remember that you are using real money when you invest on the stock market, and show suitable caution.

The novice investor is usually, and sensibly, given the advice that he should experiment with a trial portfolio first. In that way you can follow the day-to-day gyrations of selected shares, noting that even if one does well, the portfolio as a whole may not benefit if another is falling out of bed. It should also bring home to the tyro the way in which shares move in sympathy with the general stock market; it is little use holding a share which has dazzling attractions and expecting it to soar ahead if every other share is falling back. Similarly it should be instructive to see how far individual shares benefit from a general rise in the level of the stock market. The beginner can also note the reactions of shares to relevant information, such as company results or the movement of share stakes. It is very important to notice at this early stage that the price of a share does not instantly adjust to changes in sentiment towards the company concerned. It is more likely to be a gradual adjustment of expectations, as greater and greater numbers of investors appreciate the benefits, or disadvantages, of some new element in the equation.

As an example of this, I have shown the graph of the shares of Peninsular and Oriental Steam Navigation Company, whose delightful name is usually diminished by an unsentimental stock market to a brusque 'P & O'. The past few years have been extremely busy ones for the company, seeing off a bid from the conglomerate Trafalgar House, announcing a merger with Sterling Guarantee, buying OCL and Stock Conversion and taking over European Ferries. Now a combination of transport and property interests, the image of the company has been transformed in the stock market's eyes from that of a stodgy, uninspiring shipping company into a go-ahead, well-managed conglomerate. To a great extent, much of this change of attitude is due to the work of one man, chairman Sir Jeffrey Sterling, an indication of how important

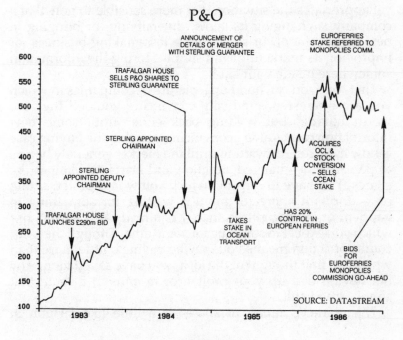

P&O

SOURCE: DATASTREAM

monitoring changes in the composition of company's boards of directors can be to the private investor.

Note how the rise in P & O's share price was pretty gradual, once Trafalgar came out into the open. It takes time for the stock market to 're-rate' a company, to revise its collective opinion. That time is important for the private investor. It is true that some price-sensitive information is often available to the big institutions before the general public, however much that may be against the spirit of the Stock Exchange's rules. But even if important news is announced publicly during the day through the Stock Exchange's Announcements Office, it won't be until that evening, or possibly the next morning, before the private investors, mulling over their papers, notice what is going on. You shouldn't believe that will automatically make action on your part too late but, as with tips, if the price has already moved substantially, consider first whether there might not soon be a reaction to that share move.

You may find yourself able to react with greater knowledge and alacrity to new information on a company's affairs if you have already been doing some groundwork. Many of the more sensible investors keep an eye on far more shares than they actually hold in their portfolio. It is little use holding a share, knowing it is a marvellous investment, if no one else yet appreciates the situation. Far more sensible to note that a company is changing its spots, diversifying, or bringing in new management, or selling off a loss-making business, or improving its marketing, and simply storing the information somewhere inside your skull.

That way you can build up a picture of companies in which you are interested, gradually convincing yourself they are worth buying, but holding back either until some new information comes along convincing you that the buying case is now cast-iron, or waiting until the market generally begins to perceive the changed situation and starts nibbling at the shares. You have to consider which you would prefer; sitting on a dormant share for months waiting for something to happen, or buying after a share has already had a small rise which you expect to continue for some time. Though the latter course of action means you may be paying a little more than when you first thought of the idea, you have saved money by not having tied up your capital for months in a share that simply stood still.

The market's rating of shares is a little like fashion in

clothing. Those who first experiment with a new style are the ones taking the risk, facing ridicule from their more staid contemporaries for daring to stand out from the crowd. The crowd moves more sluggishly, often slavishly responding to the fashions that are dictated to them by the press and the clothing industry. Once they latch on to a new style though, it rapidly spreads until the early pioneers are swamped by a large movement in which they no longer stand out; they have to content themselves with the knowledge that they were first. But by now they should be contemplating moving out to something new before the style becomes rather passé. The last few to hang on to the trappings of an outmoded fashion face as much ridicule as those brave enough to attempt it first.

So it often is with shares. The cannier investors buy just as they sense that the crowd is becoming interested, as they realise that the 'sleeper' is about to awaken and become fashionable. They use the movement of the crowd into the share to benefit substantially themselves, selling out just as they feel the trend could be coming to an end, 'leaving' – as the saying goes – 'something for the next man'. Some of those 'next men' are going to find they have jumped on the bandwagon just a little too late. As Adam Smith puts it in *The Money Game*: 'When everybody finally believes in a stock, there is almost no one left to sell to.'

Fashion is important in the stock market. For within the general movement of the market as a whole, sectors and individual shares do come in and out of vogue. This season's sector might be food retailing, software companies or engineering; it might be broader than that, with consumer-related shares, for instance, all finding favour on hopes of lower interest rates, or companies with large overseas earnings in demand as a result of weakness for the pound.

It is important to realise how important this can be, particularly as the all-important institutional investors tend to have their favourites. In 1985, for instance, the stock market as a whole rose 16%. But that average concealed some very sharp differences for particular sectors. Retailing shares climbed some 40%, helped by a rash of bid battles, while those investors who were heavily into electronics suffered a 30% loss in the sector. Many shares did either much better or much worse than this, of course. The 'Slush Puppie' drinks makers Somportex, for example, saw their shares rise over 600% while those of the BBC home computer group, Acorn, plummetted from 400p to just 40p during the year. So bear in mind that it is possible to lose money even when the general stock market is climbing and feasible, although difficult in practice I have found, to pick shares that rise while most around them are falling back.

One way of monitoring the ebbs and flows of sentiment for individual sectors of the stock market is through the weekly 'Leaders and Laggards' column tucked away in the back pages of the *Financial Times*, that area of the paper that is such a rich mine of information for the shrewd investor. A very sensible exercise is to rank the sectors by number, monitoring them from week to week, and noting which are climbing and which are falling out of fashion. As I warned earlier, do remember that the odd sector is dominated by only one pre-dominant company. Even if you don't have the time or the patience to follow the sectors so closely, it should become apparent from regular reading of the financial press which areas the big institutional money is flowing into.

This is where the private investor's fears of being unable to compete with the giant institutions can be turned into a pos-itive advantage. True, the institutions may have the better service from the stockbrokers, they may be meeting the man-agement of companies all the time and they may have access to wonderful research. But having decided to move heavily into a new area, they have all the balletic agility of an oil tanker. Their sheer size makes it impossible for institutions to get hold of all the shares they want in just one transaction. But if the funds simply kept buying until their needs were satis-fied, the prices of the shares would sky-rocket. It would not be too helpful to the performance of their funds if such clumsiness in dealing sent their favoured shares soaring. They need to bide their time where they can, picking up a few shares here, a few there, waiting for sellers to appear. It isn't always the case, but generally it takes an institution ages to build up large stakes in a company from nothing. Many of their deals may simply be adjustments in the size of existing holdings, but for a giant like the Prudential Corporation, or the Post Office Pension Fund, to buy a substantial number of shares in even the largest of companies is going to have a marked effect.

The massed ranks of fund managers usually find them-selves talked about, behind their backs of course, as so many unthinking sheep, acting with the herd so they can't be seen to stand out. Like all generalisations, it is too sweeping. There are a good many bright fund managers around. But there are also people with extremely mediocre talents looking after large sums of money; the 'buggin's turn' method of promotion is used just as much in the institutions as in other areas. The private investor shouldn't find it too difficult to keep an eye on the sheep, noting which general direction they are moving in, and shifting nippily to get there before most of them.

Having said that, here's one contrary piece of advice: some of the more intelligent and successful fund managers claim they owe much of their enviable performance record to their habit of moving against the herd. This 'contra-think' idea used to be quite widely held by brokers too. But it could only really hold true when the institutions held less power. Now their movements are so gigantic that the herd cannot fail to move the stock market with it. Fund managers moving against the trend may find they can buy or sell shares in large quantities more easily than they would otherwise be able to do. For them, that is a great benefit, but it is not something that will necessarily help the private investor. Unless you are convinced the crowd is simply travelling in the wrong direction, try to use its momentum to your own advantage.

As an example of the way in which it can take the institutions, and the market in general, ages to appreciate a new development, take the newspaper sector in advance of the Reuters flotation. Reuters was set up as a news agency owned by many of the leading newspaper groups, but its business was revolutionised by its provision of financial information. The Reuters 'Monitor' service, providing instantaneous price information worldwide through video screens, also has a dealing facility and is reckoned to have made possible the fantastic growth of the world's foreign exchange markets.

The plan to sell shares in Reuters in mid-1984 was widely publicised in advance, and not only in the financial press. There were innumerable articles about the merits, or more commonly the disadvantages, of the sale in the general news pages too. It didn't take too much intelligence to see the great financial rewards of the sale that would flow to the existing owners of Reuters – the newspaper groups. The sector had really been rather lacklustre until the beginning of 1983. Newspapers were seen as being rather dull, racked by industrial disputes, and not very profitable. But taking into

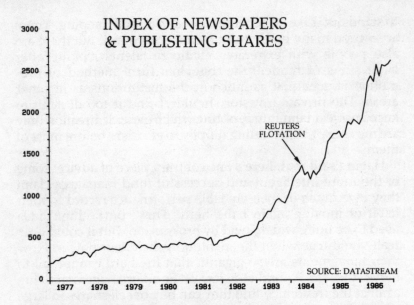

INDEX OF NEWSPAPERS
& PUBLISHING SHARES

REUTERS
FLOTATION

SOURCE: DATASTREAM

account their interests in Reuters and the shares of the newspaper companies looked far more attractive. Yet it took the
sheep an eternity to wake up to the fact that they shouldn't be
waiting until the sale of Reuters itself, but should be buying
the newspaper companies in advance of that sale. Anyone investing in the newspaper sector at the start of 1983 would
have seen the shares in it double in the run-up to the Reuters
sale. For a while they then meandered. But there was then a
substantial re-rating of Reuters itself, which in the first nine
months of its life on the stock market nearly doubled in value.
That of course helped to push the newspaper groups, which
still held large chunks of Reuters, still higher.

The fun was by no means over for the sector. The move of
Times Newspapers to Wapping and the revolution that
wrought in the newspaper industry, with its resultant heavy
rationalisations, kept the pot boiling long after the Reuters
flotation was forgotten about.

Your eyes as an investment tool

'Put all your eggs in one basket and – watch that basket.'
Andrew Carnegie

I would strongly recommend that your first share purchases
are in companies whose business you can fully understand.

In fact, the more familiar you are with what a company does, the better. It might be that the company you work for is quoted on the stock market. Whether or not any provisions have been made for employees to purchase shares through established schemes, you may feel that the confidence and new-found success you can feel around you each day is simply not yet being understood or appreciated by the stock market. Or it may be that one of your competitors is proving to be too successful for comfort. If you understand why, and think that success likely to continue, why not try backing your judgement? The more you comprehend the activities of the company whose shares you are buying, the more you are likely to realise the risks and be willing to accept them.

But even if you can't do this, it is extraordinary how much important information the private investor can pick up simply by looking about him. Take the main chains of high street shops for instance. Are customers thronging them every day? Are there queues at the tills? If not, is that because of staff efficiency or simply lack of demand? How effective are the displays in the shop? Has the company changed the store layout recently, or refurbished the premises? If so, does it make for a marked improvement?

All this may sound very trivial, but believe me it is not. It is one thing reading umpteen articles on the changing nature of retailing; but actually going into the shops and seeing what is happening is every bit as important. It is only then that you can appreciate the marked changes many companies have introduced in their style and methods of selling. Hepworths' introduction of 'Next', selling co-ordinated clothing to women, sparked off a revolution in retailing with a wave of copy-cat shops being set up throughout the nation's high streets. The shift by Hepworths from being a staid and very traditional supplier of menswear, into the far more competitive womenswear market was a giant leap which paid off handsomely and very promptly. So successful was it that the company's name was changed to 'Next'. It was a move which could easily have been observed first-hand by any investor, who might also have noticed the sluggishness with which Marks and Spencer responded to the challenge in the high street. Again, it was not the financial pages that proved the most fruitful area of study in the early days, but rather the fashion and leisure pages, for it was there that the most valuable discussions of the companies' plans were printed.

[103]

NEXT

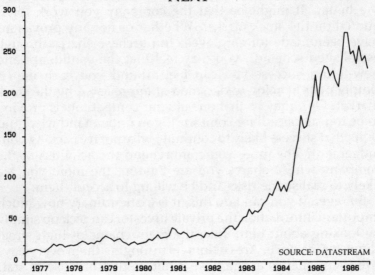

SOURCE: DATASTREAM

The importance of these changes in high-street retailing had profound repercussions elsewhere. The private investor following fashion trends should also have been considering the implications for the manufacturers, especially those traditionally linked to M & S. It was also worth finding out which design companies were benefiting from what was going on. Trips to the supermarket, the department store, the DIY superstore and even the newsagent should all be part of your research process. You should take note of what is happening when next you buy a pair of shoes, or a suit, in fact anything at all. Look at the company's advertising. How effective do you find it? How often do you spot its vans or lorries? What year were they registered? Are they clean or do they look run down? Whose products do you buy, and why? Ask your friends their opinion about various products and demand to know why they think the way they do.

Buying a share simply because you like a company's products or because you like the way it does business is not necessarily going to make you money. After all, if every other investor thinks that a company is wonderful, then the share price will already reflect that opinion. Being the last investor on the scene is no good at all. The opinion of the crowd is vital in stock market investment. You need to find something that

[104]

everyone else has either failed to appreciate yet, or something that the herd is only beginning to wake up to.

As an example of the differing performances of two companies with a very big presence in the High Street, let us take Acorn and Amstrad, both in their way rather extreme examples, but nonetheless useful for that. Acorn came to the stock market in 1983 and was initially strong on the back of market appreciation of the merits of their BBC home computers. The company grew to become one of the largest in its field in Europe but was mortally wounded by the sharp decline in the home computer market in 1984. Early the following year, it submitted to a rescue package from the Italian office equipment group Olivetti. Anyone with more than a passing interest in computers could not have failed to notice the extraordinarily savage price war among the home computer companies in which Acorn was forced to participate, a victim of changing consumer taste.

The consumer electronics group Amstrad is a very different kettle of fish. Chairman Alan Sugar has always professed to be a marketing man first and foremost, providing the public with what they want rather than foisting technically-wondrous equipment upon them. The company came to the market in 1980 at the equivalent price of 1½p (really 8½p adjusted for various rights and scrip issues of which more

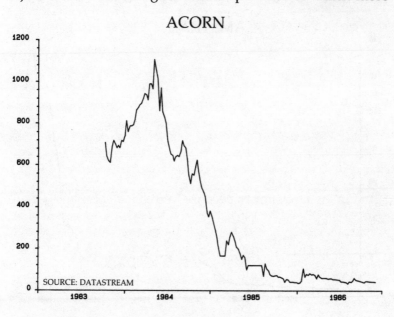

ACORN

SOURCE: DATASTREAM

later). Its early success was in the hi-fi field where the company produced tower systems, looking like expensive Japanese racked stereos, but much cheaper because they were really just one unit. But even though the company captured 40% of this market in the UK and profits rose from £1.4m in 1980 to £9.1m in 1984, the shares appeared stuck at around 20p.

City sentiment was hit by a cash-raising exercise, particularly as this was to provide the capital for Amstrad's move into home computers. Bearing in mind the problems other, better established, firms were having in the same area, the Square Mile's scepticism was perhaps understandable. However, Amstrad's products bucked the trend, helped by the fact that they were sold as complete units – all the buyer had to do was to add a plug and turn the machine on. These were computers for people, not boffins. Yet the success Amstrad was quite evidently having in the High Street was still not appreciated by the market. In 1985, the shares could still have been bought for 15p and those who did so had to kick their heels while they waited for the crowd to cotton on to what was happening.

The catalyst for the share price was the launch of the company's cheap word processor (on which this book was written). Initial scepticism turned to amazement at the public response, not only in Britain, but throughout Europe. The

AMSTRAD

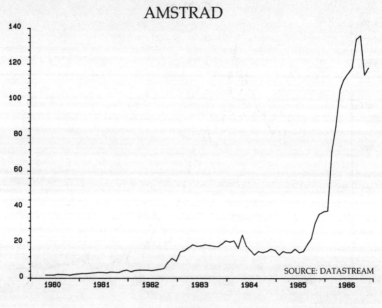

SOURCE: DATASTREAM

comparatively dormant market for word processors came alive and so, finally, did the share price. Helped by the announcement of profits of £20m, it took off. The takeover of the computer interests of Sir Clive Sinclair in the spring of 1986 for a mere £6m demonstrated conclusively the triumph of the marketeer over the boffin. Its peak was reached almost on the very day that the company unveiled details of its range of personal computers designed to be compatible with IBM's, yet a fraction of the price.

Although the public response again seemed good, many investors were content to take profits of up to ten times their original investment, there were initial delivery problems with the machine and many analysts felt the company had bitten off more than it could cope with in tackling the giant IBM in its lair. Again it took some time for confidence to return.

Exceptional though Amstrad's performance was, the reasons for its startling rise were evident to anybody with an eye to see what was happening in those shops selling computers, or who kept an eye on the computer press. Money can be made on the stock market by noting carefully what is going on around you and using that knowledge in conjunction with more basic financial research. When you come across what you think is a golden opportunity, do ascertain first that you haven't stumbled across something already well-known to the rest of the investing community. But don't necessarily be deterred by the apathy or scepticism of other investors. If you are convinced your hunch is right, that it is backed up by the evidence of your own eyes and that the numbers look alright, then perhaps you have discovered another golden opportunity in advance of all those highly-paid analysts in the City.

The company's figures

'With all the analysts and all the research and all the statistics and all the computers, it is still possible to be 51% wrong, and you can do better than that by flipping a coin.'
Adam Smith, *The Money Game*, 1968

However involved you become in the stock market, you will benefit from being able to understand the figures shown in a company's Report and Accounts. Many firms now make a great effort to show the relevant numbers in rather simpler form than previously, using charts and graphs to assist the bewildered shareholder. Some seem to have gone rather too far with this simplification process though and an investor who is clued up on interpreting figures produced by companies might find something of interest in the body of the Report and Accounts that the company has somehow failed to draw attention to in its summaries.

If you want a gentle immersion into the world of Report and Accounts, I suggest you get hold of the latest set produced by the London-based brewers, Young & Co. For the past few years Youngs, with its shareholders apparently dedicated to boosting the company's profits, has produced within its Annual Report a simplified version of the Profit & Loss Account and Balance Sheet. This explains, in plain English, the main elements of the figures and is obtainable from the Company Secretary, Young & Co's Brewery, The Ram Brewery, Wandsworth High Street, London SW18 4JD (01-870 0141). One recent set of Accounts also contained reproductions of some of the adverts the company used on its debut in the United States, including one headed 'Young's is a brewery run by brewers, not accountants'. At the very back of the Report and Accounts is a little note: 'These Accounts are produced by Accountants not Brewers!'

The profit and loss account The P and L account will show the company's income and expenditure for the year, show where the profits have gone and compare them with the previous year. **Turnover** or **sales** shows the total value of the company's sales for the year, before any deductions are made. **Trading profit** is a figure for the company's sales less the expenses it has incurred in making those sales – payment for raw materials, employees' wages, rates, electricity and so on. The profits of **associated companies**, in which our company has a stake larger than 20% but less than 50%, are also entered, in the appropriate proportion. The profits of **subsidiaries**, in which the parent has a stake of over a half, are completely consolidated into the main figure.

The company must make provision eventually to replace its plant, machinery, vehicles and other **fixed assets**. It does this by providing a figure for **depreciation**, earmarking a certain amount each year against the day when it will have to buy new plant or machinery. This figure is the amount by which

[108]

the company believes the value of its fixed assets is declining each year. Having made this, and any other necessary deductions, especially interest charges, the company declares its **pre-tax profits**.

As said earlier, shareholders should also pay close attention to **net profits**, those profits that belong to them. In addition to the whacking payments in tax, a company may also first make various other deductions, such as its payments to shareholders of its subsidiary companies, and the payments on various forms of preference stock it may have issued. What is left is the shareholders' proportion of the profits. As we have seen, this is rarely all paid out in the form of dividends (see p. 68), as some is retained to be ploughed back into the business. Divided by the number of ordinary shares in issue, though, the figure gives us the earnings per share (see p. 71), which is so prominent in investment calculations. The company might already have calculated this figure for you, though if their tax payments vary significantly from 35% you may want to work out a separate figure for yourself.

There may also be a figure somewhere for **extraordinary items**, a profit or loss derived from some abnormal activity which is not expected to recur. This might involve the sale of property or some other asset, heavy redundancy payments, benefits or losses from movements in the exchange rates, or just some bewildering bookkeeping adjustment. Sometimes companies put extraordinary items in with other trading profits, or 'above the line'. If items really are extraordinary, they are one-offs and should not recur in the following year. Including them above the line merely serves to distort the pre-tax profits figure and can give a misleading idea of a company's true position.

The balance sheet This is the other important set of figures contained in the Report and Accounts. Whereas the profit and loss account shows the year's trading performance, the balance sheet shows the company's financial position on one particular day, that of the last day of its financial year. It will point out the company's **assets** and **liabilities** at that date. There are two types of assets: **fixed assets** are, as we have seen, such things as land, machinery and the buildings – the on-going fabric of the company and should have been adjusted to take account of depreciation; **current assets** are of a less permanent nature, such as cash, money in the bank and investments. Current assets also include less realisable assets; **stocks** and **work in progress** values what the company is currently manufacturing and the materials it has already bought in for future manufacture. It also includes goods made, but not yet sold. Current assets will also have a figure for **debtors**, the amount that is owed to the company.

Set against its assets, a company will list its **liabilities**, which will include money owed to its **creditors**, taxation due, dividends recommended but not yet paid, the amount owed on various loans, and so on. **Current liabilities** are those which fall due within one year of the balance sheet date.

There may also be some contingent liabilities, which the company knows it will have to face in the future. These might be shown in the proliferation of notes that accompany the accounts. These notes should be read as assiduously as the main body of the report as this will be where the company tries to hide anything it would rather not draw undue attention to. **Goodwill** occurs when the company has paid out more than an asset was worth on purchasing it.

Net assets are simply the surplus of assets over a company's liabilities and, taking into account only that which is attributable to shareholders, gives us the **net asset value** when divided by the number of ordinary shares in issue.

The figure for a company's net assets are sometimes referred to as the **shareholders' funds**, which indeed they are. Companies now give a separate section in their accounts over to shareholders' funds to demonstrate how the firm's assets are financed. The figure is useful for working out how heavily borrowed the company is; the ratio of net debt (simply the company's borrowings less the cash it has in the bank and in the form of liquid assets) to its shareholders' funds is known as its **gearing** and represents the extent of its borrowings. Expressed as a percentage, the higher the figure, the more heavily in debt is the company.

Elsewhere in the Report and Accounts, the interested reader will find a five-year review of the company's progress, and a **source and application of funds** section which shows where the company's funds have been generated and how those funds have been spent.

There have been several attempts made to bring in an accounting standard which would show the effects inflation has upon a company's affairs. Companies depreciating their assets over the standard number of years discovered, particularly in the years of rampant inflation, that the cost of replacing those assets had soared, and that they had thus failed to make adequate provision for their replacement. **Current cost accounts** try to show what the real replacement cost of assets is and provide for realistic depreciation. But CCA accounts have been the subject of much heated debate, and many companies refuse to produce such figures.

Each set of Report and Accounts has to be accompanied by an **auditors' report**. This should be examined in case the auditors have made any qualifications to the figures. They might disagree with the way in which the company has treated a particular item in the accounts. Perhaps this disagreement is largely technical, but the qualification could be more serious, hinting at irregularities in the way the company has been going about its business or indicating serious financial difficulties that might not have been made adequately clear in the Report and Accounts. The auditors have to declare that the accounts give a 'true and fair' view of the state of affairs of the company. Unfortunately, set against this responsibility is the difficulty the auditors might face in actually accusing the company concerned with lying to its shareholders. Auditors are employed by the board of directors of the company and some critics feel they are often rather lax in criticising the directors for just that reason. In the main though, their responsibilities to shareholders should outweigh any other considerations.

You might find it useful to keep your own records of the salient points of a company's figures over a few years, which could include sales, pre-tax profits, earnings per share, gearing and net asset value. Determining trends may become easier if you break each year into two, entering figures for the interim half-way stage as well as for the full year. (The Extel Cards will give you the relevant information for interim figures if you can't find it elsewhere.) In measuring percentage changes of profits, sales, etc., make sure you compare figures for the same half of the year. Many businesses are seasonal in nature, and it may be misleading to compare the performance in the latter part of a company's year with that of the earlier part.

In drawing up their figures, companies can be quite 'creative' in the way they treat the hard numbers. Profits can be massaged or slimmed in a variety of ways without distorting the 'truth'. This is particularly true of companies frequently involved in making takeovers. So it is worth once again cautioning the investor not to trust published results slavishly, and worth his while gradually to increase his knowledge so that he can look behind the window-dressing. The accountants who audit the figures may be entirely satisfied that there are no irregularities, and under the present state of affairs, they are happy to declare that both the traditional *and* current cost accounts for any one company are 'true and fair'. But how can they both give a 'true and fair' picture when they provide widely different figures for profits, earnings and assets? Some accountants and analysts are suggesting that the emphasis should be shifted to monitoring the movements of cash, a real, not paper, asset. For the foreseeable future, however, the stock market looks likely to ignore such calls and continue concentrating its attention on the traditional account figures.

9

A FEW VARIETIES OF SHARE

*'Bulls make money and bears make money, but pigs seldom
do.'*
Wall Street maxim

The stock market likes to categorise wherever possible, a tendency that has been exacerbated by the new Stock Exchange trading system. On SEAQ every company has been sorted out into one of four classes. The **alphas** are the crème de la crème, the top 100 or so companies which are the biggest and most actively traded on the stock market. They have a minimum of ten market-makers and all deals done in alphas on SEAQ are reported and published on the screen within five minutes. Although investors may not be able to see this information, most of the quality daily newspapers now have separate lists of the alpha stocks, together with the volume of shares traded during the session. About three-quarters of equity turnover is done in alphas.

The next category, not surprisingly, are the **betas**, about 500 shares with market capitalisations generally in excess of £100m. These should all have at least five market-makers. Taken together, alphas and betas account for around 90% of UK equity turnover.

The majority of companies are **gammas**, some 3,000 of them, where the reporting requirements are less strict. The prices market-makers show on their screens are, in alphas and betas, firm to other Stock Exchange members. Gamma prices may be indications only and market-makers might deal only in very small numbers of shares. Trades in betas and gammas are not published until the following day.

The lowest of the low are the 'deltas'. These tend not to be ordinary shares, but odd things like fixed interest stocks in tiny companies and they are dealt on a matching-basis only, where investors must wait until the market-maker can locate someone willing to do the other side of the business.

Being the most actively traded, competition among market-makers in the alphas is pretty tough. As a result the prices are fairly keen, with spreads between the buying and selling prices usually a little under 1%. The risk for the market-makers is far greater in the gammas where spreads could be as high as 3%.

These categories are relatively new to the market. But there are other, older ways in which shares are compartmentalised and I thought it would be helpful to look at the attractions and disadvantages of six different sorts of shares: the blue chip, the smaller company, the penny share, the growth stock, the high-yielder and the resources stock.

Blue chips As we saw earlier (see p. 67), blue chips are simply the biggest companies quoted on the stock market. The name is said to derive from the colour of casino gambling counters. Some firms, such as ICI, GEC, BP and British Telecom are very obviously blue chips. But as there isn't a true definition of a blue chip, it is difficult to know at what level to draw the line. Those with a market capitalisation of more than £500 million can probably count themselves safely in the hallowed list. Any alpha share, or company in the 100-share index, could probably be labelled blue chip.

The most important investment characteristic of these giants of the stock market is their safety and stability. So large are they that the investor can go to bed at night undisturbed by nightmares that the company in which he has his money invested is going to disappear in a puff of smoke. In fact, it would be very rare for a blue chip to get into difficulties without receiving some sort of assistance from central government, no matter what the professed attitude of the ruling party might be to the principle of free markets. For this reason, blue chips are often known as 'widows and orphans shares', namely those that are considered safe enough for even the most risk-averse of investors. That does *not* mean, however, that you can't lose money in them.

One advantage of blue chips is that they are easy to deal in. No investor reading this book is likely to find his broker telling him that he can't deal in the number that he wants, but then this is probably true for virtually all but the very smallest of companies. The above average activity in the blue chips also ensures that there is a narrower jobbers' turn involved than in some of the smaller shares. There is usually no shortage of information on these stock market giants, for virtually every stockbroker looks at them and virtually every large institution will hold their shares. You are consequently unlikely to be able to 'second-guess' the crowd, for in blue chips the sheep reign unchallenged.

Despite the concentration of the stock market on the affairs of the blue chip companies, they *can* prove a fruitful hunting-ground for investors. The tobacco, paper, retailing and financial services conglomerate BAT Industries, for instance, always seems to have a dull reputation in the stock market, as evidenced by its PE ratio which is well below the market average. The reputation came about when the company's profits figures were stuck in the doldrums for years. But they took off again in 1981 and the shares soared from under 100p to 400p in under three years. The company diversified away from tobacco, making the PE rating look too cheap. This set the institutions buying until they thought it of fair value, but BAT kept spoiling things for them by producing results far better than expected, thus reducing its PE ratio sharply again. This made the shares look too cheap once more and set off another round of buying. A poor year in 1985, partly as a result of currency movements, convinced the sceptics that they had been right all along and the price came tumbling back to 270 pence before a realisation that they had blundered caused an abrupt change-around of sentiment and the shares leapt almost 200p in under a year. And all this in a 'widows and orphans' share.

One of the most favoured blue chips among small investors must be Marks & Spencer, a share where investors can play at

MARKS & SPENCER

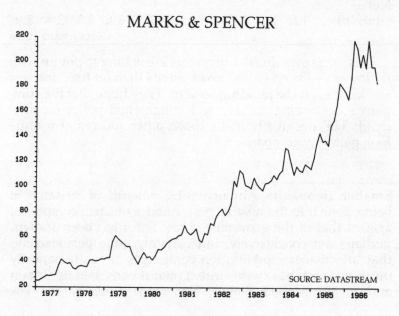

SOURCE: DATASTREAM

being analysts every time they go shopping. The track record of Marks is much like the store, sound and dependable. Profits, earnings and dividends have increased steadily each year. The trend on profits has been for an average 14% annual rise, while earnings and dividends have both climbed by 16% each year during the decade. The shares rose six-fold over the period, giving investors a satisfactory capital gain. It is interesting to look at their income as well. An investor buying shares in 1986 at 200p would get a net (not gross) yield of 2%, hardly an enticing rate. But things were little different back in 1977. Then a net dividend of just under a penny for a basic rate taxpayer would have produced a yield on shares bought at 30p of 3%. Yet Marks, like most other large companies, has increased its dividend in each of the following years so that the investor is by 1986 receiving a net payment of 3.9p on each share. While that may only be 2% at the prevailing price he gets a more satisfactory net yield of 13%, the gross equivalent of 18%, giving the investor considerable cause for feeling smug.

MARKS & SPENCER – GROWTH RECORD

	1977	1978	1979	1980	1981	1982	1983	1984	1985	1986
Pre-tax profit (£m)	102	118	162	174	181	221	239	279	304	366
EPS (p)	2.1	2.5	3.3	3.6	3.8	4.6	5.2	6.3	6.9	8.4
Net div. (p)	1.0	1.1	1.3	1.7	1.9	2.3	2.6	3.1	3.4	3.9

SOURCE: PHILLIPS & DREW

This helps explain why investors are willing to put up with far lower yields on equity investments than on fixed interest stocks or even the building society. They hope that the company's continuing success and enlightened policy on dividends will eventually make those other sources of income look paltry by comparison.

Smaller companies An increasing amount of research is being done into the relative performance of small companies against that of the giant blue chips. For it has been shown, perhaps not conclusively, but certainly quite persuasively, that the smaller capitalisation companies have dramatically outperformed those with large capitalisations, both in Britain and in the United States. The work done by the UK stockbroker Capel-Cure Myers into 'The Small Company Effect' reckoned that this held true even if one made adjustments for the greater risks inherent in investing in smaller firms' shares. Their conclusions should offer hope to those private investors who believe that they suffer a consistent disadvantage in comparison with the pampered institutions.

Capel-Cure Myers found three likely causes of this interesting phenomenon. First, they reckoned that there is a problem of marketability with smaller shares, noting that for many institutions the difficulties of buying shares in sufficient quantities and the administrative hassles involved with such small companies was simply not worth while. This is not a problem for the private investor.

Secondly, they felt that shortage of information has a lot to do with it. Stockbroking analysts simply don't look at such companies because they are so small and not held by institutional clients. As a consequence it is only when results come out that the progress of such firms can be appreciated. For the private investor willing to do a little research of his own, again this should not be an overwhelming handicap.

Thirdly, it was felt the large institutions simply aren't willing to take on the extra risk involved in buying the shares of smaller companies. They have, after all, to report to their trustees or clients and could be embarrassed by having invested in a crop of failed companies. But CCM's research seems to show that 'the returns of the winners more than compensate for the losers', so perhaps this should not be too great a hurdle for the private investor.

Once smaller companies become a respectable size, the institutions start taking an interest, acting as a further stimulus to the share price and enabling the companies to grow still further. Anyone considering investing in smaller companies, though, should be careful to spread his risk as widely as possible. While smaller companies as a whole may outperform the stock market, that does not necessarily mean that one or two particular shares will do well. You should also be aware that there are likely to be very few market-makers in the share. That, together with the fact that dealings take place less frequently, means that it will take far smaller transactions to move prices, both on the way up and the way down. If the stock market is going through rough waters, it could prove difficult to sell shares in very small companies. At such times, if you still believe them to be attractive, it might be far better to ride out the storm and, if anything, consider taking the opportunity presented to top up on your holdings.

Penny shares There is one misconception about the stock market that must have cost private investors dear over the years. That is the totally erroneous idea that if a share only cost a few pence, a so-called 'penny share', it must be some sort of bargain. In fact as far as a potential investor is concerned, it matters not one jot to the relative merits of two companies that one might have one million shares in issue at a price of £12 each, and the other, 100 million shares in issue priced at just 12p. Both have a market value of £12 million and if their earnings are the same, they will have the same PE ratio. It is that you should consider when evaluating the merits of a company, not the actual level of the share price.

That said, many investors who realise this still have a preference for penny shares. Some, irrationally, find it nicer to be able to buy a greater number of shares at a time even though the total cost may be exactly the same. But the others are searching for massive capital gains, and taking on massive risks at the same time. For most penny shares are the dregs of the stock market, companies on their last legs, halting briefly on the way down before disappearing into oblivion. Occasionally, however, the stock market may have misjudged a penny share. New management, reorganisation of a previously chaotic business or the attentions of someone after cheap assets – all could have a dramatic effect on a penny share's price. Some of the most neglected companies may be little more than 'shells' and these are watched avidly by the stock market buzzards, for an entrepreneur wanting a stock market quote may quietly and unobtrusively buy up the shares in such a company to inject his own business interests into it – the famed 'reverse takeover'.

When discussing tipsheets, we saw some of the risks of these low-priced shares: they are more difficult to deal in, their price can move ahead quickly on only a little buying interest, the spreads between the buying and selling price tend to be wider than for 'heavier' shares and the risk involved is far greater. Having said that, you may feel confident enough to invest a small part of your available cash in a penny share or two if you think you have spotted a special situation that the stock market must sooner or later cotton on to. If so, you must have patience. You may find you have to sit on your shares for months or even years before anyone else sees what you can see and helps to spread the word.

High yielders The yield on a share will decrease as the price of that share rises and vice versa (see p. 70). If a share price has fallen heavily in response to a downturn in the company's fortunes, the yield could look outstanding compared with the market average. Many investors keep a weather eye out for such shares, situations where the management may feel the pessimism of the stock market has been overdone and try to keep the dividend at previous levels, rather than cut back until the company's business recovers. There could be a very sound reason for the market's shunning of the shares and these high-yielders can often, like penny shares, prove extremely risky for the investor.

But some are basically sound businesses and, should the company's fortunes revive, investors will still receive the high yield on their original purchase, together with any subsequent capital gain. These sorts of shares, often referred to as 'recovery situations' can be, like the penny shares which of course some of them are, sleepers which lie dormant for some time before interest in them is reawakened. If you have a Personal Equity Plan then you may find high-yielding shares an attractive proposition.

If you are tempted by the current yield of a share, do remember that dividends can be cut by a company's board should they so wish. Such an action could precipitate a fall in the price of the shares, as investors who had held on only because of the high yield sold out. The other serious problem with 'recovery situations' is that many of them never do recover, but instead become terminally ill and eventually have to have the last rites read over them. Yield is, to some extent, a measure of risk and, as with penny shares, investors diverting funds towards high-yielders and recovery plays, should take care to invest wisely and spread their risk widely.

Growth stocks The very opposite of high-yielders, growth stocks tend to pay minimal or even non-existent dividends. They could still be in the early years of their life, needing to husband all their available financial resources to plough back into the business. They need to go all out for growth, to establish their niche in the marketplace and make their name. But they don't have to be new companies. Concerns as large as Sainsbury and Glaxo have been tagged as growth stocks in recent years, with earnings increasing far faster than the stock market average. But it is obviously easier for a company in its younger days to grow at a rapid rate. Firms which already have a large proportion of available market share will find it much more difficult to continue growing at the same breakneck pace, a difficulty which makes the performance of Sainsbury all the more remarkable.

Growth stocks will have high PEs, with the market expecting that the strength of future earnings will justify the high prices at which the shares are trading. That faith may or may not be justified, but investing in growth stocks can be daunting to the investor more used to shares cruising at less rarified heights. While the PEs of high-yielders may be in single digits, some growth stocks have PEs in excess of 30, even when calculated on estimated future earnings. The trouble with such 'hot' stocks is the 'Icarus effect'; those that fly just that little bit too close to the sun find themselves plummeting to earth with nothing to halt their fall. There can be few more stomach-churning rides than that experienced by an investor in one of these shares when the market suddenly turns against it. The suddenness of these dramatic falls for highly rated companies which go 'ex-growth' is compounded by the fact that many are operating in bewildering high-tech areas. For all their professed sophistication, many of the

J. SAINSBURY – GROWTH RECORD

	Sales £m	Pre-tax profits £m	Earnings per share p	Net dividend p
1977	664	26	3.0	0.7
1978	811	28	3.1	0.8
1979	1007	33	3.2	0.9
1980	1227	44	3.8	1.3
1981	1531	62	5.8	1.8
1982	1876	83	10.1	2.4
1983	2202	100	10.7	2.9
1984	2575	130	12.5	3.8
1985	2999	156	15.6	4.5
1986	3414	193	18.2	5.5

SOURCE: PHILLIPS & DREW

SAINSBURY

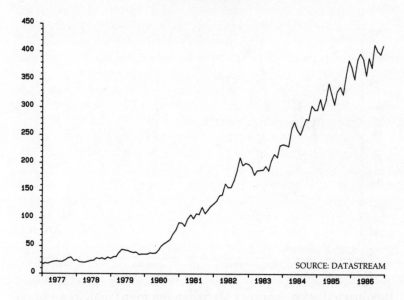

SOURCE: DATASTREAM

traders in the City may know only a little more about the company's business than the inexpert private investor, trusting that faith alone will keep the shares rising, and leaving the important questions unasked until it is too late.

In May 1985 the City greeted results from software company, Micro Focus, with stunned disbelief. Against all the expectations, including that of the company's own broker, profits had not continued to grow. In fact they fell sharply, from £2.8 million to just £721,000. So savage was the response to the figures that Micro Focus's share price was more than cut in half in a matter of hours, a cautionary tale for those who place their faith in 'growth' stocks. Despite this, a report by brokers Fielding, Newson-Smith in 1985 concluded that high-technology stocks had generally strongly outperformed the market. Although there were some disasters, the gains for those that were successful outweighed them. For anyone making shrewd investment decisions there are, reckons the broker, enormous potential rewards.

Bearing in mind the example of Micro Focus, you may find it safer only to consider investment in those growth stocks whose business you can understand and where you believe you foresee a consistently expanding market in the years to come.

[121]

MICRO FOCUS

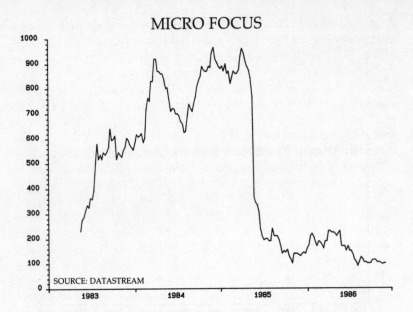

SOURCE: DATASTREAM

Resource stocks Another area of investment which can prove extremely speculative in nature are the shares of companies hunting for raw materials, whether it be oil, gold or other precious metals, or even rubber, tea or kryptonite. In recent years, the increasing importance of the North Sea to our economy has been accompanied by a proliferation of new companies involved in its development coming to the stock market. Some are broadly spread operations, but many of the newcomers are involved in the chancy business of oil and gas exploration and their fortunes may depend upon making a strike in just one small area. These tend to be small companies and the prices of their often volatile shares will move in line with the market's expectation of a successful 'find'.

The higher risks involved in investing in such companies are undertaken in the hope that the eventual rewards will prove far greater than for more pedestrian manufacturers or retailers. Investment in resource stocks really ought to be treated very cautiously by private investors unless they have specialised knowledge of the industry involved. This is particularly true if they are in far-off lands. But greed often overcomes common sense and fingers that get burnt often return to the fire for second helpings.

One volatile company, an oil explorer called Atlantic Resources, was avidly pursued by private investors in 1984.

[122]

Atlantic were drilling in the Irish Sea and the attractive idea that there might be wealth there similar to that found in the North Sea, with the consequences that would have for the Irish economy, stimulated the imagination of the locals. For many, it was their first venture into the stock market and Irish stockbrokers, unaccustomed to handling real cash, were bewildered by the number of punters walking in off the streets brandishing bundles of used notes which they wanted to invest in Atlantic Resources. Brokers being brokers, they were of course able to accommodate these impulsive investors.

The investing fever surrounding Atlantic became like some latter-day Ealing comedy, for those who bought shares weren't simply content to monitor the price of their investment in the newspapers each day. Instead many took to the sea in boats, heading for the drilling rig to see for themselves what was happening. The drilling operations were under constant observation from the punters for signs of 'flaring off', the indication of a strike that would make the shareholders of Atlantic Resources considerably richer. Anyone working on the rig suddenly found himself with an overabundance of friends and never short of a drink. Inevitably there were stories of corruption, with drill-workers said to have been paid large sums of money to signal the results of the tests to nearby yachts. All great fun while it lasted, but as in so many other resource companies, a great many fingers were singed, and not from the heat given off by flaming oil either.

10
THE TRICKS AND TREATS OF SHARES

Rights issues

'Warning – shares can seriously damage your wealth.'
Anon.

Most investors will sooner or later find with dismay that one of the companies in which they own shares is launching a rights issue. This is a means by which a company with an existing stock market quote can raise extra capital, possibly with a view to making future acquisitions of other companies, or perhaps to help fund an expansion programme or simply in an effort to reduce a high level of borrowing.

The Companies Act insists that all existing shareholders are offered the chance to contribute to this fund-raising programme, in which they are offered more shares in the company in return for providing extra cash. There is, however, no obligation on the part of any shareholder to subscribe to his 'rights' under the issue, but his holding in the company will decrease proportionately if he does not do so.

Each shareholder should consider carefully what action to take when his company announces a rights issue. It may be that the extra money is very evidently necessary and that the past record of the company has been so good that investors can be confident the rights cash will be put to good use. In other cases it may be that the company is struggling, and that it believes it would be easier to raise money from its shareholders than from any other source; indeed it may have found it almost impossible to raise money from anywhere else. There are also some rights issues which are merely opportunistic; the amount a company can raise is directly related to its share price. If the price has been strong, the board may feel it would be timely to raise finance 'on the cheap' before the shares fall back. Boards of directors aren't always considerate to the shareholders on whose behalf they manage their companies.

The dismay many investors feel when a company announces a rights issue is easy to understand. It necessitates, should the rights be taken up, finding extra cash to invest; it is usually accompanied by a fall in the price of the shares; and it raises complications which may prove irritating to the shareholder who likes an easy life.

Our old friend Morpheus Engineering has ten million shares in issue, currently standing in the stock market at 155 pence. Its finance director, a chap with ambitions for the company and keen to make a mark himself, reckons Morpheus needs three million pounds to finance expansion. Rather than borrow it, he, together with the board, decide to have a rights issue to raise the money.

They announce they are raising £3 million by offering shareholders one new share at 120 pence for each 4 they already hold. In the jargon, this would be a 'one-for-four rights at 120'. Each existing holder of shares in Morpheus will be offered the new shares, but although they will end up with five shares for every four they now own their proportionate holding in the company will not change, for after the issue Morpheus will have an extra 2.5 million shares in issue, twelve-and-a-half million rather than the previous ten.

Irrespective of any reaction to the news of the rights issue, the shares of Morpheus will not remain the same price after the issue as before. The theoretical price the shares will have after the issue, is easily calculated:

Old holding	4 shares @ 155p	620p
Rights entitlement	1 share @ 120p	120p
New holding	5 shares worth	740p

This would place the value of each share at 148 pence (740 divided by 5). This is the so-called 'ex-rights' price. Assuming that the price of Morpheus's shares does not change in the interim, they will be adjusted from 155 pence to 148 on the day the shares are declared 'ex-rights', in line with the timetable for the issue that will have been sent to shareholders with the other documents detailing the issue. On that day, trading will start in the 'new' shares to which shareholders are entitled. These are called 'nil-paid rights' as no money has yet had to be produced. With Morpheus now trading at 148 pence, each of the nil-paid rights which entitle shareholders to a new share on payment of 120 pence ought to be worth 28 pence.

They will trade in this form for the few weeks before the rights call is due, at which point anyone holding the nil-paid rights must stump up 120 pence on each one, or forfeit their entitlement to the new shares. During this period the shareholder must decide what action to take. If he chooses not to take up his rights, he should sell them in the nil-paid form, or he will simply be throwing money away. Neither course will necessarily make any difference financially. Our shareholder has 800 shares. If he subscribes for the rights his position will be:

BEFORE RIGHTS ISSUE		AFTER RIGHTS ISSUE	
800 shares @ 155p		800 old shares @ 148p	£1,184
Value of holding	£1,240	200 new shares @ 148p	£296
		Value of holding	£1,480
		less cost of rights	£1,240
		(200 × 120 pence = £240)	

If the shareholder takes up his rights, the value of his holding will have increased merely by the amount he has had to pay for these rights. At 120 pence on his 200 new shares, that amounted to £240. No commission or stamp duty is payable by a shareholder taking up his rights. If the shareholder instead disposed of his rights entitlement, this would be the position:

BEFORE RIGHTS ISSUE		AFTER RIGHTS ISSUE	
800 shares @ 155p		800 old shares @ 148p	£1,184
		Proceeds from sale of 200 nil-paid rights @ 28p each	£56
Value of holding	£1,240	Value of shares & proceeds	£1,240

So the decision as to whether to take up the rights or not should depend upon the view of the shareholder as to the future of the company, and whether he wishes to participate to the same degree as before through his shareholding. It may simply be that he hasn't the spare cash available at the time of the rights issue and so has to sell his rights entitlement.

Few rights issues are taken up by all shareholders and the expectation that some will be selling shares usually leads to a drop in the share price of any company that announces it is raising money in this way. It isn't always the case. On rare occasions, a company is so highly regarded by the stock market that the shares will climb on the news, but such behaviour is pretty infrequent.

Whatever the response of shareholders, the company will in any case get the money it is seeking by arranging to have the issue underwritten by the big institutions. In return for a fee they guarantee to buy those shares not taken up by shareholders. In most cases they are barely troubled by this and are keen to have the income from underwriting, which as far as they are concerned is generally money for old rope. But from time to time a share price can react so adversely to a rights issue that it falls below the level at which the new shares are offered. There is no point in shareholders taking up their rights if they could buy the shares more cheaply in the market and so, for once, it is the turn of the fund managers to go around with long faces after they are compelled to buy them by their underwriting commitment.

During the time the nil-paid rights are trading, there may be considerable activity in the shares. As long as the shares trade above the rights price, the nil-paid rights will have a 'premium' in the market, which in Morpheus's case was 28p. As the shares fluctuate, so does that premium. If Morpheus's old shares rose quickly to 185, a 25% rise, the nil-paid would have to rise with them. But with the right to buy shares at 120p, they would now be worth 65p each, a gain of 132% to anyone who bought them earlier at 28p. The more volatile movement of nil-paid shares, downwards as well as upwards, makes them attractive to the more speculatively minded of investors. They are said, in the market jargon, to be more highly 'geared' than the normal shares.

A company will usually announce its rights issue at the same time as its results, hoping that the trading news will soften the blow and give the board a chance to justify its fund-raising exercise. It may be that the new shares issued do not qualify for the forthcoming dividend payment and investors should check this when making their deliberations over the rights issue.

Companies are not free to announce rights issues quite whenever they please. The Bank of England organises a 'rights issue queue' and each company in the queue has, in true British fashion, to wait patiently for its turn. If, in the meantime, the stock market falls, the company may simply let its allocated space go by without making its move, feeling it advantageous to wait for a more propitious moment. In organising the queue, the Bank of England is concerned not only to prevent companies saturating the City by announcing their rights issues in a bunch, but is also attempting to mesh such calls on investors' money with other fund-raising exercises such as the issue of new government stock, or the latest big privatisation sale.

Vendor placings

The massive size of the British Telecom sale in 1984 meant that the Bank of England had to put a stop to rights issues of any consequence for some time. During this period another means of raising capital from the stock market was employed by several companies – the vendor placing. It is a method which can be used when a company needs cash in a hurry, perhaps when suddenly presented with the opportunity to make an acquisition, and it involves the firm's financial advisers arranging to sell, or place, a block of ordinary shares at a discount to the current price, to various institutions throughout the City.

Unfortunately for private investors, the size of these vendor placings seems to be on the increase and in many cases they now involve a significant jump in the number of shares in issue. This places the private investor at a disadvantage; because of the speed with which vendor placings take place, he does not get a chance to subscribe to any of the shares and sees his stake in the company decline as a consequence. In substantial vendor placings, shareholders have subsequently to approve an increase in the share capital of the company. But even if all the aggrieved private investors on the company's share register vote against the move, those big investing institutions who will have benefited from being granted shares in the placing will usually be able to steamroller the resolution through.

[128]

Occasionally, enlightened institutions will persuade companies that all shareholders ought to be able to participate in vendor placings. In this case a claw-back scheme will operate in the event of small shareholders showing sufficient interest. Many companies back their argument in favour of vendor placings by saying that private investors are usually reluctant to provide extra capital anyway, so why go to the trouble and expense of rights issues? A similar argument could be used against the continuation of democracy, given the level of apathy at even the most vital of general elections.

When they involve such large increases in the number of shares, vendor placings go against the spirit of the legislation on companies, which insists that all shareholders should be treated equally. The increasing prevalence of vendor placings is to be regretted, but a display of dismay is unlikely to be forceful enough to halt that increase. For they are significantly cheaper to a company than rights issues, and the speed with which a vendor placing can be carried out removes the cloud which the extended process of a rights issue can place over a share price. Even though this might make a shareholder better off in reality than he would be if the company had announced a rights issue instead, one can't help lamenting the popularity in the City itself of vendor placings and the blind eye that is being turned towards the interests of the small investor.

Scrip issues

Surprising though it may seem, companies don't always ask shareholders for money when offering them shares. Sometimes they give them some for free! There's a catch, of course, for scrip issues, which are also known as capitalisation, bonus or free issues, are really nothing more than a book-keeping exercise and don't benefit shareholders financially. They can occur when the reserves the company has accumulated (as shown in Shareholders' Funds in the balance sheet) are looking top-heavy when set against the issued share capital. In an effort to make the issued share capital appear more representative of the capital actually used in the business, a company can 'capitalise' the reserves by issuing a greater number of shares.

[129]

Theoretically at least, a scrip issue will have no effect on the value of the shareholder's investment. Should a 'one-for-three' scrip issue be announced, each shareholder will receive one free share for every three he already holds. But because no money is actually being injected into the business by this procedure, the price of the shares has to be adjusted so that every four shares have the same value as three previously held. The adjustment is made when the shares go 'ex capitalisation'. If the shares stood then at 120 pence, making three worth 360p, after they went ex cap their price would be 90p each, with the four together still worth 360p.

Although theoretically a scrip issue should have no effect on the value of an investment, in fact it can often prove beneficial to the share price. Even though there is no logic to it, the market believes that investors tend to prefer investing in companies which don't have massive share prices. Thus a company making a scrip issue may in fact be helping to stimulate demand for its shares, simply by making the price of each share lower. It may sound barmy, but there *is* usually a rise in a company's share if a scrip issue is announced. It is also possible that the book-keeping operation indicates the company is anticipating further rises in profits and wants to reorganise the balance sheet in advance.

The investor should realise that all the investment calculations made before the capitalisation will still produce the same figures afterwards. The company's earnings and assets remain the same, but are now worked out on the greater number of less highly-priced shares. Dividends are also reduced proportionately so there should be no extra benefit there.

You shouldn't be alarmed, therefore, if you suddenly notice that your shares have halved or worse overnight. Hopefully you will discover that a scrip issue has taken place and the experience will convince you of the soundness of paying attention to the documents which come through the door. If you do get certificates relating to scrip issues, take care to guard them as carefully as you do all the others.

It is important for investors keeping records of their share transactions to adjust their original purchase price after a scrip issue or rights issue. A failure to do so, particularly if a company has more than one or two such issues over the life of an investment, could mean you have no idea of how your shares have done. In our example of a scrip, where four shares replaced three, the original price paid for each share needs to be adjusted downwards by multiplying by three-quarters.

There is one useful wrinkle if you find all this rather a chore. The compilers of the price pages in the newspapers have to cope with all this as well. The share prices on the day a company goes 'ex-rights' or 'ex-scrip' will be adjusted by the market. No problem there. But the papers need to adjust their figures for the shares' highs and lows as well. Providing the shares haven't moved to either extreme that day, simply note what proportion the current highs and lows are of the previous day's figures. That will be your scrip or rights factor, to within the odd decimal place at least.

Bids, mergers and takeovers

There is nothing more certain to cheer the heart of an investor than the news that one of the companies in which he has an interest is the subject of a takeover bid. All thoughts of supporting the company he 'owns' through thick and thin usually take second place to the contemplation of the quick and often substantial profits that can result from a takeover. For one firm to gain control of another, it needs to acquire more than 50% of the shares, a position which will then give it a majority of the shareholders' votes. But most firms making a bid approach will be keen to gain not just a majority stake, but full control over the other company's affairs. In order to tempt all the existing shareholders to sell out, they may have to make an offer on extremely generous terms, which might be far above the price at which the shares were previously trading. When you realise that on occasion such offers can cause the value of an investor's holding to double almost instantly, it isn't difficult to understand the excitement of shareholders involved in such situations.

Although bids are supposed to be closely kept secrets, the announcement of a takeover attempt may not come as a complete surprise to shareholders. Some may indeed have bought their shares in the first place because they felt the company to be a likely takeover target. There may have been persistent rumours about a bid surrounding the shares for some time, encouraging shareholders to believe such a move to be a possibility. But in any case, it is unlikely that a bidding company will make a move completely out of the blue. It will more probably build up a stake in the target first. As we saw earlier, any stakes of more than 5% in a company have to be declared. When the announcement of such a stake is made, the potential bidder will usually play his cards close to his chest, murmuring that the stake is being taken as a 'long-term investment'. But then a predator is hardly likely openly to admit his intentions to mount a full-scale bid, or the shares would climb in advance to an unaffordable price.

Rather than make this softly-softly approach, a potential bidder may make a 'dawn raid' by asking his broker to buy as many shares as he can as quickly as he is able. These dawn raids began to get out of hand in the early 1980s and a raider is now restricted to buying 15% of a company's shares in this way. After a week's pause he may attempt to increase that stake to just under 30% but may proceed no further without making a full-scale bid. His actions are constrained by the intricate rules of the City's Takeover Panel, whose aims include making sure that all investors receive equal treatment and opportunity in takeover situations.

Shareholders who have seen the price of their shares rise either on the building of a stake, or on nothing more than rumours of impending action, should be aware that an anticipated bid may not materialise, and that the price of the shares could thus fall substantially as hopes of a bid evaporate. Selling before this happens could give you a substantial profit but will, of course, mean you see no benefits if the bid does arrive.

In a few cases when a bid is announced, the board of directors of the target company may welcome the newcomer and agree to the terms of the offer. This could be because the two firms have already spent some time behind closed doors discussing it in advance, finally thrashing out details acceptable to both sides. In the case of such an 'agreed bid', things should flow fairly smoothly, with the board endeavouring to convince its shareholders of the logic of the deal. The details will be announced in the press and a formal offer document, together with the recommendation of your board, will be sent to you. The offer, like that for any bid, could be in the form either of cash or shares in the bidding company, or perhaps a mixture of the two. It may be that the two firms choose to term the deal a 'merger', which should help to mollify the feelings of the target company's board, but is in reality usually no

[132]

different from a takeover. You have two courses of action open to you. Either you can sell your shares in the market, where their price will probably be within a few pence of the bid terms, or you can instead 'accept' the bid, opting for shares or cash as you see fit. If you have a massive portfolio, note that accepting cash for your stake counts as a disposal for Capital Gains Tax purposes; taking shares doesn't.

The level of acceptances of the bid will be revealed from time to time in the press. You should always wait until shortly before the day specified as the 'final' date for acceptances, in case another bidder comes onto the scene. But once the bidder declares his offer 'unconditional', which can be done once he has gained more than 50%, you have little to gain by waiting any longer, however much you may disapprove of the bid or its terms. Once the bidder has received acceptances for over 90% of the shares, it can compulsorily acquire those of investors still holding out.

Even if you miss the 'final' date, you may not have missed the boat. Bidders often extend these dates and should in any case be happy to take further acceptances. But you should try to avoid being one of just a few minority shareholders if, say, the bidder could only get his stake as high as 75 to 85%. He will have effective control of the company and your shares will be almost untradeable, so you may as well throw in the towel.

Much more fun than agreed bids, from the spectator's point of view at least, is the contested bid. Bid battles can be splendidly acrimonious and often afford great ringside entertainment. A board finding itself the target of a takeover bid may resolutely set itself against the offer. This may be because it objects to the bid in principle, or merely to the terms that are being offered which it might feel are derisory. It's also worth remembering that the bidding company will probably be planning to take a new broom to its potential purchase. In this case your board of directors may be fighting to keep their jobs and perhaps using the intervening period to write themselves lucrative severance payments in case they fail.

Even contested takeover bids used to be rather gentlemanly affairs. But the gloves came off when the merchant banks advising companies started using massive advertising campaigns in an attempt to sway the opinions of investors, tactics which came of age with conglomerate BTR's bid for Thomas Tilling in 1983. If you want to learn how to present statistics in a misleading light, some takeover adverts should prove a fruitful source for your education. Such was the scope for misrepresentation, with essential facts being omitted or charts drawn rather too imaginatively, that the poor beleaguered Takeover Panel felt forced to restrict adverts to dry statements of fact or to mere presentation of corporate image. Even so, each side will bombard you with documents putting the case for the bid and against it. So frequent can these missives become that you might find your postman pleading with you to make your decision and help bring the battle to an end.

It won't be you, but the institutions, who will eventually decide whether the bid will succeed. It used to be the case that if a board under siege could demonstrate good reasons why it should be left in control of a company, the institutions might rally to its defence. But these days fund managers are concentrating so heavily, and short-sightedly, on the short-term performance of their funds to the detriment of the longer term, that they are more likely to take the money and run. They will hold out before making a decision for as long as possible, not only to demonstrate their power and influence, but also to see which way the wind is blowing. You should be able to follow the progress of the bid in the press, and note what course of action is being recommended there.

There may be a general expectation that the bidding company will raise its bid if it doesn't receive enough acceptances to its original offer; or it may be that the market is hoping for another bidder to appear on the scene and liven things up a bit. The besieged board may have spent the intervening period looking for a White Knight to rescue them from the clutches of the evil predator trying to destroy their company, in which case their approval could come with the new bid. Or it may be that the new challenger is yet another Black Knight, even more loathsome to the board than the first bidder.

If the market *is* expecting further action, the share price should rise in anticipation of one or more fresh bids which, if they materialise, will be at higher levels than the first. A shareholder who has accepted an earlier bid shouldn't worry – he must be sent details of any revised bids and can usually withdraw any earlier acceptance he may have made at any stage until a bid is declared unconditional. Should a bid fail to receive sufficient acceptances then it will lapse, and those who have already accepted will simply have their share certificates returned to them.

[134]

Even though an investor's main motivation may be solely the search for profit, he should still question the motives and logic of any bid. It might be that the bid target is in an area of business which the bidder feels will be beneficial to add to its existing range of activities. Some conglomerates indulge in purchases of companies in areas in which they have hitherto had no experience simply because they feel they can run them more competently than the existing management.

Investors should be wary of acquisition-hungry tycoons who revel in the wheeling and dealing involved in bid battles and who may indulge in such activity as much for their own self-aggrandisement and as an ego-trip than for any sound business reasons. If shares in the bidding company are being offered in return for your stake you should be certain that you want to hold those shares before accepting a bid. You always have the alternative of selling your holding in the stock market. If you can't find adequate advice in the press, then do consult a stockbroker. He will know the mood of the City and be able to set out the advantages and drawbacks of each of the possible courses of action.

One fly in the ointment that can affect a bid is the possibility of a reference to the Monopolies and Mergers Commission, a body which is supposed to guard against takeovers that would act against the public interest, highly debatable though this may be. Like any committee, the work of the Monopolies Commission is far from swift and if the Secretary of State for Trade and Industry decides to refer a bid, their deliberations are likely to take at least six months, even if they eventually decide to allow a bid to proceed. The bid will automatically lapse on referral to the Commission and after it reports to the Industrial Secretary and he has made his decision, the bidder can always decide not to renew its takeover attempt.

The possibility of Monopolies Commission interference may be signalled to the investor by the share price. If it is stubbornly sticking some way below the bid price, it could be because market opinion is expecting a referral. The number of occasions on which the Monopolies Commission is called into action very much depends on official government policy. Of late, referrals have been made solely on considerations of the effect on competition, rather than because a bid may offend certain interests or because it comes from overseas.

Smaller companies are more likely to receive bids than the giants. It is rare for blue chips to be taken over, simply because there are so few companies around with the resources to mount such an operation and because such bids stand much more chance of receiving the unwelcome attentions of government. However that didn't stop the takeover of the Imperial Group or Distillers or British Home Stores. High asset values can attract bids, as can lazy management in charge of an otherwise sound business. Keep an eye on changing share stakes, particularly watching out for the 'investments' being made by companies known to be particularly predatory, and especially the aggressive conglomerates.

The king of these must be Hanson Trust, which has made a speciality of buying up what can only be described as 'low-tech' companies. Its profits have risen each year since its birth in 1964 and Hanson has grown from a market capitalisation of one million pounds to five billion. Although there has been internal growth, Hanson's extraordinary record owes much to its ability to spot badly-run and frequently very dull companies and turn them round. Frequently this involves selling off parts of its acquisitions. Within months of acquiring SCM, for instance, the American manufacturer of Smith-Corona typewriters, Hanson had more than recouped the purchase price through selling off various divisions and yet it still had the typewriter and other industrial businesses left within the

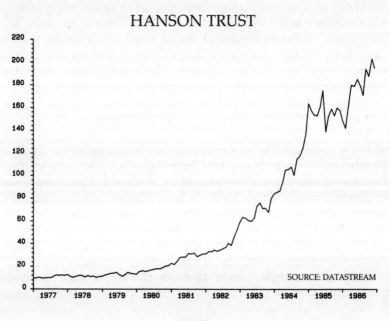

HANSON TRUST

SOURCE: DATASTREAM

[136]

group. Other acquisitions along the way have been Ever-Ready Batteries, the UDS stores group, London Brick, and Imperial Group. Its areas of operations now are diverse: meat processing, textiles, tobacco, leisure, consumer goods, construction and so on.

However, any company can boost its profits figures by buying another. If profits of £100m are made by the original company and it swallows another making £25m, profits will automatically have been boosted by 25%. This is why it is so important to concentrate on the earnings per share figure. In Hanson's case, this has not performed quite as well as profits, rising an average of 25% against an annual 32%. The differential has seemed bearable for shareholders.

HANSON TRUST – GROWTH RECORD				
	Sales £m	Pre-tax profits £m	Earnings per share p	Net dividend p
1977	477	24.4	1.1	0.4
1978	605	26.2	1.1	0.5
1979	658	31.2	1.7	0.5
1980	684	39.1	1.7	0.7
1981	856	49.7	2.3	0.8
1982	1148	60.4	2.9	1.0
1983	1484	91.1	3.4	1.2
1984	2382	169	5.7	1.9
1985	2675	254	8.0	2.4
1986	4310	464	10.7	3.2

SOURCE: PHILLIPS & DREW

If you are on the receiving end of a bid, bear in mind that even if your board accepts a bid, the first offer made may not be the last. Don't be too eager to take quick profits by selling in the market. Some speculators make a habit of buying shares when a bid first breaks cover, hoping for a counter-bid, but reckoning that even if further, more lucrative, offers don't appear they will generally be able to satisfy themselves with the terms of the first bid, should it be completed.

Although in many cases a failed bid will mean a drop in the price of the shares of the target company, that isn't always so. If the potential bidder were shrewd, he might have spotted some important attraction in the company that the market as a whole had overlooked. His attentions may wake others up to this potential, and the management which has successfully seen off the bidder may find a new level of support from investors, such as we have seen P & O found after they had seen off Trafalgar House.

Even the possibility of a takeover approach may give a company's managers greater incentive to strive to increase profits. The higher they are able to keep the share price in the stock market, the more expensive it will be for someone to mount a bid for their company.

In this country at least, takeovers usually work to the good of the company, with lazy or inefficient management being elbowed out by those who are more competent. The rules on takeovers insist that the last shareholder to accept a bid should get as good a deal as the first. This isn't the case in the United States, where takeover battles can be extremely ugly. 'Greenmailers' buy up large stakes in companies in a form of corporate blackmail, hoping to frighten the victim into buying them out at a huge profit. The companies themselves try to make themselves unattractive to raiders by inventing ploys such as 'poison pills' and 'shark repellent', methods by which the finances of the target firm can be adjusted to make the company virtually indigestible. Colourful though this may be, its effects weaken companies rather than strengthen them, and there can be few investors in the British stock market who are not thankful that such behaviour is largely restricted to the other side of the Atlantic.

11
NEW ISSUES: THE PRIVATE INVESTOR'S FREE LUNCH

'The shares are a penny, and ever so many are taken by Rothschild and Baring.
And just as a few are allotted to you, you wake up with a shudder despairing.'   W. S. Gilbert, *Iolanthe*

If anyone ever tells you there's no such thing as a free lunch, they are talking through the top of their head. In the City there are many ways of making money where almost no risk is involved. But for the outsider the problem is in grabbing a piece of the action, which is usually jealously guarded.

The chance to participate does present itself with new issues, however, when companies launch their shares onto the stock market for the first time. For while those companies want to raise as much as possible from the sale of their shares, they and their advisers must also make sure that the issue attracts sufficient demand. To do that, the share price must be set low enough to tempt investors to take up all that are on offer. Pricing new issues correctly is a fine art, some might say an impossible task and, erring as they so often do on the side of caution, the prices fixed by the issue's sponsors are frequently seen by investors as extremely attractive. With a limited number of shares on offer, the demand from those hordes of investors who think they've spotted a good thing can lead to a massive oversubscription. With only a part of the pent-up demand satisfied, the shares could open on their first day of dealings at a substantial premium to the offer price at which they were sold to those few lucky enough to be granted the original shares.

Such fixed-price issues bring out packs of one of the Stock Exchange's animals – the stag. Whereas the stag in nature is a noble beast, in the City these creatures are considered to be a sort of vermin. For the stag is an investor who doesn't play the game according to Queensberry Rules. Instead of putting in an application for the number of shares actually required, a stag, reckoning the shares will open at a premium, applies for enormous quantities. Knowing that if the demand is great enough, applications have to be scaled down, these stags apply for far more than they can really afford. They expect to sell their shares almost immediately to take a quick profit, so the risk involved is fairly short-term.

The Stock Exchange and the merchant banks who handle new issues try their utmost to curb the stag's activities. For while the banks do want to see widespread demand for the new shares, they would prefer that demand to come from genuine investors who want to buy the shares for the long-term. The stags become ever more cunning in their attempts to outwit the merchant banks. They might put in one extremely large application or opt for scores, maybe even hundreds, of smaller ones. They will apply not only in their own name, but in the names of all the members of their family, including the pets. They may use completely fictitious names and have even been known to use the names of the recently deceased.

Enormous effort is called for in stagging, writing out all those application forms in longhand, using different coloured pens and trying to vary the style of handwriting. Some of the more professional stags actually go as far as employing others in their task. But the fun really comes in trying to sneak in the many application forms without detection. The small-scale stag, with just a few forms, may content himself with posting each in a different postal district. But the king stags have to leave their decision whether to apply or not until the last moment, to make certain the issue looks likely to be success-ful. As a result, the merchant bank handling the sale could open its doors on the final day an offer is open to find queues of 'investors'. Each will deposit an envelope under the watchful eyes of the bank's employees, then rush to the back of the queue and try to assume a different personality the next time he comes through, perhaps theatrically acquiring a squint or even going so far as to affect a limp.

On the last day for applications you may see stags scurrying through the City with suitcases crammed full of their forms and cheques. With a very large issue it is easy to mix with the crowd. It's a slightly bigger problem when the issue is small and there are only a few investors who have bothered to hand in their application forms at the last minute; if there are only a dozen people in the queue it's difficult to pass unnoticed on the fourth or fifth trip.

The banks are now trying ever harder to put an end to these stagging activities, particularly on the very public issues, such as British Telecom, TSB and British Gas. In each case, it was made clear on the prospectus that multiple applications were illegal and scores of officials were deployed to try to weed out those breaking the rules. Prosecutions of the worst offenders followed. Even if the bank doesn't go that far, it may decide to cash all the cheques which are sent in, for instance, rather than only the successful ones. This is a course of action which can cause problems for the stag who has written out cheques for far more than he could possibly afford. If they are really playing dirty they might then send out new ones made out to the fictitious names the stag has used; pity the poor stag trying to cash a cheque at his bank made payable to Mickey Mouse or Donald Duck. It is also feasible that the bank will 'confiscate' those shares bought by a stag before they are sent out.

However, efforts to weed out multiple applications can never be completely successful on a popular issue. Those investors who have no wish to bend the rules but who are keen to get hold of a large number of shares will apply for far more than they need, in the expectation that their application will be scaled back. This is a sensible policy on successful issues but you could come badly unstuck if the issue flopped and you got all the shares you asked for. Gold cards, which give the facility of large overdrafts at fairly low rates, are one of the more useful tools the new issue applicant can have.

Although the City officially frowns upon the stag's activities for distorting the true picture of demand for a share, the benefits from stagging are frequently so apparent that many of those working in the Square Mile participate. Most stockbrokers will go in for stagging, as will the fund managers, many of their funds, and even some of those sanctimonious bankers. However, most employees are not allowed to buy shares in a company which their firm has helped to bring to the stock market.

The faintly hypocritical attitude of the City establishment towards stagging – 'don't do as we do' – should not put you off the activity, providing it isn't specifically banned. Whether or not you will find it worth all the effort, only you will be able to discover.

New issues – the mechanics

Applying for a new issue, if you are a serious investor who merely wants to buy the shares for the long term, is really terribly easy, as all those who bought shares in British Telecom, British Gas and TSB discovered.

A prospectus has to be published whenever a company decides to come to the stock market. Although you should be able to get copies from the company's broker or banker, assuming the stags haven't snapped them all up, most will also have to be published in at least two national newspapers, one of which is certain to be the *Financial Times*. Employees of the company may be eligible for special treatment and they will be given the fabled 'pink forms' on which to apply for their shares, but everyone else must use the form in the paper or in the prospectus.

If the company is applying for its shares to be traded on the main stock market, it will normally have been trading for at least five years and will have to issue 25% or more of its share capital to the public. To encourage smaller companies to look to the Stock Exchange for funds, a thriving second-tier market was set up in 1980. Companies coming to the Unlisted Securities Market, as it is called, need only have been trading for three years and may issue as little as 10% of their shares. The financial information they give can be less fulsome too, and less advertising needs to be undertaken.

When published, a prospectus can look fairly daunting. But it will kick off with a general bit of waffle about the company, which may be all you want to look at, particularly if there has been a lot of press comment about the issue in advance. The private investor will most commonly meet with two types of share launches, the fixed-price 'offer for sale' and the more complicated 'tender offer'. With the former, the price at which the shares are to be sold is established in advance. Tender offers are basically auctions, in which investors are told the minimum price at which they can bid. The merchant bank will determine at what level to fix the price. It is often difficult to decide at what price you should tender for shares sold this way. Press comment should give some idea of expectations, but if you decide you definitely want the shares, pitch your offer higher than you need to or, if the form allows for it, agree to pay the so-called 'striking price' at whatever level it is fixed.

[142]

Even if you offer to pay more than the eventual striking price, you will only end up paying the same price as other investors.

For both fixed-price offers and sales by tender, all the work the potential investor need do is fill in an application form and attach his cheque. But if you are stagging the issue, this is where the hard work starts. There are two big advantages for investors applying for new issues. Firstly, no stockbroker's commission is payable and secondly, being new shares, no stamp duty is due on the purchase. The only cost will be the basic consideration, the number of shares multiplied by the price, and a first or second-class stamp.

Investors have only a matter of a few days after publication of the prospectus in which to make up their minds. Again the press should be able to give some idea of the demand for the shares that is developing in the City. Check if the stockbroker to the company has a record of successful flotations. If you work in or near the City, walk its streets and see how many discarded copies of the prospectus you can see littering the pavements with the application forms torn out. Take extra care applying for new issues if the market as a whole is looking shaky, but note that when shares are in buoyant mood there are times when virtually any newcomer to the market will be welcomed with open arms. Even in good times, however, you can never be sure of the success of a new issue, as those subscribing for the heavily-publicised Virgin Group discovered.

Many investors fail to get shares because they make a silly mistake on their application or forget to sign the cheque or fill it out correctly. Do make sure you have done everything as asked on the form and use a pin, not a staple, to attach your cheque.

Once the cheque and application form are sent off, there is no going back. You have made a firm commitment and will know no more for a couple of days, when the issuing house will announce the extent to which it has been oversubscribed, or undersubscribed, and the basis of allocations to investors. Many are heavily oversubscribed. Despite their aim to give shares to all investors, such was the demand for TSB that the bank had to resort to a ballot to weed out one million potential shareholders. When Superdrug came to the market in 1983 there were applications for 95 times the number of shares available. In such cases, applications may be scaled down drastically or placed into a weighted ballot. You may end up with so few, you will be sorry you ever bothered, like the thousands of investors who received a mere 100 Britoil shares in one of the government's least successful privatisation issues.

The smaller your application, the more favourably you are likely to be treated on the whole, one reason why stags prefer to make many tiny applications rather than one large one. This is especially true of privatisations where the government wants to spread the ownership of the shares as widely as possible.

The new shares should start trading about a week after the prospectus was originally issued, although timetables do vary. Your shares, plus any balance cheque if you have been scaled down, ought to arrive that morning. If you're unlucky, your original cheque will be returned to you. If the issue was particularly heavily oversubscribed, there could be a substantial premium as unsatisfied investors, especially the big institutions, move into the market to buy more shares. Superdrug climbed above 300 pence in its first day's trading, pleasing investors fortunate enough to have been granted shares in the issue at 175 pence. If the sale has been by tender, it is far less likely that there will be dramatic dealings on the first day as much of the pent-up demand will have evaporated once the issuing house established the striking price.

Your shares will arrive in the form of a 'renounceable allotment letter' which you should guard carefully. If at any time you want to sell the shares before the proper certificates are issued, which takes a few months, you simply sign the form of renunciation on the allotment letter and send it to your broker. After the problems resulting from early dealings in British Telecom, some stockbrokers will not now deal in new shares until they have the renounced allotment letter in their possession, particularly for new clients.

If the stags have come out in force on a new issue, their early dealings, as they dump the shares they have been granted, could keep the price depressed. Once they have disappeared back into the forests, the shares could start climbing. Consider carefully, even if you did stag the issue, whether it might not be worth hanging on to your new shares. Although stagging can give investors an extremely quick profit, it may be small in relation to that to be made by sticking with the shares.

In the back of your mind should always be the possibility of misjudging the potential of a new issue. Stags can have their fingers very badly burnt if an issue proves unpopular. They may be saddled with all the shares they applied for, and those shares could then start trading at a substantial discount to the offer price. So don't go overboard on new issues. You should realise that it needs only one flop to wipe out all the profits a stag has made on several previous successful issues – but then even a free lunch can occasionally give you indigestion.

New issues – placings

Thanks to the idiocy of the policy-makers at the Stock Exchange many smaller companies are now coming to the market, not through an offer for sale or tender, but through a placing, with the new shares earmarked for the favoured clients of the company's brokers and bankers. You or I are hardly likely to be among that number. Instead, the institutions will snap up most of the shares available. You may be lucky enough to pick up a few scraps in a placing if it is your stockbroker arranging the sale.

The restricted nature of placings often ensures a substantial premium develops once shares begin trading. For it may prove impossible to satisfy the needs of the institutions and they may see the commencement of dealings as their only chance to get an acceptable chunk of the shares, forcing the price much higher. Conversely, you stand a better chance of getting shares in the original placing if others consider the issue an unattractive one.

New issues – privatisations

It is usually the lot of a government to find its populace grudging, not to say reluctant, to hand over their hard-earned money to their rulers. Has there ever been a popular tax? Yet time after time the public have crammed the pavements outside big City banks, jostling and shoving their way to the front of a queue in order to hand in cheques destined for the

[145]

government's coffers. Privatisation is a government policy that has not only been electorally popular but has swollen government revenues and improved the outlook for tax cuts at the same time.

However, it was fairly late on into the privatisation programme that the Conservative Government decided to try and actively extend the degree of share ownership among the public. The 1979 election manifesto gave no hint of what was to come. Yet the idea of removing companies from the stifling grip of the Treasury and sending them out to face free market competition appealed to the incoming government. Management would no longer be able to rely on being bailed out at every turn and this, ran the argument, would compel them to be efficient.

Initially there was little thought of promoting wider share ownership. Companies like British Aerospace, the first to be privatised in 1981, Cable and Wireless, Britoil, Associated British Ports, Enterprise Oil and Jaguar were sold in much the same manner as any other issue, with the institutions picking up the vast majority of the shares.

But British Telecom was so large that the government needed to involve the public as well, mounting such an enormous advertising campaign that you would have to have been a particularly insular individual not to have noticed what was going on. Even so, the final response from the public took everybody by surprise. Nearly three million people applied, many of whom had never before owned a share in their life. The heavy demand meant applications had to be scaled back, but smaller investors were favoured in the rationing of shares.

Like any other seller, of course, the government is concerned that each issue should succeed. But although it and its advisers would like to find a price on each sale which meets with sufficient demand to sell all the shares and ensures they then start trading at a modest premium to the issue price, it has rarely been successful in its aim. The partly-paid shares in British Telecom costing 50p began trading at nearly double that price, leading to accusations that the Conservatives had once more sold the taxpayers' property on the cheap to its 'friends in the City' and that it had forgone about £1.3 billion in the process.

Despite the immense premium on the shares, it had only been two months previously that the big investing institutions had been showing indifference to British Telecom very much at odds with their enthusiasm just a few weeks later. Had the price been set much higher, there was a danger the institutions would have given British Telecom a wide berth and, for all the interest shown by private investors, the issue could have floundered.

While opponents of privatisation talked of the shares trading at double their cost as dealings got under way, that wasn't strictly true. For the real cost of the shares was 130p, not 50p. In terms of the fully-paid price, which is the way the market in general had to view BT, the premium was a rather less dramatic one-third above the cost of the shares.

Also ignored by critics of the sale was the fact that the government was the biggest shareholder in BT, still retaining 49% of it. As the price soared in the stock market, the government's stake became ever more valuable.

There have been other privatisations which have been criticised for being sold too cheaply, such as Jaguar and Amersham International, oversubscribed 22 times. But others, which investors and critics would sooner prefer to forget, were terrible flops. Worried about the enormous premiums seen in some of the fixed-price sales, the Government tried to sell shares in Britoil in November 1982 through a tender offer. It was an unmitigated disaster. Just 30% of the shares were applied for and it took more than six months for the shares to reach the 215p which the unlucky investors had had to pay for their shares. The sigh of relief was short-lived, for the price very soon afterwards collapsed again. The second sale of Britoil shares was even worse; in partly-paid form they halved in just three months. Enterprise Oil, another tender, was also a signal failure. British Gas is about the only one where the opening premium seemed reasonable.

The government was quick to learn the lesson of BT and within weeks ministers were extolling the virtues of wider share ownership whenever anybody left a convenient soapbox around for them to climb onto. Like their aim of giving everybody the right to own their own home, a popular electoral issue had been discovered almost by accident. Even after a flood of early sellers had taken their profits, the government could claim that the number of private shareholders in Britain had nearly been doubled by BT to around three million. The fact that that number is now approaching ten million is largely thanks to the government's efforts and heavy advertising expenditure.

The government has raised more than £10 billion in a little over six years and cynics would say that that is the main reason for extolling the virtues of wider share ownership. Although most of the privatised companies have prospered in the real world, can the transformation of hugh public monopolies like British Telecom and British Gas into huge private monopolies really be said to help foster a competitive environment? Smaller companies coming up against BT in the market place have had cause to lament its greater freedom since privatisation. Electoral ploy, or policy of principle? Whichever it is, the government shows no inclination of giving up on the idea yet. It has been fortunate that the sales have been on the back of one of the longest-ever bull markets in shares. It remains to be seen how keen the new army of shareholders will be on the government if that bull market cracks and the value of their savings comes tumbling down.

Employee share schemes

Of all the privatisation issues, that of the National Freight Consortium must surely be the most successful. This distribution and transport company was sold as a management buyout in 1982 for £6½m with shares widely distributed among employees. Of the 25,000 who work for NFC, well over half have bought shares in the company, probably the most successful investment any of them will ever make. While the profits of the company have more than trebled since, the shares have risen from an original £1 in 1982 to £35 by 1986.

Like many other companies NFC hopes that employees owning shares will identify more closely with the company and understand more readily how to boost its profitability. In a recent survey, around a quarter of all shareholders said that they had received them from a company scheme. The Department of Employment has calculated that a fifth of British companies have some form of employee share ownership or profit-sharing scheme, a proportion which rises to well over half when you consider large, publicly-quoted companies alone.

These share schemes used to be held in some contempt. ICI has given shares to its workers for years, but so uninterested in retaining them were most of the employees that local stockbrokers would park outside the factory gates on the day they were distributed in order to take them off their hands. Possibly as a result of the privatisation campaign, this attitude seems to be changing.

The majority of schemes make employees put a limited amount, between £10 and £100 a month, in a special building society account for five years, at the end of which a bonus is added. The lump sum can be used for buying shares at a price set five years earlier, retained for another two years, or alternatively, the savings can simply be withdrawn. There is no tax to pay if the option is taken up and the shares bought, but on selling them CGT rules apply in the event of more than £6,600 capital gain being made in that year. Obviously, employees will only be tempted to exercise their option if the shares have risen in the intervening 5 years.

12

THE BABY MARKETS

The USM – how to make your million from the stock market

'When you buy a stock you may have a chance at a very nice percentage gain. But the marvel of market capitalisation, of public ownership, has already given the principals sixty times their money.'

Adam Smith, *The Money Game*, 1968

At the turn of the decade, the Stock Exchange took a bold step forward when it brought into being the Unlisted Securities Market. It had been dismayed at the infrequency with which new companies were using the stock market as a source of capital and came to the conclusion that this was largely due to the onerous requirements and the burdensome cost that a Stock Exchange listing entailed.

The USM was introduced as a second-tier market, where companies who would not qualify for the main market could issue shares. They did not need such a long trading record, could part with fewer shares and the information they had to give about their company could be sparser too.

The advent of the USM was a godsend to many of Britain's entrepreneurs, providing the shot-in-the-arm many needed to keep their businesses expanding and enabling them to place a value on their enterprises. The owners of new, often quite speculative ventures, suddenly found that there were queues of potential investors wanting to buy a share of the action. The Stock Exchange had headed off one of the major worries of the entrepreneurs, that of losing control of their brain-children, by allowing companies coming to the USM to issue as few as 10% of their shares.

No matter how successful an investor in the stock market you may be, your return is always going to bear a very close relationship to the funds you commit. Even if you beat every other punter hands down, to make your million from dealing in shares you will have to start with a tidy sum. The really quick way to making a million, or two, is not to deal in other people's shares, but to create your own.

Suppose you start up a business with £10,000 of your own savings, and a little help from your local bank manager. Maybe it is a shop with a new retailing style that you open just round the corner from where you live so that you can stroll to work in the morning, and pop home for lunch. Perhaps word of mouth soon spreads and shoppers begin to make a detour to seek out your shop. Pretty soon your go-ahead bank manager is crying out for you to open another shop, with his help of course. You do so, and are rewarded with similar success. Gradually, as you realise that your retailing ideas are popular with the public everywhere, and not just a flash in the pan, you expand further until you have a chain of forty or so shops, all flourishing, and a profit of around £200,000.

By this time, you have worked yourself pretty much into the ground. You've been paying yourself what you consider a pittance, keeping every last bit of available cash in the business to finance expansion. Then your bank manager, who has been doing very nicely from your business all this time, as have your accountant and your solicitor, suggests you have a chat with a stockbroker about the possibility of a quote on the Unlisted Securities Market.

Your situation may then be transformed completely. As you stroll around the floor of the Stock Exchange on the first day of dealings in your shares, you reflect that it was only a few months previously that you were worrying you were paying yourself too much money. Now you have sold a substantial proportion of your shares, picking up well over £200,000 in the process. It's a little upsetting to you that your stockbroker and merchant banker seem to have set the issue price of your shares too low, for the price has raced ahead already as investors try to pick up more shares than they were able to get in the offer for sale.

Still, as the price rises, your residual holding increases in value. At the last count, your shareholding was worth roughly £1.5 million. And the company now has plenty of cash and won't need any financing for some time to come. Not bad at all.

Since the advent of the Unlisted Securities Market, stories like that have become almost commonplace. By the end of 1986, 600 millionaires had been created by floating their companies

[151]

on the new market. Many are merely paper millionaires, holding the title because their shares are worth more than the magic figure. If they tried to sell their holding, the share price would collapse as outsiders' confidence vanished and they could find themselves with rather less than they might have hoped. But they won't sell out. The USM millionaires have, almost without exception, a tireless dedication to the business which they have founded and immense faith in them.

The aim of the Stock Exchange was that companies quoted on the USM would gradually expand until they felt they wanted to graduate to the main market. Quite a few have done so. Others have felt the USM perfectly adequate for their needs. Several others have never had the chance, for not all of the new shares have prospered. The list of companies coming to the stock market for finance through the USM shows a wide variety of trades; computers and attendant software, catering, dance studios, tourism, shoe repairing, horticulture, retailing, entertainment, video production, homes for the elderly, electronics and brewing are only a few. Cast your eye down the prices page of the *Financial Times*. The USM shares have their own symbol. You might be surprised at how many names you recognise: Body Shop, French Connection, Owners Abroad, Garfunkels, Cecil Gee, TV South, Aspinall's, Ruddles, Merrydown, Air Call, Miss World, Intasun, Acorn computers – all started their market life on the USM.

For the private investor, there is no difference between the main market and the USM as far as the dealing procedure is concerned; commissions are exactly the same. The differences lie in the general attitudes towards the main and USM markets. Private investors are frequently warned that the USM is a risky area in which to place their funds. To some extent this is true. There are probably a few more failures here than on the older stock market. But that isn't too surprising. The companies on the USM are younger, and at a more delicate stage of their growth than their more mature cousins. Despite their number, the total market capitalisation of the USM is under £6 billion – around the size of the General Electric Company and a fraction of the size of British Telecom or British Petroleum.

As we've seen so often, that greater risk is offset by some splendid returns. The ratings, or PE ratios, of most USM companies are significantly higher than similar enterprises quoted on the main market. For many, though, their incredible expansion has ensured great capital profits for those investors who backed them when they first sought a quote. The same investment rules apply as for other shares, but you should be prepared to find USM shares far more expensive, as measured by PE ratios, than on the main market. In times when the stock market is prospering, this may not matter, but there can be some pretty hairy shake-outs in USM companies when things turn sour – Micro Focus only transferred from the USM to the big board a matter of months before plummeting in so dramatic a manner. Their shares are dealt in less frequently on the whole than companies on the main market and it takes fewer sellers to depress a price heavily. Again, contrarily, it takes fewer buyers to make a price shoot ahead.

No private investor should be deterred from USM shares. The market has many of the advantages we have already seen possessed by smaller companies, in particular the dislike of the big institutions for dealing in such tiny shares, and the sparseness of research work by the big stockbrokers. If you find yourself becoming a USM devotee, there is one magazine covering the market in detail which you might find useful. Called *The USM Magazine*, it is available from 1 St John Street, London EC1M 4AA (£95 p.a.). There is also a daily tape service, giving subscribers up-to-date information on market movements and results which might go unnoticed by the newspapers, together with comment on the attractions of newcomers to the market.

And if a friend comes to you asking for finance for a project he or she has in mind, don't be too hasty in turning them down. Anita Roddick had been shown the door by her bank when she turned to her friend Ian McGlinn, borrowing £4,000 to help her start up her second shop selling natural-based cosmetic products. His investment earned him nearly half a million pounds when Body Shop came to the USM and his remaining holding in the company, which has now progressed to the main market, is worth well over £10 million!

The Third Market

'I don't say I've ever sold Central Park or Brooklyn Bridge to anybody, but if I can't get rid of a parcel of home-made oil stocks to a guy that lives in the country, I'm losing my grip and ought to retire'
P. G. Wodehouse, *Money for Nothing*, 1928

So successful has the USM been that the Stock Exchange has just established yet another new market. The Third Market is for the shares of young, unquoted companies that are too new or small for either the main market or the USM. The Stock Exchange gives little to this new market except its name and the fact that it is a Recognised Investment Exchange under the new investor protection legislation. The onus for controlling and policing the various companies on the Third Market lies, not with the Stock Exchange, but rather with the sponsoring stockbrokers, who have to be members of the Exchange.

The requirements are rather less stringent than on the USM. Third Market companies must normally be incorporated in the UK and must have a minimum of one year's audited accounts under their belt or at the very least show that they have fully researched projects or products which will generate revenue within the next year. To keep costs low, companies coming to the Third Market need do no more than place one box advertisement in a national newspaper.

The Third Market began life in January 1987 and one study reckons that by the end of its first year, some 200 companies may have their shares dealt on it. Some of them will have been trading in the past on the largely unregulated Over-the-Counter market, while others will be raising equity capital to the public for the first time. Most of the licensed dealers who operated the OTC have become members of the Stock Exchange in order to take advantage of the Third Market.

Third Market shares are all 'gammas' and the sponsoring brokers must, in most cases, ensure that at least two market-makers will be dealing in the shares. Obviously the companies whose shares are dealt in on this market are in the early stages of their development, making them fairly speculative investments and thus a good deal riskier than more mature companies quoted on the USM or main market. Interestingly, Business Expansion Scheme companies can be traded on the Third Market without in any way affecting the tax relief granted to investors. The ability to claim income tax relief at top rate if BES shares are held for five years or more has proven a sufficient incentive for many investors to back new companies and the ability to invest in BES shares on the Third Market is to be welcomed. However, no matter how attractive the BES may seem, you should never buy shares simply because of the tax relief; always ask yourself first whether you would consider making such an investment if it did not come under the BES umbrella.

The over-the-counter market – an artistic licence?

'It can take years of hard work to build up a nest-egg of savings. It can take hardly any time at all to lose it to somebody who sees no need to work for his money when he could get hold of yours.'   Securities & Investments Board

When British Telecom, TSB, British Gas and other big new issues began trading, you may have seen advertisements in the press giving you the chance to deal in the shares 'free of commission'. These were placed by licensed dealers who operate outside the Stock Exchange's authority on a rather more informal basis. These operators are a good deal less reticent in their attempts to attract clients than their more staid counterparts at the Stock Exchange. Although strictly it is accurate to claim that deals can be done 'free of commission', that is not necessarily of any benefit to the investor. For investors using licensed dealers are paying 'net' prices, as are the big institutions when they deal on the main stock market. The Over-the-Counter dealers get their income in much the same way as Stock Exchange market-makers, by creating a difference between the buying and selling price of shares in which they deal. It's still a form of commission, even though it is more difficult for the investor to see just how much he has been charged.

Checking out the OTC dealers at the time of the British Telecom launch, I found that it would actually have cost me more to sell my shares 'free of commission' through one of them than by using a bona-fide stockbroker. So do work out all the sums before agreeing to deal. I have even noticed one firm that claims to deal free of commission adding on a 'handling charge' of several pounds!

[155]

Dealing in shares quoted on the stock market isn't the main business of the OTC dealers. The shares in which they deal usually aren't quoted on the Stock Exchange at all but are traded 'over the counter'. There is no physical counter; the OTC is another telephone market with no trading floor. Before the advent of the Third Market, a company might go onto the OTC because it was too small or too young to qualify for a listing. Now that the Third Market exists, investors would need to ask probing questions about why the company's shares are not traded there. The market in OTC shares is very, very thin and in some cases there is only one market-maker in the shares, a very dodgy situation if you are one of many people wanting to unload their investment. In that instance, the 'price' of the shares could mysteriously collapse. Such disadvantages aren't usually made obvious by OTC dealers, who specialise in hard-sell techniques, badgering potential investors over the telephone until they capitulate. Unlike the practice at the Stock Exchange, OTC salesmen are paid on a commission basis. They need punters to deal if they are to survive. One firm even penalises its dealers if their clients dare to give them selling orders.

Some OTC dealers use big share issues to attract potential new clients, calling them up later with suggestions for investments that might be completely unsuitable for the investors' needs or circumstances. If you are ever rung up out of the blue with what sounds like a marvellous investment idea, then never agree to anything there and then. Always ask for time to think about it so that you don't get carried away by the salesman's enthusiasm. Most OTC dealers not only make markets in shares, but also have substantial holdings of those shares themselves, making them even more eager to sell them on to you. Check which regulatory body they belong to. It is likely to be FIMBRA – the Financial Intermediaries, Managers and Brokers Regulatory Association, although the firm may have registered with the SIB directly. If you have any doubts, then ring FIMBRA or the SIB and check them out.

You shouldn't confuse this country's OTC market with the far more sophisticated and popular market of the same name in America. There is no connection between them at all. It is true that despite the unsavoury nature of parts of Britain's OTC market, some of the companies traded there have done extremely well, with a few graduating to the USM. But there are some very high risks involved in obtaining those high returns, both on the OTC and on the Third Market.

You should beware of any tempting blandishments from OTC dealers operating from abroad. These people, who used in the main to operate from Amsterdam, now seem to have spread to places such as Spain, Luxembourg and Cyprus, and frequently advertise their free newsletters in English newspapers. These contain some fairly uncontentious investment advice for a little while and then suddenly go overboard on the attractions of a 'wonder share' that only they have discovered. This will usually coincide with a high-pressure telephone call explaining how rich you can become if only you follow their advice. These shares frequently have developed miracle devices that will change the face of the known world, be it technology, medicine, or bio-technology. Or perhaps they are about to do some wonderful deal or discover gold or some other precious metal or mineral in enormous quantities.

Whatever they tell you about the shares, it is likely that they will be the only people making a market in them, which means they can manipulate the price to whatever level they want. They tempt gullible investors by telling them how much the shares have gone up over the past few weeks and by insisting that to delay is to throw away money, virtually guaranteeing massive percentage rises over the next few days alone. They will also dangle the carrot that nothing you do through them will ever be revealed to the tax authorities. Everything sounds wonderful until you try to sell any shares. Then the problems begin and fairly soon you realise that you have invested your money in some extremely expensive, yet totally worthless, pieces of paper. As these boiler room operations base themselves in countries with very lax investor protection regulations, you are unlikely ever to see your money again.

The more a salesman promises you, the more wary you should be of the goods he has to offer. If you are ever tempted, then re-read the SIB's booklet, *Self-defence for Investors*, the financial equivalent of having a bucket of cold water thrown over you.

[157]

13
FIXED INTEREST

'Gentlemen prefer bonds.'   Andrew Mellon

I've concentrated exclusively so far on ordinary shares and thus may have inadvertently given the impression that they are the most important instrument traded on the Stock Exchange. That isn't true, for in terms of actual money transacted, it is the fixed interest stocks that see the most business. Although only some 10 per cent of all transactions carried out on the Stock Exchange are in fixed interest securities, the value of the dealings in them is extraordinary, being more than 60 per cent of all the turnover on the Exchange. Over a billion pounds worth of fixed interest securities change hands each day. The most prominent of these are gilt-edged stocks, securities issued by the government to help pay for its borrowings. At the end of December 1986, the total value of all UK shares was something like £1,100 billion while the total capitalisation of gilts was around £130 billion. The reason that the value of gilts transactions is so high, and the number of deals done is so low is that the market is dominated by the institutions, by banks and building societies and by insurance companies and pension funds.

Unlike equities, which will pay out a variable dividend, or none at all, fixed-interest stocks will offer investors a predetermined yield. The major difference between fixed interest investments on the Stock Exchange, and the building society or National Savings, is that they are traded and their price will vary, like shares, according to the demand for them.

Fixed-interest securities should be thought of as loans, which they are. The borrower, be it the government, local authority or a company, agrees to pay a set amount of interest to its creditor, usually for a set number of years, at the end of which time the amount borrowed will be paid back. You won't get much of a buzz from fixed-interest investment, but it is suitable for a great many investors who want to reduce the risk they are taking on. Both the income and the original capital are guaranteed which, provided the borrower doesn't go bust, offers a greater degree of safety and security.

REAL RETURN ON STOCK EXCHANGE INVESTMENT
(GROSS INCOME REINVESTED)

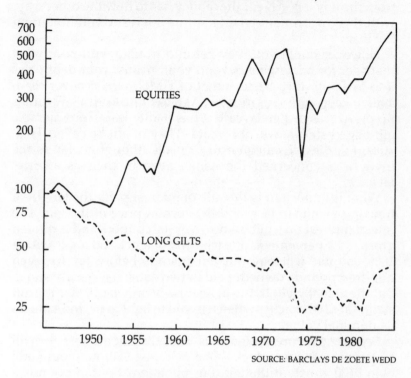

SOURCE: BARCLAYS DE ZOETE WEDD

Gilt-edged stocks

The borrower least likely to default on its debts is the government of Britain. It never finds that taxes, no matter how heavy, raise enough to keep the country bowling along, so HMG has to resort to borrowing to make up the short-fall. You may well have contributed something to the Public Sector Borrowing Requirement before, by buying into one of the National Savings schemes. From the government's point of view, though, these are pretty small beer. In the short-term it borrows from the City's money markets by selling Treasury Bills. But the very nature of government makes it necessary for most of its borrowing to be for the longer term. It does this by issuing its own stock, known because of the security it offers as gilt-edged.

In some ways this is very similar to the way companies raise money, for the government only receives cash when it first

[159]

sells the stock. After that, even though the stock is traded daily, no more income from it goes to the Exchequer. In fact, from the day it is issued, the money has to flow the other way, with the government paying out its interest commitment on the loan.

However much you may get into trouble with your bank manager for borrowing beyond your means, your debt pales into insignificance besides that of HMG, which never manages to keep within its income. As it can't just run a few things up on Access or Barclaycard it has had to issue innumerable gilt-edged stocks over the years. They might be called Treasury, Funding, Exchequer or Consols, though as far as the investor is concerned the name given to them is an irrelevance.

What is important is the rate of interest paid, the length of time the loan is to last, and the current price of the gilt. The rate of interest on a gilt is known as its 'coupon' and is quoted gross, as a percentage of each £100 of stock. So a gilt with a 10% coupon will pay out ten pounds before tax for each hundred pounds owned, paid in two equal half-yearly sums. But the actual yield to the investor will only be 10% if the gilt stands at £100 exactly, when it is said to be at 'par', the same as its nominal value.

Because gilts are traded, it is unlikely that an investor will be paying par for a stock. If he paid just £80, he would still own £100 worth of the gilt. But the interest of ten pounds a year would give him a yield, not of 10%, but rather of 12½%. Similarly if the gilt cost £120, there would still only be ten pounds of interest paid out, giving him an effective yield of just 8.33%.

GILTS – VARIATION OF YIELD WITH PRICE		
Price of gilt £	Coupon (interest rate p.a.) %	Gross interest yield %
80	10	12.5
100	10	10.0
120	10	8.33

The yields available on gilts, and indeed on any fixed-interest stock will vary with the levels of interest rates generally. If interest rates are falling, government stocks will rise in value as investors chase the attractive yields available there. Conversely when interest rates are rising, the prices of gilts will fall. It is important to understand this see-saw effect and to realise the prices of gilts move not only to mirror the changes in interest rates, but also in response to the supply and demand for each particular stock.

The whole business of gilts is terribly bound up with mathematics. Yet despite the precision necessary for the gilt-edged market and the calculations made to umpteen decimal places, the actual prices are still quaintly quoted in *fractions*, sometimes as small as thirty-seconds or sixty-fourths.

If you cast your eye down the British Funds section of the prices pages in the *Financial Times*, you will notice, next to the coupon of each gilt, a date. This is the year in which the stock will be repaid in full by the government. Listed in the order in which they mature, starting with the nearest dates, gilt-edged stocks are divided into four categories: shorts, having a life of less than five years; mediums with between five and fifteen years to go; longs with more than fifteen years till redemption; and undated, where the government has no obligation to repay by any fixed date. Also available are index-linked issues where both the interest paid out and the amount repaid when the loan matures, will rise in line with inflation.

Sometimes the gilt is listed with two dates, such as Treasury 11½% 2001–4 which is to be redeemed sometime between the two dates given.

The gilt-edged market is not one renowned for its jocular nature. Just occasionally, though, someone forgets themselves and indulges in a moment of levity. When the government announced the issue of Treasury 13% 2000, the stock was soon christened 'Grecians' after a well-known hair dye which no doubt has its adherents in the market. Exchequer 12½% 1990 is sometimes called 'the Dog' because, for its first few months of life, it was such an appalling performer. But that's your lot as far as amusement from the gilt-edged market goes.

Going for gilt – choosing a gilt-edged stock

There are over five score government stocks and any investor buying a gilt should consider very carefully which suits his purpose. Even though seeking advice from a stockbroker is pretty sensible, there is no reason why, if you are mathematically inclined, you shouldn't make the decisions yourself. As an investor, you certainly ought to know something about the sector and how it works.

For a private investor, gilts have several advantages over other sorts of security. In addition to the safety they offer, dealings are for 'cash' settlement and sellers of gilts will receive their money almost immediately. From July 1986 capital gains tax has been abolished on dealings in gilt-edged securities. Income received from government stocks, though, is still liable to income tax. Lastly, the level of commission charged on deals in gilts is lower than for equities (see Appendix B for pre Big Bang rates). The absence of any stamp duty on gilt purchases makes them still cheaper to deal in.

With so many gilts to choose from, you should closely examine the last two columns given in the *Financial Times* listings for government stocks. The first gives the interest yield, or running yield, which will tell you how much income you will receive each year gross as a percentage of the current stock price. Unless you buy your gilts from the Post Office, interest will, as with shares, be paid to you after basic-rate income tax has first been deducted.

As we have seen, the yield does not remain constant, but varies with the price of the gilt. Although its price from day to day will depend on the general level of interest rates and the performance of the gilts market as a whole, over time its price will gradually tend towards par, or £100 – its nominal value. For at its redemption date a gilt's owner will receive the sum originally lent to the government and a hundred pound's worth of stock will be valued by the market at £100. If a gilt stands at a discount to its par value, it will obviously appreciate as redemption approaches, whatever the fluctuations of the market in the interim. If it is at a premium to par, it will have to decline in value.

The Gross Redemption Yield, also given in the FT each day, calculates this effect. This yield, which is hideously complicated to calculate yourself, takes into account not only the interest paid on a gilt, but also the movement in the capital value of the gilt as it moves towards par at the redemption date. Even if you do not intend to hold the stock for its full life, gross redemption yields are useful, being the yardstick for valuing gilts relative to each other in much the same way as PE ratios are employed in the equity market.

In assessing which gilt is the right one for you, you need to consider how long you are likely to want to hold the stock and your own tax position. While a non-taxpayer may be delighted to find the gilt with the highest yield, an investor paying tax at the top rate will be less content with it. Highest-rate taxpayers are going to be far more interested in low-coupon gilts where the amount of income, on which tax at the highest marginal rate has to be paid, is as low as possible while capital appreciation, which could be free of tax, will be avidly sought.

For those investors who pay tax at lower rates, it is a matter of preference how income and capital are mixed. You should always bear in mind, though, that gilts are traded. You may know what the yield on your gilt is to thirteen decimal places if you hold it until it is finally redeemed. But if you suddenly find you have to sell it to raise money urgently, the price in the market may be significantly out of line. Despite the ultimate safety of gilts, they often undergo wild fluctuations on the way to maturity.

It is worth knowing that as a small investor you may be able to 'wash' your bonds. A gilt will rise in price as the six-monthly ex-dividend date approaches, much like a high-yielding share, and drop by the amount of the dividend on the xd date. For large investors, this will give them no advantage, for that part of the price rise that is a result of the interest build-up will be taxed as income; gilts are dealt in at an underlying price plus so much accrued interest.

However, those who have gilts holdings of less than £5,000 nominal *can* buy just after a dividend has been paid, watch them grow fat on accrued interest and then sell just before the xd date, thus grabbing a nice capital gain instead of having to receive taxable dividends. The higher the dividend, the greater the growth. As you are going to need to give this some attention, you would be best advised to carry this out in conjunction with your broker.

Gilts in action

The government doesn't deal with the Stock Exchange directly when it sells gilt-edged stock. Its dealings are handled by the Bank of England, which issues a prospectus and sets a minimum price for each new issue. This is usually offered by tender, with investors bidding the price they are willing to pay. The striking price for a gilt need not be the nominal or par value at all. Nor need all the stock be sold at once. The Bank can hang on to the rump and sell it in the market whenever it feels circumstances are propitious, the so-called 'tap' system.

Your reason for investing in gilts might not necessarily be just because you are looking for a safe and secure income. You might have your own view on the direction of interest rates and want to try to take advantage of it as it affects the gilt-edged market. It tends to be the longer-dated gilts which are the most volatile, for the shorter ones will be heavily influenced by the proximity of the repayments, and thus gravitate towards par. However, this isn't always the case, particularly if interest rates are moving around quickly, and the advice of a stockbroker will always prove useful.

It's worth pointing out at this stage that, unlike shares, gilts don't need to be bought through a stockbroker. Many of the available gilts are also on the National Savings Stocks Register and can thus be bought through the Post Office. This can have two advantages for investors; first, it is much cheaper than dealing with a stockbroker, being less than half the cost, and secondly, the interest is paid to you gross. This is most convenient for non-taxpayers but can be useful for others in that they have the use of the money until they have to hand it over to the Revenue. The main disadvantage, and it is a big one, is that your order may not be carried out for several days and you have no control over what price you may eventually pay or receive.

Simply because you are lending money to the government by buying gilts, knowing that your capital is safe with a guaranteed income on top, does not mean that you will actually be making money. For as with other forms of investment, inflation can eat away at gilts like a canker, eroding the real value of an investor's holding. You need to consider carefully whether gilts are offering a real return, above the present and likely rate of inflation, before committing yourself.

The survey by de Zoete & Bevan on the performance of gilts

and equities concluded that an investment of £100 in gilts made in 1918 would now be worth a mere £3.30p in real terms! That compares with an equivalent of £414 for equities. However, like building societies, the last few years have been more satisfactory, with gilts yields exceeding the rate of inflation by several points and thus giving a positive real return.

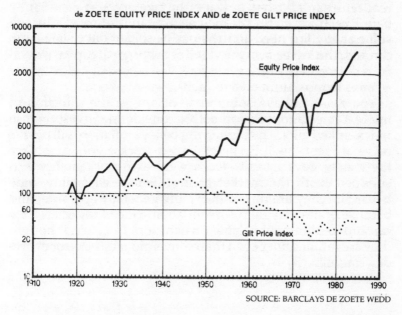

de ZOETE EQUITY PRICE INDEX AND de ZOETE GILT PRICE INDEX

SOURCE: BARCLAYS DE ZOETE WEDD

Index-linked gilts – a real investment?

'A penny goes a long way now. You can carry it round for days without finding a thing it will buy.' Anon.

If preserving your capital against the ravages of inflation is your primary aim as an investor, then you could find index-linked gilts a major attraction. They were introduced by the Government in 1982 and both capital and income of an index-linked gilt are increased in line with the Retail Price Index. Conventional gilts will, at their maturity, be redeemed at their nominal value of £100. Index-linked gilts, however, have their par value adjusted to take account of the rise in the RPI in the interim. At maturity you get back not £100, but one hundred pounds multiplied by the change in the RPI over the period. If a gilt has just five years to run, and inflation averages 8%,

[165]

then its repayment will be around £147 for each original £100 of stock held.

But the coupon, or rate of interest, paid out each half-year will also be increased in line with the rise in the RPI. If you glance down the list of index-linked gilts, you'll see that the coupons are tiny, of 2 or 2½% each. Even though these are real returns, adjusted upwards to take account of inflation before each payment, the income from index-linked gilts will still be very low. Because they achieve most of their return through the increase in the value of the original capital invested rather than the interest, which will be taxed, index-linked issues are most attractive to high-rate taxpayers.

You need to have some view on the future direction of interest rates and inflation before considering investment in index-linked gilts. The higher you believe inflation will be, the more attractive will be index-linked stocks. For some time these new government stocks were extremely stodgy and subdued, with the market giving them a reasonably wide berth. But they are now rather more generally accepted, and because of the play on future inflation which they offer, they can prove extremely volatile on occasion. In general though, they are rather duller even than conventional stocks for every-day trading.

14

'GIVE YOUR MONEY TO ME. I'LL LOOK AFTER IT.'

Unit trusts

*'My boy . . . always try to rub up against money, for if you
rub up against money enough, some of it may rub off on you.'*
Damon Runyon, *A Very Honourable Guy*

The excitement of direct stock market investment isn't for
everyone. Many who crave participation in the market, but
who want less hassle and risk, opt instead to have their money
looked after for them by the managers of unit trusts or investment trusts. Both work on the same principle. Many investors
entrust their cash to professional fund managers who pool the
resources of the many into one giant portfolio. Each investor
has a stake in the resultant whole but, having picked his fund
has no further say in its running. This not only means that there
is less work for the investor to do, but also that a far greater
range of investments can be covered than would otherwise be
possible. There is a vast range of funds, many of which
specialise in particular areas of the market or in overseas
markets, and the fund managers can offer expertise which it
may be impossible for the individual investor to acquire easily.

Unit Trusts are known as open-ended funds, for the simple
reason that if more investors are buying into a fund than are
selling, new units can be created to meet this demand. Each
investor's holding is made up of a number of units which give
him a proportionate share in the value of the entire fund. The
price of each unit, which is valued at the end of each trading
day, is simply the total value of a particular fund's holdings
divided by the number of units in issue. Because of this, the
price of the units does not depend upon the supply and
demand for them from investors, but solely upon the success of
the fund's investments.

Investment in such funds reduces an investor's risk. The far
greater size of its portfolio ensures a unit trust spreads risk
more widely than a small punter would be able to do with his

handful of shares. One big advantage of unit trusts for the little chap is that he can make smaller investments than would be feasible with shares. Indeed some unit trusts can be bought on a savings plan; for as little as £10 or £20 per month an investor can accumulate units until his holding begins to look quite significant. An investment of £20 per month in the median UK general unit trust over the five years to October 1986, for instance, would have grown to £2,045, a profit of £845. Over the ten year period it would be worth £6,900, a profit of £4,500 against an increase of only £1,400 if it had gone into the building society.

Investing in unit trusts is very simple. The telephone numbers of the groups administering them are included in the tables of daily prices given in papers like the *Financial Times*, *Times* and *Telegraph*. One phone call will secure you your units or start up your savings scheme.

Of course the management groups which administer unit trusts don't do so out of the goodness of their hearts. Altruism is not a virtue widely prevalent in the City. The way charges are levied aren't, at first sight, terribly simple. But they are worth looking at. Far too many investors assume benevolent fund managers are charging a pittance for their service and wonder why, even though the market has been rising, they don't seem to be showing much of a profit on their units.

A unit is priced by working out its market value. For a fund of two million units, a total value for the fund's assets of £6 million would mean that each unit ought to cost three pounds. An initial charge of around 5% is built into the price of each unit and an annual charge ranging from 0.5 to 1% of the fund's value is levied upon you and taken from the trust's income.

Unit trusts, like every other form of market investment, have their equivalent of the 'jobber's turn'. They cover their dealing and administrative costs, and make a little profit, by charging more for their units than they will pay an investor who is selling them back to the management house. Most unit trusts are 'authorised' by the Department of Trade, which allows for spreads between the 'bid' and 'offer' price of as much as 13.5%. The average unit trust wouldn't do very much business on that basis, and most have a difference between the buying and selling price of around 7%. These spreads are quoted wherever the unit trust prices are listed, the most comprehensive being in the *Financial Times*.

Investors will need to see the value of a fund rise by at least 7% or so before they are seeing any profit on their units. Unit-holders may see not only a capital profit from a rise in the value of their units, but also income from the dividends received by the trust. Some trusts pay this income out, after deducting their management charge, while others allow investors to reinvest the proceeds in further units, an option which is usually made slightly more tempting by allowing a small discount.

Unit trusts – should you trust them?

Unit trusts are the private investors' playground, yet the extent to which they are understood by many of those investors using them is often pitiful. Many trusts have undoubtedly been extremely successful and this success has encouraged not only further interest from the public at large, but also from the management houses who recognise a good thing when they see it.

It used to be the case that picking a unit trust was a fairly simple affair; there were, after all, only a handful of them around. A potential investor could look for a reputable 'stable' of fund managers and choose from their general trust, their growth trust, their income trust or, if he felt particularly daring, their international trust. But with £30 billion under management, the choice has become completely bewildering. There are some 1,000 trusts to choose from and the vast difference in performance of different funds only underlines how important the investor's choice is. There is no evidence to suggest that Unit Trust Brokers, who charge a fee for advising on unit trust investment, are any better at picking than private investors. Recently 'Funds of Funds' have been allowed, unit trusts that invest in other unit trusts, making the task of picking even more difficult.

The array of trusts is made still more confusing by the heavy-handed marketing many employ, their adverts being frequently so misleading that they only just remain this side of the law. There is a distinct similarity between much unit trust advertising and that for the tipsheets. You will rarely see an advert for a trust group that makes any mention at all of the poor performers, though there are almost certain to be some. The impression gained is that the trust group has only ever managed winners. But if a management house has several unit trusts under its wing, it isn't too surprising if at least one has performed reasonably well, simply by the law of averages. It will be on this one that the advertising will concentrate. And it may be that its performance will be shown, not over the past five years say, but over some period chosen simply because it gives a flattering image of the fund.

If you don't treat these adverts with a good deal of scepticism you might have cause to regret it. Don't just concentrate on the percentage rise in a fund's value. Note how the fund has performed in relation to the market. If that figure isn't given, you ought to be on your guard. For instance, many funds show their growth since the stock market crashed in 1974, but since then every single fund can show staggering percentage gains. Even if the management group is being completely straight with the figures it presents in its advertising, remember that these are past performance figures and do not necessarily offer a guide to the future success of the funds.

When casting an eye at unit trust advertising, and when considering investing in trusts, remember that it is far easier for a young fund to perform well, particularly if it is part of a large management house. Part of the reason for this is its smaller size; it will be able to deal quickly and easily and can subscribe for small placings of new issues which wouldn't be worthwhile for larger funds. However, small funds investing in obscure overseas markets might find they lack the quality of broker contact that the bigger players can get, which is a severe disadvantage in those markets.

Because the fund is new, most management groups will make an effort to ensure that it gets off to a good start. The hot tips will be bought for the new fund which will be receiving a greater-than-usual amount of management time. It is also fairly common for investments to be booked late to a new fund, with its managers delaying in order to see if a share rises before adding it to the portfolio; if it doesn't then the purchase can always be lost in one of the more mature, larger funds. All this won't worry you if you've owned units since the off, but ought to make you a little more cautious if you're thinking of investing in a fund just as its early growth begins to slow.

There is also a regrettable tendency in the advertising of unit trusts to show the increase in funds' values by showing the rise in the trust's offer price, the level at which investors *buy* units. It would be more truthful to take the original offer price, and compare it with the present *bid* price, for that is the only fair way of representing the gain that investors in the unit trust would have been able to achieve.

You may feel that the spreads on unit trusts, of around 6% or 7% between the buying and selling price, are wide enough. But things aren't always as they first appear, and it is possible for the management of trusts to play around with the spreads. Most unit trusts are sold on what is said to be an 'offer basis'. For example, if the fund and the market in general are rising, then it is probable most deals in the unit trust will be purchases by the public. If the asset backing of our fund – let's call the trust group Albion Investments – is three pounds a unit, then the price quoted to investors could easily be 300p bid, 318 offered. Most unit trusts are sold on what is said to be an 'offer basis'. In this case, they would therefore sell at 318p. But suppose the mood of the market turns sour. Then the managers at Albion might feel their investors could start ringing in with sell orders. Although they are honourable gentlemen, and have never felt it necessary to penalise their investors by having a spread on the trust any wider than 6%, they know that the Department of Trade allows spreads as wide as 13.5%. It is the work of but a moment to slide the unit trust's spread within that maximum permitted band. By putting the trust on a 'bid basis' they can quote a price of 282 bid, 300 offered, quite legitimately. The fund hasn't changed in value. It is still worth £3 a unit. The spread is still only 6%. The maximum guidelines laid down by the Department of Trade haven't been infringed. But by a sleight of hand the moving of the trust from an offer basis to a bid basis ensures that someone who had just bought units at 318 pence each can now only sell them for 282 pence, a loss of over 11%.

ALBION INVESTMENTS: FUND VALUE £3 A UNIT		
	To sell	To buy
Offer basis	300p	318p
Bid basis	282p	300p

Such a move by a fund management house discourages selling, and indeed for any investor caught by an unexpected turn of the market, can wipe out steadily mounting profits at a stroke. Unfortunately it is difficult to find out whether this is the case with any particular fund when you want to deal. The managers don't go out of their way to advertise that their funds are being sold on a bid basis. If you suspect it might be the case, demand to know before you deal.

This sliding round of the trust's spread within the permitted maximum can be further used by the management stable to flatter performance figures, but can also have an advantage for alert investors who choose to buy when a trust is quoted on a bid basis. They will benefit when it is once more quoted on the more normal offer basis, for the spread will then move upwards.

There are other moves the managers of a trust can make that affect their fund, such as 'dealing for the box', when they start dealing in their own units. Such actions ought to be made public, as should any move by a fund on to a bid basis, but we may have to wait some time before we see such enlightened legislation.

There is one piece of information which few funds will part with and that is the name of the particular manager in charge of each unit trust. Yet you are, after all, entrusting this individual with your money. He may be a wizard at portfolio management, or he may be an absolute bozo. Even though you have a good idea of the record of the management group as a whole, that is no guarantee that your fund will be looked after by a man representative of that record; unit trusts tend to be managed by the younger people in the firm. It is understandable why such personal information isn't available. For then investors would start to chase the managers, rather than the management houses. Good fund managers are hard to find and it could harm a management group if investors' money were to leave when a manager left. Nevertheless, fund managers are as keen to seek the limelight as anyone else and are being quoted more and more frequently in the financial press. If you can't locate the manager of a fund in which you are interested there, or from the management house itself, try asking your stockbroker. He will be touting for deals from the funds and will have a fairly good idea of which managers are worth following and which should be avoided at all costs.

Background information on unit trust performance can be

obtained from the magazines *Money Management* and *Planned Savings* or from the *Unit Trust Yearbook*. Look at the performance over a one, three and five year period, remembering that past performance is not necessarily an indication of future trends. Also take care to compare like with like, Japan Fund with Japan Fund, UK general with UK general, or the exercise will be futile. Make sure that the trust you are considering investing with is authorised by the Department of Trade, and if not, why not? There might be a perfectly acceptable reason, for the DTI places restrictions on funds that some of the more adventurous ones may want to escape from, even though it means they can't then be advertised in the UK. It is also worthwhile checking whether the management group belongs to the Unit Trust Association, the industry's trade body.

When you are seeking independent advice on which unit trusts to go for, remember the advice you are given may not be completely impartial. Whoever your adviser is, perhaps your stockbroker or accountant, or maybe your insurance broker, he is probably going to receive commission from the trust itself for persuading you to buy units. No doubt he is an upright and honest man for whom the offer of such cash inducements means absolutely nothing. Bully for him. Just make sure he doesn't bully you.

Investment trusts

Like unit trusts, investment trusts are funds managed by professionals which can cover a greater range of investments than can the private investor on his own. But investment trusts differ in that they are individual companies, whose shares are actually quoted on the stock market. They are known as closed-end funds, as they have a fixed number of shares in issue. Unlike unit trusts, where the price of units must reflect the asset value of the fund, the price of investment trust shares reflects the supply and demand for them in the stock market. The demand, and thus the price, does depend to a large extent, however, on the value of the funds of the investment trust and the level of dividends it pays out.

In essence, investment trusts are shares which invest in other shares. Investors deal in them in exactly the same way as other shares, with the same costs. They also have the same rights, being part owners of the companies, entitled to their share of the profits and to a say in the way the company's affairs are conducted.

Investment trusts are not really 'trusts' in the strict sense of the word and so have fewer restrictions placed upon them than unit trusts which are governed by their Trust Deeds. The managers of investment trusts may invest in whatever they like, though they may have to account to their shareholders later on if they've been too innovative. Being 'closed-end funds', they don't have to cope with the movements of cash in and out of the trust as unit trust managers do. As a result they can be rather more sophisticated vehicles altogether than the more restrained unit trusts.

Like unit trusts, investment trusts specialise in certain areas; there are trusts investing solely in the UK or in various overseas markets, in commodities, in energy, in smaller companies, and so on *ad infinitum*. Like unit trusts, some aim to give their investors capital growth and others concentrate on income.

While an investment trust's share price will tend to move in line with the company's assets, most stand at a 'discount' to the net asset value of the fund. Recently the investment trust industry has, in a widespread advertising campaign, emphasised this feature, claiming that investors have a greater value of assets working for them than the cost of their investment. Although this is true, these discounts are likely to remain for some time and an investor shouldn't expect them to disappear overnight. However, the general level of the discount of investment trusts varies over time. When the shares are in demand it can narrow considerably, giving investors in the shares a rise proportionately greater than the rise in the general market. But this works both ways. At times in the past decade the average discount on investment trust asset values has varied between 35% and 20%.

The discount on individual investment trusts can vary widely from the norm, with a few actually standing at a premium to their asset value. In recent years more and more trusts have found themselves the subject of attention from outsiders interested in getting their hands on the trusts' assets. Several companies have bought up investment trusts and then sold off the assets, raising cash more cheaply than they could have done through a rights issue. Some investment trusts have been 'unitised', becoming unit trusts. Others have been the target of big investing institutions, insurance companies or pension funds who have seen them as a way of getting hold of an attractive portfolio of investments on the cheap.

The share prices of most investment trusts are quoted daily in the financial pages of the newspapers. On the fourth Saturday of each month the Association of Investment Trust Companies publishes a table of detailed statistical information in the *Financial Times* and the *Daily Telegraph*. This shows the management, asset value, yield, and geographical composition of each portfolio together with a five-year performance record.

Also included is a figure for the 'gearing factor'. One of the most important differences between investment trusts and unit trusts is that the managers of investment trusts are permitted to borrow money. If the assets they buy with the money increase in value, the growth of the assets belonging to the shareholders will be magnified.

EFFECTS OF GEARING IN INVESTMENT TRUSTS

	YEAR 1 £m	YEAR 2 £m	INCREASE %
Asset value of fund	10	15	50
Loan stock	3	3	–
Assets available for shareholders	7	12	71

With a fixed amount of loan stock a rise in the portfolio proves more beneficial to the value of each investment trust share than if the fund were unborrowed. In this instance the assets of the fund available to shareholders increased by 71%, even though the value of the portfolio has only grown by 50%. This principle of gearing applies to every houseowner, who benefits substantially as the price of his house climbs above the fixed level of his mortgage. As with homeowning, the benefits of gearing are greatest when the level of interest rates is sufficiently low to make it attractive to borrow money. The gearing factor quoted in the monthly tables shows the percentage amount by which the net asset value of the trust would rise if the value of the portfolio of stocks and shares held by the investment trust doubled in value.

It should be realised that the benefits of gearing quickly become a disadvantage if the value of the fund is falling. For then the fixed value of loan stock becomes ever more burdensome, eating into the profits of the trust.

As with shares, very small purchases of investment trust shares will incur a disproportionate amount of commission, but the costs of buying and selling are exactly the same as for any other shares. The charges levied by investment trusts are significantly lower than for unit trusts: about 0.4% annually, against a figure of up to 1% for unit trusts and the initial 5% charge included in the price. There is no initial charge for investment trusts, but you have to pay broker's commission, stamp duty of ½% and the invisible charge of the jobber's turn.

Several investment trust groups operate savings schemes in exactly the same manner as unit trust savings plans, although they are of rather more recent origins. Among them are Foreign & Colonial, Touche Remnant and Robert Fleming.

Performance tables for the past few years show the average investment trust to have outperformed its unit trust rival. Over the ten years to August 1986, for instance, investment trusts beat unit trusts by a margin of some 25%. You might sensibly ask why the investment trust industry keeps its light so well hidden from the outside world. That is largely because investment trusts have to conform to far more stringent rules on marketing and advertising than do unit trusts. This handicaps them twice over, for newspaper editors find it far less attractive to do special features on investment trusts as they can't spend the sort of money on ads that the far more aggressive unit trust companies are willing to pour in whenever their virtues are extolled in the press.

Before you make any investment in unit trusts, you should consider this very viable alternative. The Association of Investment Trust Companies will no doubt snow you under with bumpf if you contact them on 01-588 5347.

Stockbrokers and fund management

Many stockbrokers are only too happy to look after your money for you, handling all the paperwork, providing valuations of your portfolio from time to time, taxation advice and so on. However, you are likely to need a pretty sizeable portfolio if the brokers aren't to turn up their noses at it. If you are willing to give the stockbroker total discretion to run your stock market investments he will at least countenance comparative paupers, knowing that they won't be bothering him at all hours of the night and day with trivial and distracting questions about the performance of their shares. Some of the smaller stockbroking firms might handle comparatively small sums of money in this way, but for the larger firms you are more likely to need at least five or ten thousand pounds and possibly rather more.

If you aren't willing to give discretion to your broker, but instead want him to give an advisory service where any investments or sales that are made are done after consultation with you, then you will need an even larger portfolio. Again some of the more minor stockbrokers will perform this service even for very small amounts, but for the major firms you could need as much as fifty or even one hundred thousand pounds.

Many stockbrokers now run their own unit trusts, or other forms of funds, specifically for their own clients. Those with advisory or discretionary portfolios will usually be guided towards these 'in-house' funds. From the broker's point of view it makes it a good deal simpler to manage a private client department if many of their clients can deal together through a fund in this way. Obviously the performance of such funds varies enormously, so even if you are being offered financial inducements to participate, don't rush in blindly.

On the other hand, there are some 'in-house' funds which benefit from the expertise a stockbroking firm may have in a particular area. And despite the efforts firms profess to make to keep their corporate finance departments separate from the rest of the firm, many funds have a record of investing successfully in the shares of companies to which they are the broker. Not surprising, perhaps, but beneficial none the less to those clients in the funds.

15

TRADED OPTIONS: THE PRIVATE INVESTOR'S FRIEND, OR SERVANT OF THE DEVIL?

'The safest way to double your money is to fold it over once and put it back in your pocket'.

Frank McKinney Hubbard

One corner of the stock market floor is unlike any other, an area packed with video terminals, on each of which is a bewildering jumble of numbers. One or two brokers will be nearby, eyeing them warily when another will stride up and shout something at the assembled company. They will scream back at him in return. This done, he departs, either defeated or satisfied, while the operator of the nearest computer terminal clatters on the keys until the prices of the screen are updated.

This particularly strange ritual takes place in the Traded Options Market. It is an 'open outcry' market, where every dealer is supposed to be able to hear the details of each transaction, participating if they wish. As a result a trading floor is essential and this is one market that hasn't been physically affected by Big Bang.

Even though the noise on the market floor isn't audible to the investors who use the Traded Options Market, each is aware of the pace and volatility of options, characteristics which make them suitable only for those who are active players. Unlike shares, you can't deal in an option and then lie back and forget about it. For the interested investor, however, traded options can provide a stimulating addition to an equity portfolio.

What is a traded option? The basic idea of options is simple. There are two sorts available; a 'call' option gives its holder the right, but not the obligation, to *buy* shares at a fixed price before a set date, while a 'put' option gives the right to *sell* those shares. For years there was a traditional options market available in any share listed on the Stock Exchange, but it lacked versatility. The introduction of traded options in 1978 changed that for, as the name implies, these options can be dealt in themselves by being bought or sold at any time during their lifespan. They are an extraordinarily versatile investment tool, being able to increase the speculative element of a portfolio or conversely to reduce greatly the market risk inherent in it.

Before going into details, let's look at a very basic example of how traded options work. Let us suppose that in January an investor decides to buy one call option contract lasting until June in a company called Gargantuan Industries. It gives him the right to buy Gargantuan at 70 pence, the price at which the ordinary shares are currently standing in the market. That option has cost him ten pence for each share it represents and will last for about six months.

The first graph shows how the movement of Gargantuan would affect a holder of the ordinary shares. For each 10p rise in the share price above 70p, the investor will be making a profit of 10p on each share. And for each 10p fall, he will be losing 10p on every share he holds.

The second graph shows the example of an options holder. The option gives the right to buy Gargantuan shares at 70p at any time until June. If Gargantuan is standing at 70p then that option has no intrinsic value. No one would want it if they could simply buy the shares at the same price in the market. Indeed the option would have no value at all were Gargantuan's shares at any price below 70p; the investor would lose his original investment of 10p per share. But for any value above 70p, the option would be worth something. At 80p for instance, the option which gives the right to buy shares at 70p should be worth 10p. At 90p that right would be worth 20p, and so on.

Bearing in mind that the option holder paid 10p for his investment, he will be making money only when Gargantuan is above 80p, and losing below that level. But the most he can lose is his original 10p a share, unlike a holder of Gargantuan shares who will continue losing money as Gargantuan's share price slides ever further downwards. By buying an option, an investor limits his risk. But his rewards are not limited, for the option is worth an extra 10p for every 10p by which the shares of Gargantuan increase.

When Gargantuan's shares are at 100p, the purchaser of shares at 70p will be making 30p on each share. The holder of the option will be making 20p, the value of the option (30p)

PROFIT/LOSS TO BUYER OF SHARES AT 70p

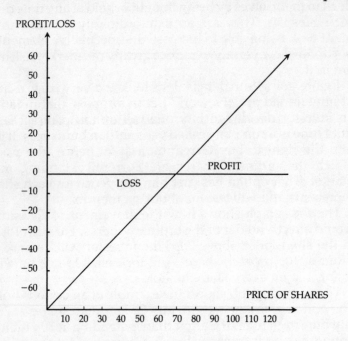

PROFIT/LOSS TO BUYER OF 70p CALL OPTION AT 10p

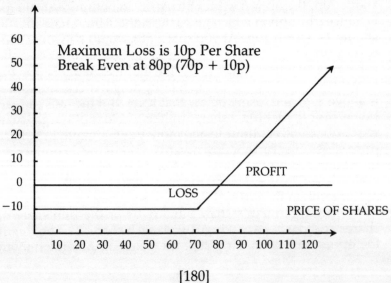

less the cost (10p). But for the option holder, that is a trebling of his original investment, while the shareholder only makes 43% profit.

EFFECTS OF CALL OPTION VERSUS ORDINARY SHARES					
Price of shares (p)	Profit/(loss) on shares (p)	% profit	Price of call option (p)	Profit/(loss) on option (p)	% profit
40	(30)	−43	0	(10)	−100
50	(20)	−29	0	(10)	−100
60	(10)	−16	0	(10)	−100
70	0	0	0	(10)	−100
80	10	+14	10	0	0
90	20	+29	20	10	+100
100	30	+43	30	20	+200
110	40	+57	40	30	+300
140	70	+100	70	60	+600

If the share climbs to 140p, this gearing element inherent in traded options becomes even clearer. At that level the shareowner has made a handsome 100% profit on his investment, doubling his money and no doubt feeling pretty smug.

But the option holder now has seven times his original stake! This example illustrates three of the important advantages that traded options can give to the private investor. First, he can gain the benefits from investing in thousands of shares by putting up cash for only a fraction of the cost that the shares themselves would cost him. At no time does he have to exercise his right to buy those shares. Secondly, because the option can be traded his risk is limited to the money he originally invested in that option which is less than the money at risk to the shareholders. If Gargantuan's shares fell to 40 pence, the option holder would have lost his entire investment. But that would only be 10p per share, whereas the shareholder who bought at 70p would be losing 30p on each share. Thirdly, and perhaps most importantly, the percentage gain on a successful option investment is far greater than would be the case from buying the underlying shares.

The investor deciding he would like to buy a call option in Gargantuan need not have chosen one giving him the right to buy shares at 70p. There will be several 'striking prices', as they are known, which in the case of Gargantuan might be 60p, 70p, and 80p. More would be added if the price moved sufficiently.

For the prospective buyer the option at 80p, still 10p above the current share price, is the most speculative and the one which will give the greatest percentage return if successful. But whereas the price of Gargantuan shares would need to climb 10p before that option had any intrinsic value, with the shares at 70p the 60p option already has 10p of intrinsic value in it. It is said to be 'in the money', while the 80p option is 'out of the money'. The option in our example, the 70p one, standing at the share price is, not surprisingly, 'at the money'.

There is still more for the option investor to decide, apart from choosing the exercise price which most suits him. Each option is dealt in in units, called 'contracts', which usually represent 1,000 shares. So a buyer of five contracts would be dealing in the rights over 5,000 shares. He would have the right to buy 5,000 shares at 70p at any time during the life of that contract. Each share for which an option is traded, or each 'class', will have various 'expiry dates' which determine how long that life will be. These are set at three-monthly intervals, the dates of which vary for each share. There are three possible cycles: January, April, July, October; February, May, August, November; and March, June, September, December. Each share, or class, will always follow one cycle and at any one time will have options quoted for three of the possible four months. An investor looking for an option to buy will be faced with expiry dates of no more than 3, 6 and 9 months.

In Gargantuan's case, the third cycle is used. At present March, June and September options are available. When the March expiry date is reached, those options will be withdrawn and the December ones will be introduced. The actual dates on which options expire are set by the Stock Exchange and will appear on the contract note for your deal. The expiry date is the last day on which an option can be traded or exercised. If you need to work it out for yourself, the Stock Exchange always set expiry dates on the antepenultimate day of the last complete account in the month! That's almost always a Wednesday, but if you're still unsure your stockbroker or the Exchange will always send you a calendar.

An investor wanting to buy a Gargantuan call option in

February might be presented with the following possible choices:

CALL OPTIONS AVAILABLE IN GARGANTUAN INDUSTRIES			
Shares standing at 70p			
	60p	70p	80p
March	13	7	3
June	18	10	7
September	23	14	10

As you can see, the in-the-money options (60p) will cost more because they contain an element of intrinsic value. The remainder of the option's price which is not taken up by its real worth is called 'time premium'. The June 60s have 10p of intrinsic value and 8p of time premium in them. Any option with some time left until its expiry will contain at least some time premium. The longer away the expiry date, the greater the premium an investor will have to pay.

There are several influences on the price of an option. The price of the underlying shares is the most important; the higher the share moves the greater will be the cost of the options. The longer the expiry date is away, the more expensive an option will be, for investors are prepared to pay more to have a longer 'run' for their money. Option holders do not have the rights to any dividends that are paid out on the underlying shares unless they decide to take up, or 'exercise' their rights to buy the shares beforehand. As a result, dividends due will depress the premium of an option. Conversely, the higher interest rates are, the greater the level of premiums will be: a call option is the right to buy shares at some particular date in the future and in the interim an investor could be earning interest on his remaining unused funds. Lastly, the more volatile a share is, the more expensive will be the option.

As an example of how the options in Gargantuan's case might perform, let's see what would happen if Gargantuan shares were at 85p on the day the March series expired. The March options would have only intrinsic value on their last day, while the June and September ones would still contain time premium.

POSITION OF OPTIONS IN GARGANTUAN AT MARCH EXPIRY

Shares standing at 85p, an increase of 21% on the original price of 70p. The figures in brackets show the percentage increase in the call option price on the figures quoted at 70p (see above).

	60p	70p	80p
March	25 (+92%)	15 (+114%)	5 (+67%)
June	32 (+78%)	21 (+110%)	14 (+100%)
September	38 (+65%)	27 (+93%)	19 (+90%)

Just to whet the appetite, let's look at what would have happened if, as every option investor must long for, there is a takeover bid for the company. After a couple of weeks or rumours of a bid in which the shares rose strongly, it finally comes just before the March series expires, at 143 pence, and is still in progress at the March expiry date.

POSITION OF OPTIONS IN GARGANTUAN AT MARCH EXPIRY

Shares standing at 143p, an increase of 104% on the original price of 70p. The figures in brackets show the percentage increase in the call option price on the figures quoted at 70p (see above).

	60p	70p	80p
March	83 (+538%)	73 (+943%)	63 (+2000%)
June	95 (+428%)	86 (+760%)	77 (+1000%)
September	105 (+356%)	93 (+564%)	86 (+760%)

From this extreme, but by no means unheard-of example, you can see that the nearer-dated options will respond most rapidly to quick movements in the share, and that the higher the exercise price, the more volatile the option. Had the bid not materialised and the shares slumped to below 60 pence then all the March options illustrated would have expired worthless.

Dealing in traded options

Suppose that in early February, an investor decided he wanted to buy some call options in Gargantuan which is standing at 70 pence, believing that the shares would perform well over the next two months. After discussion with his stockbroker, he decided to buy 5 March 70 calls priced at 7p each. This price of 7p represents the premium per share. As five contracts represent 5,000 shares, the cost to the investor would be £350 (5,000 multiplied by 7p) plus commission. All options are for cash settlement, so money must be forwarded immediately. Commission on traded options is steeper, for the amount invested, than dealings in ordinary shares. But it is significantly lower than if the investor bought 5,000 shares in Gargantuan outright (see Appendix B).

The price of the options quoted to him by the broker might have been 6 to 7, for as in so many other areas of the market, options have both a bid and an offer price. The latest details of these are available to the stockbroker via the Stock Exchange's TOPIC system. You ought to be able to deal at these prices for most of your transactions unless the market is moving very quickly, in which case the screen prices could become a little out of date. Because the options market involves open outcry, trading does not continue, as it does in shares, after 3.30. There are only six and a half hours in the day in which you can deal in traded options.

By the time the expiry date of the March options has come round, Gargantuan has indeed risen in price, to 85p, a gain of 21%. But as we have seen, the growth in the options was rather greater. The March 70 calls have risen from 7p to 15p, to a value of £750 for five of them, giving the investor a profit before expenses of 114%. The investor might find that the price quoted to him is 14 to 15p, which will reduce his profit, so he should always be aware of the importance of the 'turn' which, in the Traded Options Market, is even more significant than for ordinary share dealings.

An option holder must take some action before his options expire. Once the expiry of an option has occurred, his holding has no value whatsoever. There are probably three choices open to our investor. He could simply sell the option in the market, pocketing the profits. Or he could decide that he would like to exercise his right to those 5,000 shares. To do so, he simply informs the broker of his wishes and will be sent the normal contract note. But although the shares are standing in the market at 85p, the investor's options give him the right to buy 5,000 shares at just 70p which will cost him £3,500. The cost of the shares had he bought them in the usual way would have been £4,250.

Purchasers of call options may not only be interested in speculating upon short-term movements in share prices, but might want to buy the shares for the long-term. If the necessary funds are not to hand at the time, call options enable an investor to acquire the right to the shares and he won't have to pay the bulk of the cost until the expiry date of the option. In our example the investor paid £350 for his five options, together with £3,500 when he decided to exercise them to buy the shares. That total of £3,850 is a significant saving on the cost of buying the shares outright at the March expiry date, but proves to be more expensive than if the investor had bought the shares at the time of his option purchase.

The other alternative, if the investor believes the long-awaited bid for Gangantuan is just around the corner, is to 'walk out' his option, buying another with a longer expiry date. Using his sale proceeds, he might buy 5 June 80 calls, for instance. Or he might pocket his profit, and re-use only his original funds.

It is extremely important not to allow expiry dates to pass unnoticed. Your stockbroker should certainly let you know of any impending expiry that affects you, but you will probably have to fight hard for some comeback if he can't get hold of you. Always leave him with instructions if you plan to be away at the crucial time. However, it would be a very negligent broker who didn't sell all his client's options which still had some value on their last day of life, instructions or no.

I ought to stress that if you plan to deal frequently in options you ought to make some effort to find out if there is anyone at your brokers who really understands them. There is an awful lot of ignorance about traded options in the City, yet few brokers will admit the depth of their ineptitude. This was particularly true for the first few years of traded options in London, as the market was extremely slow to get off the ground. Now most major brokers have departments specialising in options and even the middle-rankers should have a few people who know what they're doing.

The examples of dealing in call options have only touched

upon one small aspect of the market. There is space only to mention briefly a few other areas in which the potential options investor might be interested.

Put options Private clients can profit not only from a rise in a share by using a traded call option, but can also make money from a share's decline by buying put options. These give holders the right, but not the obligation, to sell shares at a certain price, and so increase in value as the price of the ordinary shares declines, as can be seen in the illustration below.

PROFIT/LOSS TO BUYER OF 70p PUT OPTION AT 10p

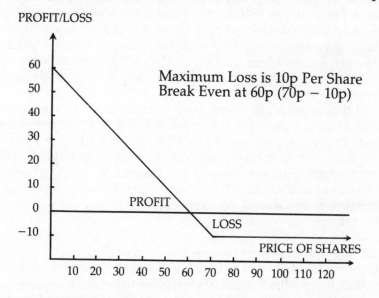

From bitter experience, I can tell you that it is far more difficult to make money from buying put options than it is from buying calls. For a start, most investors are natural 'bulls', believing that share prices ought, in the natural way of things, to keep rising over time. Even those who believe a share is due for a tumble can find it a very unnerving experience dealing in put options, willing the shares and the market to go down and not up.

In addition, unlike call options, there is a limit to the amount of profit that can be made from buying a put option. A share can, after all, only fall as low as zero. Those shares which have options traded in them are mostly blue chips and are unlikely, unless there is a complete collapse of the Western capitalist system, to see their share prices wither to nothing.

However, an investor may choose to buy a put option for reasons other than to make a simple profit. He may use puts as a hedge against a fall in the value of a share. By purchasing a put option to cover his holding, an investor can set off the loss of value of the shares against the consequent increase in the value of the put option. Even if he fully expected those shares to fall, it would be far safer using the Traded Options Market to cover himself against that fall, than attempt to sell the shares and then buy them back again lower down. Such an action could go badly wrong and the investor who chances it may find himself paying more for the shares than he received earlier from the sale. By hedging in the Options Market, he may lose the cost of the option premium, but at least he still has the shares from which he can continue to profit.

If this sounds attractive, bear in mind that buying shares and buying a put option to protect them will give investors exactly the same shape of profit/loss graph and incur exactly the same sort of risk as simply buying the call options on their own. Both limit the risk on the downside, while offering unlimited potential on the upside, and the purchase of call options alone would be significantly cheaper for a private investor.

Selling options Most private investors dealing in the Traded Options Markets will invariably *buy* options with a view to selling them later. But it is also possible to benefit from selling, or 'writing' options. This is a field which is dominated by the big institutions who can use it to generate income on investments they already own, but it can also be of use to a private investor.

Whereas the *purchaser* of a call option is buying the right to purchase shares at a certain price, the *writer* of a call option is facing the possibile liability of selling them at that price. In effect he is selling somebody else the right to buy his shares from him. Suppose someone held 5,000 Gargantuan shares and at the beginning of February decided the price was going to remain fairly stagnant for the next couple of months.

[188]

He could decide to sell 5 March 70 options at 7p each which would bring him in £350 of income, using his shares as collateral. At any time he faces the risk that a holder of a March 70 call could decide to exercise that option. If that happens, and he receives an 'assignment notice', he will *have* to part with his shares at 70p. As compensation, though, he has already received 7p a share and will be better off for having written the option provided the shares do not climb above 77p (70p plus 7p). There is little likelihood of the options being exercised unless the share price stands above 70p. Below that level no holder of the calls will want to take up his right to buy shares at 70; he could buy more cheaply in the market itself. The writer will effectively have reduced the cost of his shares by the 7p premium received.

The writer of an option can, just like a buyer, close out a position at any time. In this case, he buys the option back, thus cancelling his liability.

While the option is open, the writer will be asked by the stockbroker to lodge his shares with him so that if an assignment notice is received, the shares can be transferred to their new owner. Exercise and assignment notices are handled by LOCH, the London Options Clearing House. An exercise notice issued to LOCH will be assigned randomly by computer among the existing writers of that particular option, so it is possible that an investor will find an assignment notice for only some of the options he has written.

An investor need not actually own shares on which he writes call options. He may instead deposit 'margin' with his broker in the form of cash, gilt-edged stock, or even other shares. It is pretty risky writing 'uncovered' options – when you don't own the shares in question – and it ought not to be undertaken unless you are absolutely certain you understand what you are doing.

It isn't only call options that can be written. Put options, too, can be sold. Again this creates a possible liability. Whereas a put buyer has the right to sell shares at a certain price, the put writer might find that he is obliged to buy those shares at that price. Again he might receive an assignment notice at any time before expiry of the options, after which time he is safe. Puts are written as a way of generating extra income and as a method of acquiring shares more cheaply than is possible in the ordinary way.

A seller of 5 March 70 Gargantuan puts might receive 5p

each for them, making a total of £250. If the shares remain above 70p until expiry, holders of put options will not want to exercise their right to sell the shares as low as 70p, and the income the put writer receives will be safe. However, if the shares fall below 70p he may receive an assignment notice, obliging him to *buy* 5,000 shares at 70p. This was a possibility the put writer had taken into account and he will find he is effectively buying the shares, not at 70p each, but at 65p – the cost of the shares less the premium of 5p a share received.

This chapter has only skimmed the surface of the subject of traded options. It is possible to deal in combinations of puts and calls, either as a buyer or as a writer, or both. This is a field rich with jargon, much of it inherited from the Americans who invented traded options. The long-term options player may deal in 'straddles', 'combinations', 'butterflies', 'bear spreads', 'bull spreads', 'Texas hedges', or a medley of other possible variations on a theme.

The fact that options can be so sophisticated an area of investment should not put off investors who only want to buy call options or put options with a view to selling them later on. It matters not a jot if they don't understand the complexities of all those other option strategies. They will, however, have to sign a form when they first deal declaring that they do understand the principles and the risks involved.

Anyone who does venture into the world of traded options should remember just how quickly prices can move about. Although prices of the most commonly traded options are given in the *Financial Times* and *Daily Telegraph* every day, these might have changed significantly even before the options market opens at 9 a.m. for the next session, and should be taken only as a rough guide to the state of the market. For those who need to see the prices moving from minute to minute, I would recommend the options service on Prestel, which is linked to TOPIC and gives investors details of prices almost as quickly as the participants on the market floor get them. Press comment on options in general, however, remains woefully inadequate.

Options are by no means traded on every share. At the time of writing there were 50 shares with options traded in them, including BP, GEC, ICI, Grand Metropolitan, BT, British Gas, TSB, Marks and Spencer, Shell, British Aerospace, Jaguar, Lonhro, Racal, Bass, Beecham, BAT and Cadbury Schweppes. The list is being extended steadily. In addition to the traded options on shares, there are options on a short and a long gilt.

In addition, there are now contracts in the FTSE-100 share index, for investors who wish to trade on their view of the market as a whole, rather than on individual shares. And, since the middle of 1985, there have even been options on currencies too. The principles involved in these other instruments are exactly the same, although in practice other options have important differences in contract size and so on.

Activity in the Traded Options Market is increasing as both institutions and private individuals begin to see the benefits they offer. I would suggest that any individual who is a regular investor in the stock market takes the time to do a little further reading on options, even if he is sceptical at first. They have now reached the stage where it is possible for the tail on occasion to wag the dog, with dealings in the Traded Options Market being of sufficient size from time to time to affect the price of the underlying shares.

For once, the booklets the Stock Exchange produce on the subject are quite admirable, providing a clear, concise, and valuable introduction to the subject. For those getting heavily involved in traded options, the only book of any note on the subject published in Britain is *Trading in Options* by Geoffrey Chamberlain (Woodhead-Faulkner).

In the early days of the Traded Options Market in London, difficulties with the way they were treated for tax discouraged many investors. Now that has all been sorted out, and options are taxed as if they were shares, with the added proviso that if an option purchased expires worthless, the investor is able to treat the purchase cost as a loss for tax purposes. For the writer of options, of course, the expiry of an option with no value signifies a profit, and should be treated thus. If any options are exercised or assigned against, the entire transaction, including both the option deal and the resultant share deal, are simply lumped together and treated as one.

The booklets produced by the Stock Exchange can be obtained by writing to The Options Development Group, The Stock Exchange, London EC2N 1HP. In addition, the following stockbrokers have expressed a willingness to deal on behalf of new private clients: Bailey Shatkin Options (01-481 1712); James Capel (01-621 0011); T. C. Coombs (01-588 6209); Credit Suisse Buckmaster & Moore (01-588 2868); Fyshe Horton Finney (021-236 3111); Messel & Co. (01-377 0123);

Prudential Bache (01-283 9166); Scrimgeour Vickers (01-623 2494); Albert E. Sharp (021-236 5801); Sheppards (01-378 7000); Smith New Court (01-628 4433); Sternberg Thomas Clarke (01-247 8461).

Warrants – long-term call options

A few companies have issued, in addition to their ordinary shares, warrants upon those shares. These are another under-utilised area which could prove interesting to the private investor. In essence a warrant is a long-term option. It gives the holder the right to purchase the underlying shares at a certain price, with that right often lasting for many years. If a warrant gives the holder the right to buy shares at 100p each and the shares are standing at 150p, the warrant should be worth at least 50p. In practice, even though holders of warrants receive no dividends, it will probably cost a little more.

The attraction of warrants is that if the share rises, the warrant will rise with it and by roughly the same amount. Suppose in the above example, the warrant cost 60p. If the shares, over a period of a couple of years, rose to 250p, someone owning them would have made 100p on each one. But the warrant holder, who has the right to subscribe to the shares at just 100p will find his warrants worth at least 150p and possibly a little more if they still have some time to run. The warrant holder has made one-and-a-half times his money, while the ordinary shareholder has increased his by a paltry two-thirds.

As with options, this gearing element works both ways. A drop in the share price will hurt the warrant holder far more than the owners of the ordinary shares. Despite this, it is always worth considering buying a warrant on a share, if it exists, not only as a short-term speculation, but also for those who believe they might be long-term holders of the underlying shares. The biggest problem for the private investor interested in this field is discovering just which shares do have warrants attached. Burtons, Argyll Group, Rowntree, Ladbrokes and Redland are among those which have warrants, as do quite a few investment trusts. Your broker should be able to supply you with a more complete list.

Partly paid shares – short term call options

The effects of gearing were apparent for all to see when British Telecom were first launched onto the Stock Exchange. To make the issues more digestible, the shares began life in a partly paid form. Investors had to pay only 50p of the total 130p on each share. Those who held British Telecom shares didn't need to find the second payment of 40p until June 1985, giving them a period of grace of seven months.

This really amounted to giving investors short-term call options on BT shares. In addition to making it easier to pay for them, investors' profits looked much more substantial as a percentage figure. A holder of 800 shares had to pay £400 at the time of the flotation. The BT shares tripled by May in the partly paid form, giving the investor a profit of £800.

But had they been fully-paid shares, the investor would have had to find £1,040 for his shares. His profit at the same date in May would still have been £800. But instead of tripling his initial stake, the investor would have made 77% profit, still a handsome return, but rather less dramatic.

Surprising though it may sound, some 1,500 investors who had already paid the first two instalments on their BT shares failed to stump up the remaining 40 pence per share in April 1986. As a result their shares were compulsorily repurchased by the government. Every single one of those shareholders needed their heads examined. For even if they could not have afforded the payment at the time, they would still have received around 40p per share more from selling their holding in the stock market than the government gave them. Those shares disappearing back into the Treasury's coffers were worth £340,000 more than the government had to pay for them. If you're a shareholder, don't automatically assume that *everything* that comes through your letterbox is junk mail.

[193]

16

TAX? DON'T GIVE IT A SECOND THOUGHT

'The taxpayer? That's someone who works for the government but who doesn't have to take a civil service examination'.

Ronald Reagan

Most people reading this book will not be overtroubled by taxation on their stock market investments. Income tax is simple enough to work out. Any investment income received on shares is taxed at your top marginal rate; there is no longer any investment income surcharge. Companies deduct basic-rate tax before paying out dividends, so if you're a standard rate taxpayer you need do little else except detail on your tax return the level of dividends you've received together with the accompanying tax credits. If you are in any of the higher tax bands, you will then receive a courteous letter from the Inland Revenue informing you just how much more tax you still owe on those dividends.

The other tax which can apply to stock market investments is Capital Gains Tax. Many investors are quite unnecessarily afraid of this imposition. Yet for most, it is perfectly harmless. CGT is only levied if the net gains you realise on your investments in any one year exceed a minimum amount – £6,600 for the year 1987–8 – an amount that is increased in line with inflation in each successive budget. Losses incurred during the year should be offset against profits and tax only becomes due if that minimum figure is exceeded. You can also carry forward net losses from previous years, using just enough to reduce your gains to below the minimum limit. So as you can see, you really need to be very successful in your investments for CGT to affect you.

Even if you do exceed that limit, you will still only have to pay 30% on the excess. It's hardly punitive, yet you would scarcely credit the efforts some investors make to avoid CGT, selling shares at completely the wrong time just because it will help reduce their tax bill.

Since the tax year 1981–2 Capital Gains Tax has been 'indexed'. The minimum level at which the tax comes into force is increased in line with inflation. That part is simple enough. But the original cost of each investment is also adjusted in line with inflation so that the investor selling shares only has to take into account the increase in *real* value of his investments.

This new indexation procedure is designed to be fairer than the old system. But it is horribly complicated to work out. Luckily those who have to pay Capital Gains Tax are also those who ought to be able to afford the services of an accountant to perform all the calculations for them. However, it is a moot point whether the amount the indexation system can save an individual can possibly outweigh the extra cost incurred by making your accountant work out the necessary sums.

I won't go into details of the CGT indexation system here. Your stockbroker should be able to help you here, if you don't have an accountant. But providing your shares were bought after March 1982, all (!) you have to do is find out the Retail Price Index on the date of acquisition of the shares, find out what it was on the date of disposal, and calculate the percentage change over the period. Your original cost should be adjusted by that change and the resultant gain or loss then be worked out on that new figure, rather than on the historic cost as it appears on your contract note.

Personal Equity Plans – the marketing man's dream come true

'The mountains will heave in childbirth and a ridiculous little mouse will be born. In this case, the mouse is not only ridiculous but it has a gammy leg, a touch of mange and a wall eye.'
Fred Carr (with a little help from Horace)

If you ever wanted proof of the saying that 'too many cooks spoil the broth' you have it in Personal Equity Plans, the Chancellor's chosen path towards 'People's Capitalism'. It ought to have been possible for the collective brains of Whitehall to have come up with a sensible way of giving private investors tax relief to encourage them to put their savings into the shares of British companies. It ought to have been. But for some reason, it wasn't. PEPs were intended as a simple and tax-efficient way of investing in the stock market, with the administrative burden taken from the investors' shoulders. What was produced was a breakfast suitable only for the most undiscriminating of pigs.

Personal Equity Plans allow individuals to contribute up to £2,400 a year, or £200 a month, to a scheme managed by a registered Plan Manager. This money is then channelled into shares or unit trusts. Contributions paid into a PEP in one calendar year have to be held for the whole of the following calendar year in order to qualify for the tax benefits, which give investors relief from both income taxes and capital gains tax. Dividends or interest have to be reinvested, for if the investor makes any sort of withdrawal before the end of the qualifying period, the whole Plan collapses.

Once the initial period of 12 to 24 months is over, the Plan can be merged with other fully-qualified Plans of the investor's to help save on administrative costs.

Isn't it brilliant? The marketing men certainly think so. 'Invest in the stock market tax free' the adverts shriek at us. What they keep rather quieter about is that, for the majority of us, tax is practically an irrelevance. CGT is something that will never trouble the majority of us, so the only benefit is that income from dividends and interest is free (10% of PEPs can be kept in cash). Wow. Tax-free income. On £2,400 of stock market investments, that is likely to give the investor an extra £35, hardly the stuff of which dreams are made. Notice how the graphs in the adverts showing the fantastic benefits of PEPs seem to assume that all investors pay CGT, thus making them seem incredibly attractive.

The structure of PEPs is such that the Plan managers are finding them an administrative nightmare, having to ensure that the necessary tax is reclaimed, that everyone is given notice of AGMs and that all the documents relating to the companies within the Plans are sent to investors. As a result the costs involved in most PEPs far outweigh the tax benefits, at least in the initial years.

In addition, Plan managers have found that, far from allowing investors free rein to pick and choose which shares to invest in, as was surely the government's intention, the only way they can keep costs under control is to restrict severely the freedom of choice to investors. The simplest PEPs, designed for those investing up to £420 a year are virtually indistinguishable from unit trusts, which was most definitely not the government's idea at all when they thought up the scheme. Even the fully-fledged PEPs give investors little freedom to invest in anything other than a brief list of blue chips without paying heavily for doing so.

Another disadvantage is that they do not allow investors the ability to move into cash if they feel that the stock market is looking unhealthy. As only 10% can be held in cash, investors could be unwilling to take the sensible course of action because they will lose their tax benefits. They could thus find themselves trapped in investments which are declining in value, even though it would make more sense to sell the lot and put it in the building society. None of the adverts I have seen to date even mentions the possibility that shares can decline in value.

PEPs are a wonderful tax shelter for the wealthy who are already paying CGT, but for the rest of us they are very far from the manna from heaven that they are depicted to be in the advertisements. How much simpler it would have been to give investors income tax relief on the money invested in UK shares and leave it at that. Simplicity, unfortunately, is rarely any government's forté.

17

SHARE PERKS

'Milton Friedman says there's no such thing as a free lunch.
Maybe not, but if you own the right shares, at least you can
get twenty per cent off.' Oofy Prosser

There's an incredible variation in the way companies treat
their shareholders, even though they are the ultimate owners
of the business. Unfortunately, the well-being of the individual share owner is not always an overpowering priority for
many managements. Some seem to resent even the most
tactful questioning at the Annual General Meeting from any
shareholder whose holding is smaller than the Post Office
Pension Fund. Such a cavalier attitude may not bother you at
all, particularly if the shares are performing well and you have
no intention of allowing wild horses to drag you within
twenty miles of the AGM.

However, there are some firms which not only treat their
shareholders with a great measure of respect and courtesy,
but also add a little spice to their investment by giving them
further benefits in kind. To take advantage of the majority of
these perks, you would need to be a clothes-conscious, high-
rolling, gluttonous tippler with a penchant for travel; there
are discounts on clothing, jewellery, wine, cider and beer,
billiard tables, restaurants, dry-cleaning, race-meetings, ferry
travel, electrical goods, and even houses and cars – all available to the holders of the right shares.

I must have saved more over the years on dinner bills than I
originally paid for my shares entitling me to a twenty per cent
discount in one splendid restaurant chain. The fact that I am
also sitting on a handsome profit on those shares only serves
to help my digestion.

Most famous of all share perks must be the free tickets to the
Centre Court at Wimbledon which accompany the All
England Tennis debentures. Most exotic probably is the offer-
ing by the Romney, Hythe and Dymchurch Light Railway
Company of the right to hire your own steam train once a year
at no cost, if you happen to own 5,000 shares or more. And

European Ferries, not content with offering their well-known discounts on Townsend Thoresen ferry travel, also offer to assist in the education of your offspring at University College, Buckingham.

Not all share perks are as bountiful as these. Some are unbelievably mean – the odd bottle of wine or a couple of quid off a hotel room. Others are nice gestures – Cadbury-Schweppes give those shareholders who turn up for the AGM lunch and samples of the company's product. The lists compiled by stockbrokers Grievson Grant and Seymour Pierce detail most of the perks available and I've listed below a selection of the more interesting.

You should rarely consider buying shares simply because they have a perk attached. Unless the benefit is great enough, the merits of the shares themselves should always be your first consideration. You'd look a proper charlie being able to travel free on someone's ferry if the fall in the price of the shares meant that you weren't able to afford to get off at the other end.

Quite the most wonderful thing about shareholders' perks is the incredibly attentive service which you suddenly find yourself getting. Even the most surly waiters, shop assistants and hotel clerks will suddenly remember where they've been hiding their forelocks all these years when they see your shareholders' card. They aren't to know you've only one share; as far as they know, you might be the chairman of the company. It would spoil the fun if you were to disabuse them of the notion.

SOME UK COMPANIES OFFERING BENEFITS FOR SHAREHOLDERS

Company	Benefits	Minimum shareholding
All England Tennis (Stock not very marketable)	1 free Centre Court ticket per day for every one £50-debenture held. Entry to Lounge and Buffet Bar at Centre Court, and reserved car parking space	Two £50 (nominal) non-interest bearing Wimbledon debentures (for the 1986–90 series cost would be in excess of £8,000)

Company	Benefits	Minimum shareholding
Asprey	Asprey card giving 15% off most cash purchases from Aspreys in Bond Street and Fenchurch Street	375 ordinary shares
Burton Group	12½% discount at Burton, Top Shop, Evans, Dorothy Perkins, Top Man, Principles, Peter Robinson, Debenhams and Collier. Shareholder Card gives credit limit of £5,000	No minimum
Ciro	20% discount at some large stores where they operate jewellery counters	500 ordinary shares
Emess Lighting	25% discount on a range of light fittings	100 ordinary shares
Cecil Gee	Discounts at Cecil Gee, Gee 2, Savoy Taylors' Guild and Beale & Inman (vouchers can be used during sales)	500 shares (one 10% voucher); 1,000 shares (2 vouchers). Must be held for six months
Gieves Group	20% discount from Gieves & Hawkes	600 ordinary shares held for three months
Horizon Travel	10% discount on Horizon brochure prices, up to total value of £1,000. One booking per year. Shareholder must travel	750 ordinary shares, held for six months at date of departure

Company	Benefits	Minimum shareholding
Kennedy Brookes	20% discount at any restaurant including Maxims in London, Mario & Franco, Wheelers, etc.	500 ordinary shares
Ladbroke Group	10% discount on holidays, hotels and restaurants; 7½% discount at Laskys. Shareholders privilege card issued	No minimum
Merrydown Wine	20% discount on cases of wine and cider. Lunch and wine-tasting after AGM	50 shares
Next (formerly J. Hepworth)	25% discount on one purchase in any Next shop	500 ordinary shares
Rover Group	£100 discount on new car	1,000 ordinary held for six months at time of most recent General Meeting
Sketchley	25% discount on cost of dry-cleaning and ancillary services. Discount card issued on registration	300 shares
Trafalgar House	10% discount on most cruises, including the QE2. 15% discount at Cunard hotels in UK and Caribbean	250 ordinary shares

Company	Benefits	Minimum shareholding
Trusthouse Forte	10% discount on Leisure Gift Cheques for maximum £2,000. Can be used at THF Hotels & restaurants	500 shares

SOURCE: GRIEVSON GRANT, SEYMOUR PIERCE

18
PLAYING THE MARKET

Your portfolio

'This is a money game and money is the way we keep score. But the real object of the Game is not money, it is the playing of the Game itself. For the true players, you could take all the trophies away and substitute plastic beads or whale's teeth; as long as there is a way to keep score, they will play.'
Adam Smith, *The Money Game*, 1968

Even if you follow my advice and indulge your interest in the stock market cautiously by running a trial paper-portfolio first, the time will eventually come for your first share-purchase. I can't hammer home too strongly that you are taking on more risk by investing on the stock market than with most other forms of investment you might consider; don't use money you might need urgently. However well shares have performed in the recent past and no matter how far their gains have outstripped other possible homes for your money, there is no guarantee that the market won't start to fall just as you make your first move.

The more shares you buy, the closer your portfolio will behave to the stock market as a whole. This is an argument that is frequently employed to persuade small private investors that they would do better to think about unit trusts, and leave share investments to the professionals. Ignore these killjoys, who would be happy to see the entire market institutionalised. There is probably no easy way to insulate your investments against a fall in the entire stock market, but it is not too difficult to find large companies of sufficient quality that the risk involved in investing in a few of them is pretty small; Marks & Spencer, GEC, BAT Industries, Bass and the like are not likely to pull up stumps overnight with their directors taking the petty cash off for an indefinite holiday in the Caribbean. Any one share may perform in a different manner from the general market, but you don't need to hold very many blue chips before your portfolio will match the market's performance pretty broadly, if that is what you want. Bear in mind that Guinness was regarded as a blue chip!

But an investor is likely to be far more alert if he doesn't try too hard to reduce his risk and instead has just a few shares on which he can concentrate, realising that if he gets a new idea for an investment, he must abandon one of his existing ones; it is an excellent discipline if you can stick to it.

Try to improve your own ability to analyse shares all the time. The more you know about a company, the more quickly you will be able to react to a new piece of information which may complete the picture you have been building up for a while. Even if you rely on others for investment advice, you should recognise that it is quite an art knowing which stories are worth listening to and which should be taken with a pinch of salt.

With the sort of minimum commission rates prevailing at the moment, you really need to be thinking in terms of each shares purchase being at least £500 or charges will be eating too severely into the cost of your transactions. If the thought of spending that sort of money in the stock market on just one share horrifies you, then you probably *would* be happier looking at unit trusts. But even there, most trusts insist upon a minimum investment of £500. If this is still too onerous, you might consider one of the unit trust savings schemes where you can invest as little as £10 a month in the units, even skipping months when you are strapped for cash.

Some investors form themselves into investment clubs, groups who pool their individual funds in order to gain the benefit of a size they couldn't achieve on their own. You need to be a pretty compatible bunch to stick together and still be talking to each other at the end of a year, but if the idea tickles your fancy the best place for advice on how to set everything up is the National Association of Investment Clubs, Halifax House, 5 Fenwick Street, Liverpool L2 0PR (Tel. no. 051 236 6262).

The importance of timing

'If a decision is made not to make a decision, that is just as much a decision as a decision which initiates action.'
Adam Smith, *The Money Game*, 1968

I can't stress too heavily the importance of timing in stock market investment. You may be able to pick potentially the hottest share in the entire market, but your investment won't make you any money unless that belief spreads. The longer you have to hang on to a share that is going nowhere, the more it is costing you and the better off you would have been, simply keeping your loot in the building society. This is why so many experienced investors prefer to wait until a 'sleeper' shows signs of moving ahead before committing themselves.

Again, there is little point in buying an absolutely fabulous share if the entire stock market is about to fall out of bed. There are few shares which will remain solid as a rock when every other one in sight is sliding backwards. If the market is soggy do not assume that unchanged prices given for some of your smaller shares in the paper are correct. It could just be that no one has yet tested the price, as you could discover if you try to sell out.

Some of the older hands in the market prefer to buy on weakness, reckoning that confidence will soon return, and using the fall to pick up shares more cheaply than they will be able to do once equilibrium has returned. This sounds fine in theory, but is one of those things that is a little more difficult to achieve in practice. There's nothing quite so unnerving as a stock market falling daily. It can seem at times that there is no bottom for it to hit. But of course there is an end to it and shares duly bounce back, and all those of us who were too scared to commit our funds on the way down can only kick ourselves and glare enviously at those who showed more courage.

There is much to be said for the argument that the big investing institutions now have so much money flowing into their coffers that the market can never fall very far. Even if the funds hold back their cash for a time, they are eventually going to have to recommit it to the market, causing prices to firm again. If you have strong enough nerves, you might be willing to test this theory. Certainly those who had stomach enough to invest in the dark days of 1974 have had plenty of reason to feel pretty happy about it ever since.

Timing is important, not only in making purchases, but perhaps even more so when selling shares. Each investor seems to have his own way of doing this. Some set themselves a certain target for each share they buy, selling when this is reached. Others might hold on, selling only if the share falls 10% from the highest level it reaches. There is certainly no hard and fast rule that can ensure investors 'buy at the bottom and sell at the top'.

One of the wisest of the innumerable market maxims is: 'Always leave something for the next man.' You should never be so greedy that you are still holding a share as the market turns against it, simply because you have been trying to squeeze the very last drop of profit out of it. It was a member of the Rothschild clan who is purported to have claimed that he made his money by 'buying too late and selling too soon'. You shouldn't fret too much if you see a share that you have just sold continuing to climb. 'It is never wrong to take a profit,' say the old hands. Human nature being what it is, it may be difficult to be completely calm in such a situation but console yourself with the thought that at least you did make a profit.

Just to muddy the water still further, another old saw has it that you should 'cut your losses and run your profits'. By selling any share that falls after you buy it, keeping only those that are rising, the proponents of this system believe it is only a matter of time before you arrive at El Dorado, or find the crock of gold at the end of the rainbow or whatever. But there is no 'system' which will guarantee consistent profit in the stock market, just as there has never been a foolproof system for the roulette wheel. Good fundamental research and an advanced intuition will help considerably though.

There are those who try and avoid the problem of timing stock market investment by something called 'pound cost averaging'. This is particularly popular with unit trust investment and relies on the punter putting in a fixed amount each month, come rain or shine. When the market is low, he will be buying more units for his money and when the market is high, rather fewer. But averaging means exactly that, and someone who invests in this way is never going to do as well as the chap who can sense the right time to buy and the right time to sell.

In one of the best books ever to have been written about investment, Adam Smith provides a very necessary warning: 'The share doesn't know you own it. All those marvellous things, or those terrible things, that you feel about a stock, or a list of stocks, all of these things are unreciprocated by the stock or the group of stocks. You can be in love if you want to, but that piece of paper doesn't love you, and unreciprocated love can turn into masochism, narcissism, or, even worse, market losses and unreciprocated hate . . . if you know that the stock doesn't know you own it, you are ahead of the game. You are ahead because you can change your mind and your actions without regard to what you did or thought yesterday.' (*The Money Game*, Michael Joseph, 1968)

The one investment technique everybody manages to get right is that of 'jobbing backwards'. This involves the investor describing what he *really* meant to do well after the event, and provides endless hours of harmless amusement. It's amazing to think that no one ever loses money by jobbing backwards, but then hindsight is the one sense with which all stock market investors are incredibly well endowed.

The Index

'The market will not go up unless it goes up, nor will it go down unless it goes down, and it will stay the same unless it does either.'   Adam Smith, *The Money Game*, 1968

The easiest way to see what the stock market as a whole is doing is to monitor the index. But which one? The most commonly known is the old Financial Times Ordinary Share Index, composed of thirty leading shares. This began life in 1935 and is still the most often quoted as a measure of the movement of the stock market. Yet it is not the most valuable index for the investor as it has several considerable drawbacks. A list of only thirty shares, spread very unevenly across the sectors of the stock market, cannot possibly give a good indication of the performance of that market as a whole. The 30-Share Index also gives undue prominence to the behaviour of individual shares; a sharp movement of even the smallest constitutent will have a disproportionate effect on the whole index.

In mitigation, it ought to be said that the Financial Times Index was only ever intended to give an indication of the way the market moves each day and was never meant to be used for examining longer-term trends. Until recently the only way of doing this was by monitoring the FT Actuaries All-Share Index, which includes about 740 shares in every sector of the market and which 'weights' each one, so that movements of the largest companies have the greatest effect upon the index. But the All-Share is a pretty unwieldy beast and has never been particularly popular with private investors, despite being the yardstick by which all fund managers measure their performance.

Although pension-fund managers ought really to be planning years ahead, the institutions are becoming ever more concerned with their quarterly performance figures. Most funds have to report to their trustees – not all of whom are over-familiar with the stock market – four times a year and are consequently under pressure to out-perform the relevant indices and other institutions each time, or face the consequences. They become obsessed with the short term and the time taken up by such regular reports and meetings only serves to hamper the poor fund-manager. The cult of performance has taken hold of the City with an iron grip.

Luckily, private investors face no such problems. And while the All-Share Index may be too unwieldy for us to measure our performance against, the new 100-Share Index, introduced at the beginning of 1984, is splendidly useful. The Financial Times–Stock Exchange 100-Share Index, to give it its full title, is the first to be calculated not just daily or hourly, but minute-by-minute. The 'Footsie' as it is now generally known in the market, is composed, you will not be surprised to hear, of one hundred shares. They aren't quite the 100 largest companies, because that would give undue prominence to particular sectors, but they represent a fair selection of prominent shares right across the board. The shares included account for about 70% of the *total* market value of the entire stock market, so the index does give a far better idea of the general picture than the old-fashioned Financial Times Index. Like the All-Share, it gives greatest weight to the largest shares. The Footsie, on which futures and options are now traded, was designed almost as an 'average share' which will always have an up-to-date price quoted and it performs this task admirably.

It's the Footsie against which you should measure your portfolio's performance, for the old FT Index gives a distorted picture. No doubt the latter will be given in news broadcasts for years to come, but you should treat it only as the general indicator that it is, and not be surprised if your shares behave completely differently.

PERFORMANCE OF *FINANCIAL TIMES* INDEX RELATIVE TO ALL-SHARE INDEX (BASE 100)

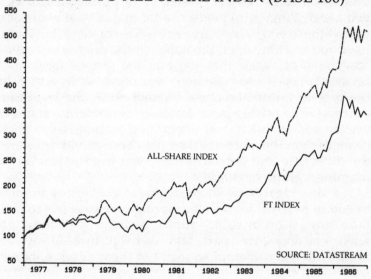

You should always view your performance record not only in absolute terms, but relative to the stock market as a whole. If your shares are doing much worse than the average, then even if the market and your portfolio are rising, you should ask yourself if you haven't picked the wrong investments. If you keep a record of the prices of shares you hold or in which you take an interest, take a few seconds more to jot down their price relative to the value of Footsie. If this ratio rises, the shares are outperforming the index and conversely a fall in the ratio means you are doing worse than the market as a whole.

The media will insist on telling you from time to time that the stock market has had its biggest-ever one-day rise or fall. This will usually be utter poppycock. A fall of twenty-odd points in the FT Index when it is standing at around the 1,000 level is only a movement of 2% after all; yet such a drop in the depths of 1974 would have wiped more than 10% off the value of the stock market, a far more momentous move. Unfortunately, an observation of percentage movements only would spoil some good headlines.

As an investor you should invariably think in percentage terms, not only when looking at the performance of indices, but also when examining the movement of individual shares. You are, after all, most interested in the profit and loss which you are making. A 10 pence rise for one of your shares may mean little to you if the share price is 500p or more, but it could have you cracking open the bubbly if the price is only 20p or so. You may notice that some of the graphs used in the financial press use the distorted logarithmic scale, rather than the regular arithmetic ones. Though rarer, the logarithmic charts give a far truer picture of price movements, giving the eye an easier task when attempting to assess percentage changes than the more usual graphs. You should be aware of the difference and note which is being used whenever you examine a graph or chart.

You should take care when looking at any figures presented to you in pictorial form. It is amazing how easy it is to give a false impression by using graphs, perhaps by distorting the scale or by only giving part of the overall picture. Always treat them with the contempt so many of them deserve, particularly when they are used to make a point in an advertising campaign or to press home a point during a fierce bid battle. More complaints are received by the Advertising Standards Authority about financial advertising than anything else bar cars and computers, and much of it stems from the way in which graphs are used to misrepresent the true situation.

19
COMMISSION AND YOUR BROKER

'A broker is a man who runs your fortune into a shoestring.'
Alexander Woolcott

All investors like to grumble about the amount of commission creamed off from every deal by their stockbroker. Brokers, for their part, grumble that they have certain fixed costs which have to be met on every deal and that they lose money heavily on the smallest transactions. Yet stockbrokers are still among the most highly paid individuals in the country. The sort of money doled to top and even middle-ranking City stockbrokers in the past few years would make many of the most lucratively remunerated industrialists in Britain weep with envy. The stockbroking industry has had to take a few pretty hard years in its stride in the past, and the degree of competition in the City post-Big Bang suggests that for many hard times could be just around the corner.

But for those that survive, it is a lucrative business. With brokers deriving most of their income from commission, the stockbroking profession has been helped enormously by the strong growth in share prices in the past decade. Commission is charged as a percentage of the value of the shares; the higher those shares are, the more commission the stockbrokers rake in. Nice work if you can get it.

Before Big Bang, virtually every stockbroking firm was far more interested in institutional clients than in you or me. Fund managers may be temperamental, awkward, blighters but one big order from them was worth a thousand deals from the retired colonels strung out along the South Coast and cost a good deal less to process too. However, the institutions have taken to the new dealing system like ducks to water and many are perfectly content to bypass the salesmen and deal directly with the market-makers.

So, almost overnight, the big City brokers have rediscovered the charms of private investors, nice docile creatures who have no qualms about handing over commission to their friendly, helpful brokers. All manner of weird and wonderful services are now offered to us.

Since the abolition of fixed commissions, institutions are free to 'negotiate' rates with their stockbroker. But if we tried to haggle over the cost of a thousand pound's worth of shares, we wouldn't get very far. We small fry have to pay the going rate.

Under the old system, investors knew exactly what they were going to be charged. If the deal was for shares worth £7,000 or less, the cost was 1.65%. Add in VAT and the 1% stamp duty and £1,000 worth of shares would have cost an extra £28.98. Since Big Bang, the cheapest of brokers would transact that deal (remembering the cut in stamp duty) for just £16.50. On the other hand, another big City firm could sting you for over £30 for exactly the same deal!

The stockbrokers providing 'deal-only' services are the cheapest. You ring up, give your order, put the phone down and wait for the administrative machinery to whirr into action. It is the equivalent of buying a hi-fi from a discount warehouse. You get what you ask for, but will have little joy if you start asking for advice as well.

If you need advice in the new world, then you are going to have to pay for it. You may want to seek a broker's opinion about a particular share, or need his advice on restructuring your portfolio or any one of a hundred things. Those offering advisory services seem to be charging roughly the same sorts of rates as before Big Bang, around 1.5% or 1.65%. Considering that they are offering the sort of service we were all used to before, this doesn't seem too bad.

Should you shop around for price? It depends on what sort of investor you are. If you never need advice of any sort then you would be silly to pay extra for a service that you never use. If you are relatively new to the stock market, uncertain about exactly what you want to do, or even if you just feel happier discussing your intentions first, then you would be mad to go to a 'deal-only' broker.

Whichever sort of broker you use, do make certain you know roughly how much you are going to be charged before you deal. Every stockbroker has a minimum commission level and it is no use doing a deal for only £500 if the chap levies a minimum charge of £20 on you. That works out at 4% commission. If your contract notes keep coming back with the words 'minimum commission' on them, you ought to consider going to a different broker. Fortunately, just as in Big Bang days, many smaller brokers have minimums of only £10.

Having said all that, commission shouldn't worry you too much. After all, we pay it in every walk of life. We unhesitatingly agree to the addition of 10% or even 12½% to our restaurant bills for the dubious privilege of having our food brought to the table. Everytime we buy something from a shop, we are helping to pay the retailer's wage bill, rates, heating, lighting and so on, as well as putting profit into his pocket. Life insurance companies go to great lengths to conceal the gigantic commission they charge on their policies. Yet on all these, we don't complain because we never see the word 'commission.'

A stockbroker, in return for his service charge, will buy shares for you at the best possible price, bill you, ensure that they are correctly delivered to you, give your name and address to the registrar of the company concerned, round up any dividends due to you, handle any tricky paperwork, ring you with the odd bright idea he might have from time to time, occasionally stop you falling flat on your face with an idiotic share idea of your own and, if he is any good, should frequently make you money. In addition, the Stock Exchange Compensation Fund insures you against loss if the firm goes under. All this for considerably less than the cost of getting a plumber to call just to have a look at a leaky washer!

Keeping too close an eye on the pennies could be a false economy in the stock market. Deal-only brokers have their place, but they may not be for you. If you are paying for advice, it is likely to be costing you only a few extra pounds per deal. By shopping around, you will find it hard to build up a sound working relationship with any one stockbroker and, in the end, this is what you are after.

If you find the big City brokers unfriendly then, as I advised earlier, look outside the Capital. Provincial firms have far more time for talking, lower costs and greater experience of dealing for the small private investor. They are also unlikely to be market-makers, so that investors dealing with them can be absolutely convinced in their own mind that there is no possible conflict of interest. There is a list at the back of the book of stockbrokers known to favour private clients.

The sure way to whittle down your capital is to deal constantly, buying and selling shares rapidly, trying to make short-term profits. It simply won't work for the private investor unless he is very, very clued up and has access to instantaneous prices. It isn't only commission that needs to be paid, but also the invisible jobber's turn.

If you have money managed by a stockbroker or other financial adviser on a discretionary basis, do make sure that your portfolio isn't being 'churned', with the broker dealing as often as he feels he can get away with it, simply because it increases his commission.

The banks are now making a concerted assault on the investment business of private individuals but, as I have said before, however convenient their service may be, can you be sure that you aren't merely putting another middleman in between you and the market? Unless you are convinced that the bank clerk you are dealing with is well clued-up on the stock market, it could be fairly dangerous using your bank instead of a stockbroker. They have to get on to a broker to handle the business for you anyway, so why bother putting them to all the effort. Do it yourself. It will be years before the banks will be able to provide the same sort of service as a full-time stockbroker at any but a few of their branches. The same obviously applies to the building societies too. Banking investment services don't appear to be notably cheap either, except on large new issues. I have always found banks slow, inefficient, haphazard and costly and it will be a long time before I risk trying my branch again to deal for me on the stock market.

I am also a little wary of share shops. Once you have entered their doors, it can be a little difficult to leave again without having transacted any business, and far too easy to do something on the spur of the moment that you might regret later. They do have a place for an investor new to the stock market who wants to discuss his first transaction in some detail and have the whole procedure explained to him. If you ever cross the threshold of such an establishment do make absolutely sure that the shop is run by a bona-fide stockbroker and not some fly-by-night outfit of which you have never heard.

Whatever the promised attractions of High Street investment facilities, I have yet to hear anyone tell me convincingly what is wrong with ringing a broker up on the phone and dealing instantly, from the comfort of my home.

20

THE PRIVATE INVESTOR
AND THE FUTURE

*'Thy bones are marrowless, thy blood is cold; Thou hast no
speculation in those eyes which thou dost glare with.'*
William Shakespeare, *Macbeth*

Wider share ownership has not necessarily improved the lot
of the private investor. Big Bang and the incredibly detailed
Financial Services Act have made things a good deal more
complicated. A perfectly satisfactory stock market was turned
on its head by a government and Stock Exchange without any
real idea of the consequences. And while tougher regulation
ought to make for safer investment, it has always seemed to
me that the tighter laws are drawn, the greater the number of
loopholes that can be found to get round the spirit of those
laws. Perhaps I am being a little too cynical, or merely nostal-
gic, in hankering for a stock market that probably was in desperate need of sweeping change.

The new City, with its vast financial institutions, may claim
to welcome the private investor. But most firms are not really
interested in the *small* investor. They are after the wealthy
individuals. They prefer to corral the minnows into unit
trusts, PEPs, insurance policies, pension plans and the like,
putting investors into convenient, easy-to-handle packages,
and giving them no voice in the way their money is invested.
Institutional fund managers may think they are very grand,
with the billions of pounds they have at their disposal. I wonder how frequently they consider just whose money it is they
are playing with.

Fortunately, there will always be people willing to transact
business for private investors at reasonable prices and who
have their interests at heart, even if they are based well outside the Square Mile. The advent of the computer in the City is
also likely to make things a good deal more convenient for
investors in the future. As I have already mentioned, there are
several software packages on the market which enable
computer owners to abandon the pastime of zapping alien

hordes and turn instead to the monitoring of share prices and portfolios. Some will perform basic analytical work for you and assist in its interpretation by presenting it in graphical form.

Services providing financial information to investors are improving steadily, with Oracle and Ceefax both providing City pages. British Telecom's Prestel Citiservice has improved considerably from its early, abysmal, days. It now offers an unparalleled array of information, consisting of share prices, foreign exchange rates, commodity prices, company results and the like. There is even a service which will monitor portfolios and one which will calculate your tax bills.

Not surprisingly, stockbrokers have begun to explore Prestel's potential. A couple allow access to their research and investment recommendations through it – at a cost of course. One has taken advantage of the interactive nature of the system and is now offering a dealing service on Prestel. Investing from the comfort of your armchair is an interesting idea, even if it does turn out to be ten times more complicated than using the telephone.

These early forays into electronic broking for the private investor are almost certainly just the tip of a far larger iceberg. For those prepared to shell out the cash, and eager to have up-to-the-minute information, it should soon be possible to provide a service to the private investor which is only slightly less sophisticated than that used by the stockbrokers and institutions themselves. Indeed there is nothing to stop you renting a TOPIC set from the Stock Exchange if you can cope with the exorbitant charges.

The advent of SAEF, the SEAQ Automatic Execution Facility, will be a fantastic step forward, with small orders automatically handled at the best possible price. There is no reason to think that in the future, private investors may not be able to tap into this system themselves.

The big investing institutions occasionally deal between themselves without using the services of a stockbroker, if one is known to have shares the other wants. Perhaps this will be possible for private investors, too, one day. A potential purchaser could simply key his requirements into the relevant computer database, which would seek out holders of the shares and bid for the wanted stock. The City might not like the idea of a sort of electronic 'Stock Exchange & Mart', but the attractions of dealing without any commission or jobber's turn might make such a system irresistible to computerised private investors.

Whether the changes that have taken place over the past few years have benefitted the private investor already involved in the stock market is open to doubt. What is certain, however, is that they have concentrated the public's attention on the stock market in a way not seen for many years and, to some extent, have helped to play a part in de-mystifying the City. Access to the stock market is becoming much easier, with many High Streets now having a bank or building society willing to deal in shares. The more outlets to the stock market there are, the less insular and exclusive the Stock Exchange will seem.

But although the ownership of shares by private individuals has soared, the level of knowledge and the amount of active buying *and* selling of shares by individuals has not greatly increased. Far more needs to be done in this direction. Many of those applying for new issues do so solely in the hope of making a quick profit, selling out within days of getting their shares, and thus missing out completely on what the stock market is really about. If the City really wants the small investor to involve himself in the stock market and if companies really do want to move away from the dominance of institutional shareholders, then much more effort needs to be made to rid prospectuses, rights issue documents and the like of incomprehensible gobbledegook. Whatever the lawyers feel they have to include, surely it is not beyond the wit of intelligent merchant bankers to explain in simple language, as well as lawyerspeak, the main points of any document of importance to shareholders? Companies grumble that private investors frequently don't show enough interest in the affairs of their investment. Have they ever asked themselves how many of their shareholders can understand the screeds of bumpf that they send out?

Everyone seems concerned to end the concentration on the short-term that is such an irritating characteristic of the big pension funds and other institutional investors. Companies rightly complain that this can disrupt terribly their planning for the long-term. Private investors are not so fickle, and are far more understanding of the need for research and development programmes, and other capital costs, if the directors can show how they may bear fruit in the future. The potential for rectifying a situation which is damaging British business is at hand in the growing number of private investors willing to divert some of their savings into the stock market.

But if widespread share ownership is to become a reality, not just a transitory phase, the iniquitous tax advantages which the institutionalised savings schemes have over the private individual should be done away with. The Personal Equity Plan should be turned into something that really does encourage people to take a stake in British business, with real tax benefits for all, not just the wealthy. Only in this way will private individuals come to feel, once more, that they would prefer to hold their shares directly rather than have some anonymous fund manager do it all for them.

APPENDIX A

The Top 40

The forty largest companies in the 100-Share Index
ranked by market valuation (July 1987)

		Market value (£m)
1	British Petroleum	22,564
2	British Telecom	17,286
3	Shell Transport & Trading	16,711
4	Glaxo Holdings	13,047
5	ICI	9,991
6	BAT Industries	9,734
7	British Gas	9,712*
8	Marks & Spencer	7,463
9	Unilever	6,329
10	Hanson Trust	6,292
11	General Electric	6,129
12	BTR	5,724
13	National Westminster Bank	5,429
14	Grand Metropolitan	5,019
15	Barclays Bank	4,485
16	Cable & Wireless	4,266
17	Beecham Group	4,167
18	J. Sainsbury	4,065
19	Prudential Corporation	4,044
20	Wellcome	3,878
21	Rio Tinto-Zinc	3,619
22	Bass	3,496
23	Great Universal Stores	3,440
24	Allied-Lyons	3,249
25	Lloyds Bank	3,103
26	Guinness	3,045

* Fully-paid

27	Boots	2,845
28	P&O	2,818
29	Land Securities	2,769
30	Tesco	2,762
31	Reuters	2,739
32	Reed International	2,592
33	Sears Holdings	2,588
34	Royal Insurance	2,496
35	Cons Gold	2,412
36	BOC Group	2,381
37	ASDA	2,273
38	Pilkington Bros	2,240
39	Dee Corporation	2,183
40	Trusthouse Forte	2,159

APPENDIX B

Commission Rates in force before
Big Bang (included only for the purposes of
comparison with current 'negotiated' rates).

ORDINARY AND PREFERENCE SHARES

On first £7,000 consideration 1.65%
On next £8,000 consideration 0.55%
On next £115,000 consideration 0.5%
(Lower rates apply for larger deals)

GOVERNMENT STOCKS

Shorts: stocks with less than five years to final redemption
   Charged at discretion. Big clients may pay nothing; private clients
   will probably be charged the same as for mediums.
Mediums: stocks with between five and ten years to final redemption
   On first £2,500 consideration 0.8%
   On next £15,500 consideration 0.125%
   On next £232,000 consideration 0.0625%
   (Lower rates apply for larger deals)
Longs: stocks with over ten years to final redemption
   On first £2,500 consideration 0.8%
   On next £15,500 consideration 0.25%
   On next £232,000 consideration 0.125%
   (Lower rates apply for larger deals).

LOAN STOCKS AND DEBENTURES

On first £5,000 consideration 0.9%
On next £5,000 consideration 0.45%
On next £40,000 consideration 0.35%
On next £50,000 consideration 0.325%

TRADED OPTIONS

£1.50 per option contract *plus*

   2.5% on first £5,000 consideration (option money)

   1.5% on next £5,000 consideration (option money)

   1.0% on the excess

Minimum on transactions of over £20 option money is £10 overall, with minimum of £5 on the option money portion.

APPENDIX C

A list of stockbrokers known to be willing to take on new private clients.

For obvious reasons, no comments have been given upon the respective merits of the brokers but I can assure you, from my own experience, priority in the alphabet is no guarantee of excellence.

LONDON

Broker	Tel. no.	Broker	Tel. no.
S. P. Angel	588 3427	Greig, Middleton	920 0481
Brewin Dolphin	248 4400	Hall Graham Bradford	
Campbell Neill	920 9661		628 7961
James Capel	588 6010	Hoare Govett	404 0344
Capel-Cure Myers	236 5080	G. H. & A. M. Jay	248 0081
A. H. Cobbold	920 9441	Keith Bayley Rogers	
E. J. Collins	588 7666		623 2400
Henry Cooke Lumsden		Kemp Mitchell	628 8991
	628 0411	Laurie Milbank	606 6622
T. C. Coombs	588 6209	Le Mare Martin	628 9472
de Zoete & Bevan	588 4141	Lyddon & Co.	628 5573
J. M. Douglas & Eykyn Bros		Northcote & Co.	628 8121
	248 4277	Parsons & Co.	588 4302
Earnshaw Haes	588 5699	Guy Puckle	628 6591
Foster & Braithwaite		Quilter Goodison	600 4177
	588 6111	Schaverien & Co.	251 1626
Southard Gilbey McNish		Schweder Miller	588 5600
	638 6761	Charles Stanley	638 5717
Godfray, Derby	638 0767	Stock Beech	638 8471
Goodbody & Dudgeon		Strauss Turnbull	638 5699
	628 4131	Sternberg Thomas Clarke	
Greene & Co.	628 7241		247 8461
		R. J. Thompson	588 2790

Broker	Tel. no.	Broker	Tel. no.
Tilney & Co.	638 0683	Walker Crips Weddle Beck	
Vivian Gray	638 2888		253 7502
		Russell Wood	236 3761

COUNTRY BROKERS – ENGLAND

Broker	Tel. no.	Broker	Tel. no.
Avon		Wise Speke	0642 248431
Bath			
Godfray, Derby	0749 76373	**Cumbria**	
Bristol		*Bowness*	
Greig, Middleton	0272 24013	Neilson Hornby Crichton	
Heseltine Moss	0272 276521		09662 2141
Hillman, Catford, Board		*Carlisle*	
	0272 291352	Keith, Bayley, Rogers	
Laws & Co.	0272 293901		0228 20299
Stock Beech	0272 20051	Stancliffe, Todd & Hodgson	
			0228 21200
Bedfordshire			
Bedford		**Derbyshire**	
R. N. McKean	0234 51131	*Derby*	
		Stevenson & Barrs	
Berkshire			0332 47451
Newbury			
Heseltine Moss	0635 41385	**Devon**	
		Barnstaple	
Cambridgeshire		Milton Mortimer	0271 71199
Cambridge		*Exeter*	
Charles Stanley	0223 316726	Milton Mortimer	0392 76244
Peterborough		*Plymouth*	
Buckmaster & Moore		Westlake & Co.	0752 20971
	0733 311611	*Torquay*	
		Whale, Hardaway	
Cheshire			0803 22441
Warrington			
Ashton Tod McLaren		**Dorset**	
	0925 572671	*Bournemouth*	
		Farley & Thompson	
Cleveland			0202 26277
Hartlepool		Jolliffe Flint & Cross	
Cawood Smithie	0429 72231		0202 25682
Middlesbrough		Robson Cotterell	0202 27581
Cawood Smithie	0642 712771	*Dorchester*	
Stancliffe, Todd & Hodgson		Richardson Chubb	
	0642 249211		0305 65252

Broker	Tel. no.

East Sussex
Eastbourne
Laing & Cruickshank
0323 20893

Essex
Colchester
E. F. Matthews   0206 549831
Westcliff-on-Sea
Henry J. Garratt 0702 347173

Gloucestershire
Cheltenham
Heseltine Moss   0242 571571
Henderson Crosthwaite
0242 514756
Gloucester
Heseltine Moss   0452 25444

Greater Manchester
Bolton
Llewellyn Greenhalgh
0204 21697
Bury
James Sharp   061 764 4043
Oldham
Mills Dutton   061 624 4651
Rochdale
Pilling, Trippier   0706 46951
Stockport
McLellan Ballard
061 480 3906

Hampshire
Southampton
A. H. Cobbold   0703 333292
Winchester
A. H. Cobbold.   0962 52362

Hereford & Worcester
Hereford
Henderson Crosthwaite
0432 265647
Worcester
Henderson Crosthwaite
0905 29551

Humberside
Grimsby
Fowler Sutton   0472 50232
Hull
Fowler Sutton   0482 25750
Stancliffe Todd & Hodgson
0482 226293

Lancashire
Blackburn
Hanson & Co.   0254 59611
Blackpool
James Brearly & Sons
0253 21474
Marsden W. Hargreave Hale
0253 21575
Burnley
Charlton Brett & Boughey
0282 22042
Lancaster
Hanson & Co.   0524 32582
Lytham St Annes
Marsden W. Hargreave Hale
0253 722166
Preston
Hanson & Co.   0772 556248

Leicestershire
Leicester
Hill Osborne   0533 29185
Wilshere Baldwin
0533 541344

Lincolnshire
Lincoln
Hill Osborne   0522 28244

Manchester
Arnold Stansby   061 832 8554
Ashworth Sons & Barratt
061 832 4812
Bell Houldsworth
061 834 3542
Charlton, Seal Dimmock
061 832 3488
Gall & Eke   061 228 2511
Henry Cooke, Lumsden
061 834 2332

Broker	Tel. no.

Pilling, Trippier
061 832 6581

Merseyside
Liverpool
Ashton Tod McLaren
051 236 8281
Blankstone Sington
051 227 1881
Milnes Lumby Bustard
051 236 9891
Rensburg & Co.
051 227 2030
Neilson Hornby Crichton
051 236 6666
Tilney & Co.   051 236 6000
Shrewsbury
Tilney & Co.   0743 51374
Southport
Charlton, Brett & Boughey
0704 32282

Norfolk
Norwich
Barratt & Cooke   0606 24236

Northamptonshire
Northampton
Cave & Sons   0604 21421

North Yorkshire
Harrogate
Cawood Smithie   0423 66781
Stancliffe, Todd & Hodgson
0423 66071
Scarborough
Hill Osborne   0723 372478
York
Hanson & Co.   0904 22085

Oxfordshire
Banbury
Harris, Allday, Lea & Brooks
0295 2103
Oxford
Heseltine Moss   0865 243581

Broker	Tel. no.

Somerset
Taunton
Laing & Cruickshank
0823 54351
Wells
Godfray, Derby   0749 76373

South Yorkshire
Barnsley
Stancliffe, Todd & Hodgson
0226 82268
Doncaster
Hanson & Co.   0302 23223

Sheffield
Nicholson Barber
0742 755100
Walter Ward   0742 22292

Staffordshire
Hanley
P. H. Pope   0782 25154

Tyne & Wear
Newcastle-upon-Tyne
John S. Smith   0632 326695
Wise Speke   0632 611266
Sunderland
Stancliffe, Todd & Hodgson
0783 657575

West Midlands
Birmingham
Chambers & Remington
021 236 2577
Fyshe Horton Finney
021 236 3111
Gilbert Jeffs   021 643 7861
Griffiths & Lamb
021 236 6641
Harris, Allday, Lea & Brooks
021 233 1222
Roy James & Co.
021 236 8131
Margetts & Addenbrooke
021 236 1365

Broker	Tel. no.
Murray & Co.	021 236 0891
Sabin, Bacon, White	
	021 236 5591
Albert E. Sharp	021 236 5801
Stock Beech & Co.	
	021 233 3211

Coventry
Daffern & Stephenson
0203 25352

Wolverhampton
Coni Gilbert & Sankey
0902 28711

West Sussex
Chichester
Heseltine Moss   0243 786472

West Yorkshire
Bradford
E. Midgley   0274 728866
Rensburg & Co.   0274 729406

Broker	Tel. no.
Halifax	
Broadbridge Lawson	
	0422 67707

Huddersfield
Battye, Wimpenny &
  Dawson   0484 21718
Robert Ramsden 0484 21501

Leeds
Broadbridge Lawson
0532 443721
Howitt & Pemberton
0532 439011
Redmayne–Bentley
0532 436941
Wise Speke   0532 459341

Wakefield
Broadbridge Lawson
0924 372601

Wiltshire
Salisbury
Alex Love, Rogers
0722 335211

COUNTRY BROKERS – SCOTLAND, WALES, NORTHERN IRELAND, CHANNEL ISLANDS, ISLE OF MAN, EIRE

Broker	Tel. no.
Scotland	

Edinburgh
Bell, Lawrie, MacGregor
031 225 2566
Capel-Cure Myers
031 225 2171
Parsons & Co.   031 226 4466
Torrie & Co.   031 225 1766
Wishart, Brodie
031 225 2813
Wood Mackenzie
031 225 8525

Glasgow
A. C. Anderson
041 221 2048
Campbell Neill   041 248 6271
Carswell & Co.   041 221 3402

Broker	Tel. no.
Greig, Middleton	
	041 221 8103

Laing & Cruickshank
041 333 9323
Parsons & Co.   041 332 8791
Spiers & Jeffrey 041 248 4311
Stirling, Hendry
041 248 6033

Aberdeen
Horne & Mackinnon
0224 640222
William Murray 0224 641307
Parsons & Co.   0224 29345

Dumfries
Bell, Lawrie, MacGregor
0387 52361

Dundee
Chalmers Ogilvie 0382 26282

Broker	Tel. no.
Parsons & Co.	0382 21081

Wales
Bangor

R. A. Coleman	0248 353242
Cardiff	
Heseltine Moss	0222 34061
Lyddon & Co.	0222 48000
Swansea	
Heseltine Moss	0792 54907
Lyddon & Co.	0792 54068

Northern Ireland
Belfast

Carr, Workman, Patterson, Topping	0232 245044
Wm. F. Coates	0232 223456
Josias Cunningham	0232 246005
Darbishire Malcomson & Coates	0232 231617
Laing & Cruickshank	0232 221002
Newry	
Mageninis & Co.	0693 4314
Londonderry	
D. M. Wright & Partners	0504 263344

Channel Islands
Jersey

Ashworth, Sons & Barratt	0534 44191
Brewin Dolphin	0534 27391
Charlton Seal	0534 25225
Laing & Cruickshank	0534 34321
Laurie Milbank	0534 76774
Le Masurier James & Chinn	0534 72825

Broker	Tel. no.
Sheppards & Chase	0534 30185
Trevor Matthews & Carey	0534 73311
Guernsey	
Ashworth, Sons & Barratt	0481 20152
Trevor Matthew & Carey	0481 26511

Isle of Man

Ramsey Crookall	0624 3171
R. L. Stott	0624 3701

Eire
Dublin

Bloxham Toole O'Donnell	776653
Butler & Briscoe	777348
Campbell O'Connor	771773
Doak & Co.	770952
Dudgeon	777314
Goodbody & Wilkinson	773481
Maguire McCann Morrison	771341
Moore Gamble Carnegie	773914
O'Brien & Toole	778797
Solomons Abrahamson	7789264
Stokes & Kelly Bruce Symes & Wilson	770572
Limerick	
Maguire, McCann Morrison	061 44065
Cork	
Beale Sheffield	021 270828
W. & R. Morrogh	021 270647

GLOSSARY

Account
The Stock Exchange calendar is divided up into a series of accounts, usually two weeks long. Most dealings in UK shares are totted up at the end of each account with only one bill or payment falling due on Settlement Day.

Allotment letter
The document showing that its holder has been allotted a certain number of shares through a new issue or a rights issue.

ADR (American deposit receipts)
When dealing in many of the big UK shares, American investors don't bother to deal in London. Instead shares are left on deposit with US banks, while investors trade in ADRs which effectively give them the right to those shares should they want them.

At best
An order to a stockbroker to deal at the best possible price rather than at a limit, getting the highest selling price or finding the lowest buying price.

Bargain
Any deal performed on the Stock Exchange.

Bear
Someone who believes a share, or the market, is going to fall and who may try to profit from his pessimism by selling shares in the hope of buying back at a lower price later on.

Bearer stocks
Securities whose ownership is vested in their holder, and not recorded on a central register in the normal manner. These should be guarded very carefully, because the person who holds them owns them.

Bed & breakfast
Hallowed market practice of selling securities and buying them back to establish a profit or loss for Capital Gains Tax purposes.

Bid price
The price at which someone, such as a market-maker, is willing to buy a particular security.

Blue chip
The giants of the stock market, large, well-established and safe. The expression, American in origin, may refer to the blue

[229]

	chips used in casinos which were the largest denomination.
Bonds	Securities which are issued by governments or companies to fund their debt and which generally pay a fixed level of interest.
Bull	The opposite of a bear, someone who believes a share or the market as a whole, is going to rise. Such optimists are said to be bullish, while a constantly rising market is known as a bull market.
Call	A payment still due on a security which is only partly paid. There were two calls of 40p each in the case of British Telecom.
Call option	The right to buy shares (or gilts, the FTSE-100 index, or even currencies) at a certain price within a set period.
Capitalisation issue	Exactly the same as a scrip issue, a free issue of shares to shareholders in proportion to their existing holding. They become no richer as a result, the issue being just a book-keeping exercise.
Cash settlement	Deals done 'for cash' need to be settled on the following day, rather than for the more usual account settlement. Gilts and new issues of shares are generally dealt in for cash settlement.
Closing	A deal, either a purchase or a sale, which reverses one done earlier in the same Stock Exchange account. No commission will be payable on the closing deal.
Consideration	The cost of a purchase or proceeds of a sale before any charges are levied upon the deal.
Cum	Latin for 'with', so that a share quoted as 'cum' something will carry with it the rights to the forthcoming dividend, scrip issue, rights issue or whatever. If quoted 'ex' it will not carry those rights.
Dealing for new time	During the last two days of an account it is possible to deal as if for the next Stock Exchange account. The settlement date for the deal will be that applying to the new account, rather than the present one.
Debenture	Loan stock which is issued by a company, and generally secured on its assets. Debentures are quoted, like gilts, in terms of £100 nominal units.

[230]

Dividend	Periodic, and hopefully regular, payments to shareholders from a company's profits. Dividends are received net of basic-rate tax, with an attached tax credit.
Dividend cover	The number of times the net dividend could have been paid from a company's earnings attributable to its shareholders.
Earnings	Net profit after tax due to holders of ordinary shares but not necessarily paid out to them. Earnings are usually expressed as so many pence per share.
Equities	Ordinary shares, whose owners take the main risks and who are entitled to those profits left over after all prior charges have been met.
Ex	The opposite to cum, ex means 'without'. A price quoted 'ex dividend' will not carry the right to the current dividend. Similarly shares which are ex rights, or ex scrip will exclude the rights to such distributions.
Gearing	Expressed as a percentage, gearing usually refers to the extent of a company's indebtedness, being the ratio of all its borrowings to its share capital.
Gilt-edged	Another name for stocks issued by the British government.
Gross	Interest payable before the deduction of any income or other tax.
House	The market's name for the floor of the London Stock Exchange.
Index-linked gilts	Government stocks on which both the level of interest paid, and the final redemption payment, are linked to the increase in the Retail Price Index.
Institutions	A generic term covering all the pension funds, insurance companies, banks, building societies, unit trusts, investment trusts and other such investment organisations.
Investment trust	A quoted company whose business is to invest, mainly in other shares, for the benefit of its own shareholders. It differs from a unit trust in being a 'closed-end fund' and in having its own shares quoted on the Stock Exchange.
Jobber	See Market-maker.

Jobber's spread or turn	The difference between the price at which a market maker is prepared to sell a security and the price at which he is willing to buy.
Kaffirs	The market's name for South African gold mining shares.
Licensed dealer	A dealer in securities who is not a member of the Stock Exchange. He will usually make 'net' prices, including his commission in the price he quotes to investors.
Limit	An order to a stockbroker which only permits a deal to be done if it is possible to execute at a certain price or better.
Long	Someone holding shares is said to be long of them.
Longs	Gilt-edged stocks with a life until redemption of more than fifteen years.
Market-maker	The wholesalers of shares in the UK stock market. Before the Big Bang they were known as jobbers but were prevented then from dealing with anybody but stockbrokers.
Mediums	Gilt-edged stocks with a life until redemption of between five and fifteen years.
Net asset value	The amount by which the assets of a company exceed all its liabilities (including those to holders of loan stocks and preference shares) divided by the number of shares in issue. This gives a figure for N.A.V. in pence per share, and can be compared with the current share price.
Nominal value	The face value or par value of a security as opposed to its market value.
Nominee	Shares can be registered in a nominee name, rather than the real one, if they are being managed on behalf of someone else or if their holder wishes to conceal his identity. Companies now have powers to find out who is behind nominee names on their share register.
Offer price	The opposite of bid price, being the level at which someone is prepared to sell a security, in particular the price the market-maker is willing to sell to a stockbroker.

Option	The right to buy a share at a set price within a fixed period (a call) or to sell that share (a put), upon payment of a consideration known as option money.
Oversubscription	An offer of shares or other securities to the investing public is oversubscribed when the number of shares applied for exceeds the number available. This can lead to the scaling down of applications, their placing in a ballot or even their rejection.
Par	The nominal value of a security, which is generally £100 for fixed interest instruments and can be almost any amount for shares. It is of little importance for investment purposes.
Partly-paid	Securities on which only part of the full cost has been paid, with a further call or calls due to be paid by holders at a future date.
Pink forms	The coveted forms which are issued to employees and others who are given favourable treatment in the allocation of new issues of shares.
Preference shares	Shares on which a fixed level of dividend is paid, providing the money is available. They rank in the pecking order below debentures and loan stock but above ordinary shares, with dividends paid before holders of ordinary equity get their money.
Premium	A security is said to be standing at a premium when it is trading at more than its issued price.
Price-earnings ratio	The number of times a company's earnings will divide into the current price of the shares. The resulting multiple is used as a measure of the shares 'cheapness' and is one of the two most widely used investment calculations.
Prior charges	The interest and dividends payable on debentures, loan stocks and preference shares, which must be paid before any dividends can be paid on the ordinary shares.
Proxy	Someone empowered to vote on behalf of a shareholder at a company meeting.

Put option	The right to sell shares (or gilts, the FTSE-100 index, or even currencies) at a certain price within a set period. The opposite of a call option.
Redemption date	The date when fixed-interest stocks, such as gilts and debentures, are redeemed, usually at their par value.
Redemption yield	The yield on a fixed-interest stock which takes into account the annual benefit to be gained as the stock climbs towards its redemption price. If the stock stands above its redemption price, the redemption yield will be lower than the running yield.
Rights issue	An issue of new shares to shareholders, generally at a discount to the current market price, with the number of shares offered in proportion to the shareholder's existing holding.
Running yield	Alternatively known as the flat yield or current yield, this is the annual return offered by the interest or dividend on a stock trading at the current price.
Scrip issue	See capitalisation issue.
Settlement day	The day on which all deals relating to the previous Stock Exchange account must be settled. Also known as Account Day, it is generally the second Monday after the end of an account.
Shop	The stockbroker or merchant bank to a company, usually responsible for the most influential dealings in any share.
Short	Someone who sells shares hoping to buy them back at a lower price later on is said to be short of them.
Shorts	Gilt-edged securities with a redemption date of less than five years.
Stag	Someone who applies for a new issue of shares, intending to sell them almost immediately in order to make a quick profit.
Stamp duty	A ½% duty imposed by the government on the purchase of most securities. Exempt are government stocks, new issues and shares issued as a result of rights issues or scrips.

Stock	Specifically a security that is traded in units of £100, such as fixed-interest stocks, but these days the term is used to refer to shares as well.
Tap stock	Government securities of which only part of the issue has so far been sold to the public, the rest being let out on to the market as the government, through its agents, sees fit.
Technical analysis	The study of shares, and the prediction of future movements of shares and markets through the use of charts and statistical analysis.
Third Market	Introduced in 1987, this is the third tier of the stock market, intended for small companies that would not qualify for the main market or USM. The responsibility for regulation rests with the sponsoring stockbroker, not the Stock Exchange.
Tender	An issue of securities in which investors must bid a maximum price at which they are willing to subscribe. When the striking price is fixed, all those tendering at that level or above will receive shares.
Traded option	An option which can be traded throughout the course of its life, giving holders the right to buy shares or other instruments through call options or the right to sell through put options.
Undated	Government securities which have no fixed date set for repayment.
Underwriter	Someone who undertakes to subscribe for all or part of an issue of securities if it is not wholly taken up by the public, in return for which an underwriting commission is paid. The underwriter will pass on this commitment to sub-underwriters such as banks, insurance companies and pension funds, and they will also receive commission.
Unit trust	A trust formed to manage a portfolio on behalf of the holders of its units. Each unit-holder's stake in that trust is in direct proportion to the number of units he holds. The value of unit trusts depends, not upon supply or demand, but upon the value of the portfolio.

Unlisted Securities Market	Introduced by the Stock Exchange in 1980 this is a second-tier market for companies which do not want, or do not qualify for, a full listing. Although there are still regulations with which USM companies must comply, they are less strict than for companies on the main market.
Unsecured loan stock	A fixed-interest stock issued by a company, but which is not secured by any of its assets.
Yield	The return on any investment, usually expressed as a gross annual figure. For traded securities the yield is the interest or the dividend divided by the present price, measured as a percentage.
Yield gap	The difference between the average yield on long-dated gilts and on equities. Prior to the 1960s gilts usually yielded less than shares, but since then there has been a 'reverse yield gap' with the yield on shares generally substantially less than on gilts.

ADDITIONAL APPENDIX

Companies offering computer investment packages

Green Acres Software, Hook Road, Ampfield, Romsey,
    Hampshire SO51 9DB
Meridian Software (01-850 7057)
Micro Investor Software (051-342 6482/3)
PHN Software Ltd, 1 Exeter Road, Portishead, Bristol
    BS20 9YE
Seestats, 20 Rozelle Road, Parkstone, Poole, Dorset
    BH1 40BX
Synergy Software (05827-2977)

INDEX